FUN WITH THE FAMILY™

in SOUTHERN CALIFORNIA

HUNDREDS OF IDEAS
FOR DAY TRIPS WITH THE KIDS

FOURTH EDITION

LAURA KATH

&

PAMELA PRICE

The Globe Pequot Press

GUILFORD, CONNECTICUT

Text design by Nancy Freeborn
Maps by M. A. Dubé

ISSN 1541-8952
ISBN 0-7627-2195-2

Manufactured in the United States of America
Fourth Edition/First Printing

For my mom, Anna Kath, whose fortitude
on family car trips is always inspirational!
—Laura Kath

To my energetic mother, Leona Effress.
Life is always full of adventures with you!
—Pamela Price

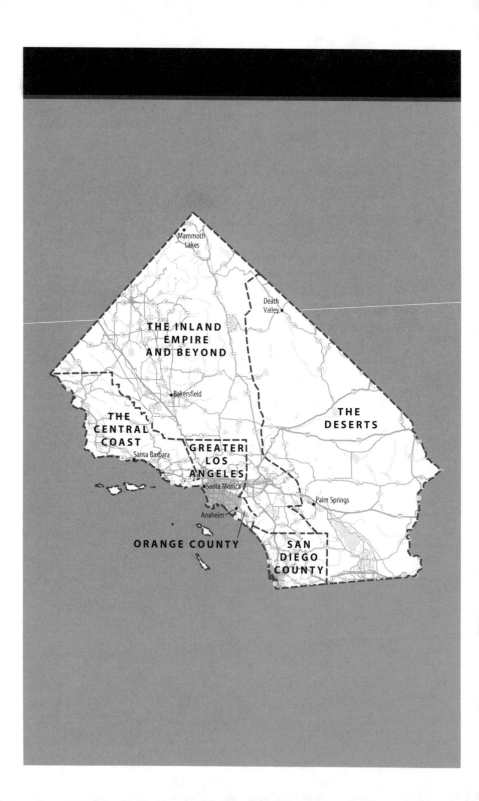

Contents

Acknowledgments

Researching the best family fun throughout Southern California could not have been accomplished without the invaluable assistance of so many generous individuals, organizations, and attractions. From the tips of our fingers to our achy feet, we gratefully acknowledge just a few of the many (and hereby apologize if we've neglected to mention anyone).

Anaheim/Orange County Visitor and Convention Bureau; The Blaze Company (Marcy Blaze, Karen Gee McAuley, and Tanisha Carden); California Office of Tourism (Fred Sater); Disneyland Resort (Robert Duell); El Capitan Canyon Resort (Donna Steinmann); Bob Gourley and family; Jane Summer Communications; Janis Flippen Public Relations; Julian White House Inn (Mary and Alan Marvin); Vern Lanegrasse, the Hollywood Chef; Le Meriden Hotel Beverly Hills; Los Angeles Convention and Visitors Bureau (Carol C. Martinez); Long Beach Area Visitors and Convention Bureau; Maris Somerville Associates Public Relations; New Otani Hotel and Gardens; Oxnard Convention and Visitors Bureau; Palm Springs Bureau of Tourism (Jeff Hocker); Palm Springs Desert Resorts Convention and Visitors Bureau (Gary Sherwin and Mark Graves); Riverside Convention and Visitors Bureau; San Diego Convention and Visitors Bureau; San Diego North County Visitors and Convention Bureau; San Luis Obispo Chamber of Commerce; Santa Barbara Conference and Visitors Bureau; Solvang Visitors Bureau; Ventura Visitors and Convention Bureau.

Pamela would like to thank Bernard Bubman who introduced her to his favorite family-friendly places around Los Angeles. Pamela thanks her son Tony for his outspoken opinions on what families will find festive in Southern California and her son Artie for his enthusiasm in exploring dozens of attractions on and off the road map. Pamela values broadcasting "wonder women" Joey English and Jackie Olden for their incredible support and travel and dining expertise. Pamela also thanks her mother, Leona Effress, for showcasing this book in her Palm Springs gift shops.

Laura especially appreciates her supportive family members and friends who are always eager to explore the wonders of SoCal attractions with her. Very special kudos to partner Brian Weeks for his "On-Purpose" coaching through her bouts of revision mania and beyond. Laura gratefully acknowledges the long-standing "author encouragement" provided by Amrit Joy, Fred Klein, Peggy Wentz, and Lee Wilkerson. Thanks to Renald Stettler and son Derek for an exciting Disneyland inspection trip. Ultimately, Laura will always treasure "the Kath Party" for providing her very first "fun with the family" car trips!

Last but never least, we acknowledge the supportive staff at The Globe Pequot Press for giving us the opportunity to write about all this Southern California fun starting back in 1994!

Introduction

Southern California is a kaleidoscope—no matter which way you turn, something amazing appears! There is just no way we can include every fun-worthy thing and place for your family in a volume this size. However, we do believe that this guide will give you and your family a very practical, yet comprehensive way to experience the Golden State, starting from the Central Coast and heading south all the way to the Mexican border.

Both of us, along with our families, have traveled thousands of miles by trains, planes, automobiles, horses, mules, and aching feet to discover the best in Southern California family fun. We are very proud of our adopted home state—Pamela originally hails from Minnesota and Laura from Michigan—and have spent more than fifty combined years as journalists researching and describing life on the "left coast" of the United States. We are thrilled to share the adventure with you!

We believe the most important element to family fun in Southern California is time. Be sure you allow yourself and the kids plenty of it. Concentrated in this golden nugget of real estate are enough activities, sights, sounds, and sensations to fill a dozen or more visits. Be sure to carefully select the elements that satisfy your family's unique tastes. Don't "kid" yourself, Southern California is not as "laid back" as you might think. Just ask any parent who has been done in by a day at an amusement park or managed to hit one of our famous freeway rush hours near dinnertime. Distance between activities can be deceptive. Five miles does not necessarily mean five minutes away. Be sure you plan "kick back" time—to relax on a beach or park bench and to soak up some of Southern California's 300-plus days of sunshine. Don't worry, we will be sure to save more for your next visit—promise!

If you and your family seek natural beauty, Southern California offers you the Pacific Ocean and its awesome beaches—some favorites include Moonstone Beach near Cambria, East Beach in Santa Barbara, Venice Beach near Santa Monica, and the pristine sands of Coronado. The mountain ranges, inland valleys, rivers, and freshwater lakes such as Nacimiento, Casitas, Big Bear, and Arrowhead are wonderful total recreation zones. Deserts such as Anza-Borrego, Palm Springs, Mojave, and Death Valley provide amazing contrasts to the palm-lined shores.

How about recreation? Participant or spectator, you can experience it all here. Teams such as basketball's Los Angeles Lakers, hockey's Mighty Ducks of Anaheim, baseball's L.A. Dodgers and Anaheim Angels, and football's San Diego Chargers offer the thrill of professional action. Needless to say, waterfront activity should rate high on your list when visiting Southern California—boating, fishing, sailing, sunbathing, surfing, and swimming are what

"California dreams" are made of. If you visit between December and April, whale-watching along the Pacific is an absolute must-see thrill. You and the kids can get into the swing of golf and tennis at hundreds of public facilities. Of course, biking and hiking trails abound to explore, yet they preserve all the area's natural beauty. Don't forget to pack a picnic basket and take time to smell the perennially blooming flowers.

You can visit natural parks full of wildlife and sea life or human-made amusement parks stocked with thrills. Southern California museums are filled with hands-on displays of fun things from archives to outer space. Be certain to include the magnificent J. Paul Getty Museum as well as the California Science Center in Los Angeles. California's history, rich with Native American, Spanish, and Mexican influences, provides your family with plenty of cultural diversity education, not to mention the thrill of deciphering foreign names—like San Luis Obispo, Port Hueneme, Ojai, and Temecula!

We have also included some of our preferred accommodations, family friendly dining, and shopping places to make your stay more enjoyable. We hope you will take the time to try some one-of-a-kind places to eat and stay that are not part of national chains. But let's be honest here—your kids would never forgive you if you didn't make a stop at a Planet Hollywood, Hard Rock Cafe, Nike Town, or Tower Records, all headquartered here.

Southern California is blessed with hundreds of annual special events—starting with January's immensely popular Rose Parade in Pasadena, right through holiday lighted boat parades all along the coast. There is always Carpinteria's Avocado Festival or the Historic Route 66 Jamboree. Since festivals have varying dates from year to year, we have included phone numbers you can call for specifics.

Southern California is like an endless summer vacation. Where else can you travel from the desert to a futuristic metropolis to some mountain snow skiing and, finally, take in the sunset at the beach—all in one day, all year-round? Would you expect anything less from the birthplace of Hollywood and Disneyland?

In this edition we have provided special sections under many area listings entitled "Where to Stay" and "Where to Eat"—describing just a few of the many outstanding establishments available for your family's enjoyment. Dollar signs provide a very general sense of the price range for each property. For meals, the prices are per individual dinner entrees, without tax or gratuity. For lodging, the rates are for a double-occupancy room, European plan (no meals unless indicated), exclusive of hotel "bed tax" or service charges.

Please keep in mind that meal prices generally stay the same throughout the year, but lodging rates fluctuate seasonally and by day of the week. Higher rates generally prevail in the summer season and holidays (when more families are on the go). Always be sure to inquire about special packages and promotional discounts.

Rates for Lodging

$	up to $50
$$	$51 to $75
$$$	$76 to $99
$$$$	$100 and up

Rates for Restaurants

$	most entrees under $10
$$	most entrees $10 to $15
$$$	most entrees $16 to $20
$$$$	most entrees over $20

Admission prices for attractions are in dollar signs, which indicate the following price ranges:

Rates for Attractions

$	up to $5 per person
$$	$5 to $10 per person
$$$	$11 to $20 per person
$$$$	more than $20 per person

Please let us know what you like about our *Fun With The Family in Southern California* guidebook. What other activities or attractions do we need to include in future editions? We really value your impressions. Write us today in care of The Globe Pequot Press, P.O. Box 480, Guilford, CT 06437.

Imagination, recreation, relaxation, nature, geography, cultural diversity, and history—complemented by a warm, sunny year-round climate—are waiting here for you. We know this guidebook will map out memorable family fun you will treasure and want to repeat; because Southern California makes every visitor feel young at heart. Enjoy!

> The prices and rates listed in this guidebook were confirmed at press time. We recommend, however, that you call establishments to obtain current information before traveling.

Attractions Key

The following is a key to the icons found throughout the text.

 Swimming

 Animal Viewing

 Boating / Boat Tour

 Food

 Historic Site

 Lodging

 Hiking / Walking

 Camping

 Fishing

 Museums

 Biking

 Performing Arts

 Amusement Park

 Sports / Athletic

 Horseback Riding

 Picnicking

 Skiing / Winter Sports

 Playground

 Park

 Shopping

 Plants / Gardens / Nature Trails

Farms

The Central Coast

The Central Coast has always been considered the northern edge of Southern California. However, there is really a midwestern feeling of friendliness and hospitality in the three geographically close yet economically diverse counties of San Luis Obispo, Santa Barbara, and Ventura. You have all the quintessential Southern California trademarks here—great year-round weather, fun-filled recreation, and attractions; and, of course, sandy beaches woven between wide-open fields planted with veggies and fruit, soaring foothills, mountains, streams, and the glittering Pacific—all presented by locals with warm graciousness. With fewer people than the megalopolises to the south, the Central Coast is much more laid-back and casual.

So much about the Central Coast says "welcome" to your family. Hearst Castle in San Simeon, spring hikes through the wildflowers of Montana de Oro State Park, the trendy beaches and shopping of Santa Barbara, kids' hands-on museums and zoos, boat cruises out to the Channel Islands, and surfing on the Rincon—or how about the simple pleasures of just hanging out in the 320-plus days of annual sunshine and basking in the waves and smiles from fellow Sunshine State dwellers and visitors? The Central Coast's two main arteries, the magnificent Pacific Coast Highway 1 and the inland U.S. Highway 101, can be your twin pathways to some of the best, and surprisingly most affordable, tastes of your Southern California dream vacation.

San Luis Obispo County

San Luis Obispo County's 3,316 square miles contain the Central Coast's most varied terrain—from windswept beaches to interior lakes, from grass-covered rolling hills to meticulously tended farmlands, plus recurring topographical evidence of seismic shifts along California's main earthquake zone, the San Andreas Fault. There are 85 miles of coastline for exploring.

1

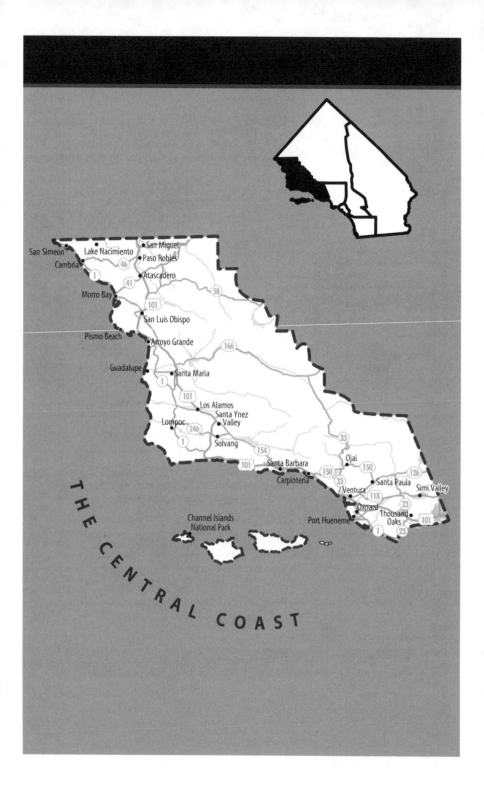

San Simeon
Lake Nacimiento
San Miguel
Paso Robles
Cambria
46
Atascadero
41
58
Morro Bay
101
San Luis Obispo
Pismo Beach
Arroyo Grande
166
Guadalupe
1
Santa Maria
101
Los Alamos
Santa Ynez
Valley
Lompoc
246
33
1
Solvang
154
101
Santa Barbara
Ojai
150
Carpinteria
150
33
126
Ventura
Santa Paula
Simi Valley
118
Channel Islands
National Park
Oxnard
23
Thousand
Oaks
101
Port Hueneme
1
23

THE CENTRAL COAST

The climate of San Luis Obispo (San Lewis Oh-bis-poe) features mild summers and winters, with patches of dense seasonal fog along the coast. Temperatures range from coastal lows in the thirties in the winter to inland valley highs in the nineties-plus in the summer. Year-round temperatures average sixty to seventy degrees, with around 22 inches of rain, mostly in the winter.

Native Americans occupied the land for thousands of years before its discovery by Spanish explorers in the sixteenth century. Two of California's famous chain of twenty-one missions are here in San Luis Obispo County, preserving the area's Spanish and Mexican heritage. The railroad arrived in the late 1890s, bringing more families and increasing the dominance of agriculture and tourism in the area. Outdoor recreation and historic attractions top the must-see list of county adventures.

For More Information

San Luis Obispo County Visitors and Conference Bureau. *1037 Mill Street, 93401; (800) 634–1414 or (805) 541–8000; www.sanluisobispocounty.com.*

San Simeon

Founded in the 1850s by fishermen and whalers, the little seaside village of San Simeon really came into its own in the late 1800s, when most of the area's land was purchased and developed by Senator George Hearst. His son, William Randolph Hearst, began construction on his fantasy "ranch" in 1919. This incredible estate, and the opportunity to visit it, has put San Simeon on the map. Most of the original village has faded, but Sebastian's General Store and Post Office is fun for kids to explore. The newer tourist town of San Simeon Acres is 4 miles south of Hearst Castle on Pacific Coast Highway 1 and plays host to various motels, restaurants, and a miniature golf course/arcade—facilities to snap you back into modern-day realities.

HEARST-SAN SIMEON STATE HISTORIC MONUMENT (ages 6 and up)

41 miles north of San Luis Obispo on Pacific Coast Highway 1; (800) 444–4445 (have your credit card ready to purchase tour tickets in advance) or (805) 927–2020; www.hearstcastle.org. Open daily, except New Year's Day, Thanksgiving, and Christmas. $$

Don't miss a chance to go on a fascinating tour of publishing baron William Randolph Hearst's real-life fantasy home between 1928 and

1951, officially called Hearst-San Simeon State Historic Monument and unofficially called Hearst Castle. See for yourself the lifestyle of someone rich and famous. Advance ticket reservations are strongly recommended.

This is the most popular attraction on the Central Coast, and there are a limited number of tickets and tour times available. If you arrive without reservations, you most likely will have to wait and might find a sold-out/standby situation (especially in the busy summer, weekend, and holiday times).

There are four different guided tours to choose from. Each is seventy-five minutes long, plus a thirty-minute bus ride to and from the castle. For first-timers, **Tour Number 1,** also called the Experience Tour, is the best bet. It includes the National Geographic movie *Hearst Castle: Building the Dream.* When you arrive at the "castle," park free at the modern visitor center just off the highway. This family-friendly center has a snack bar, gift shop, rest rooms, lockers, and a fascinating free exhibition on Hearst himself, which you can visit as you wait for your tour number to be called. You'll then board school buses for the 5-mile, fifteen-minute drive up the hill to see highlights of the 165-room "La Casa Grande"—the main house—plus three separate guest houses on the 127-acre grounds overlooking the Pacific and the surrounding Santa Lucia Mountains.

There is something for every member of your family to ogle in Hearst Castle, including enormous swimming pools, the lavish dining room (complete with Hearst's favorite Heinz ketchup bottle among the silver and china!), the playroom with billiards and trophy animal heads, incredible art, antiques, tapestries, and collectibles from around the world, plus Hearst's private movie theater with his vintage home movies for your viewing pleasure.

If you want more of a Hearst fantasy fix, take **Tour Number 2** for upper levels of the main house, the libraries, and the kitchen or **Tour Number 3** for the North Wing, gardens, and a special video on the construction of the castle. **Tour Number 4,** for more gardens, the wine cellar, and another private guest house, is offered April through October. **Tour 5** is a very special lighted evening tour lasting around two hours on Friday and Saturday during spring and fall only. The tour lasts one hundred minutes, plus a thirty-minute bus ride. Tour 5 combines the best elements of the above tours at a higher fee, but really is appropriate only for older children, teens, and adults.

Hearst Castle construction began in 1919 under the supervision of architect Julia Morgan and continued unabated for twenty-eight years, costing an estimated $3 million-plus in Depression-era dollars. Hearst then left what he referred to as "his ranch," due to poor health. After his death in 1951, the Hearst Corporation deeded the property to the state of California, which opened it to the public in 1958. Today, Hearst Castle is preserved and skillfully managed by the California Park Service.

Cambria

Nine miles south of San Simeon and 33 miles northwest of San Luis Obispo on Highway 1 is the quaint, small-town artist's haven of Cambria. This village is a welcome respite from the excesses of Hearst Castle and is a family-friendly place to stay for this part of your coastal explorations. The West Village is adjacent to Highway 1; the East Village, or Old Town, is about a mile inland. Moonstone Beach Drive is right on the Pacific and has many inns and beach-combing spots. Both parts of town are connected by Main Street. Cruise down Main Street and check out the art galleries, antique emporiums, and toy shops. The Soldier Factory in the West Village manufactures and sells detailed miniature combatants and lots of other figures made of pewter. There is a farmer's market every Friday afternoon at the Vet's Hall on Main Street. Look for olallieberry pies from Linn's Berry Farm.

Where to Eat

Brambles Dinner House, *4005 Burton Drive; (805) 927–4716; www.bramblesdinnerhouse.com. Opens at 4:00 P.M. most days and has excellent early-bird specials.* Located in the East Village, 2 blocks south of Main Street. Choose from multiple dining areas in this rambling English cottage. Friendly servers and a children's menu will make you feel right at home. Superb steaks and prime rib. A great place to unwind after a busy day of touring. $$$

French Corner Bakery, *2214 Main Street; (805) 927–8227.* Wander in, get some fresh-baked treats. Open for breakfast and lunch 7:00 A.M. to 6:00 P.M. daily. $

Where to Stay

Best Western Fireside Inn, *6700 Moonstone Beach Drive, Cambria; (888) 910–7100 or (805) 927–8661; www.best westernfiresideinn.com.* You'll find spacious rooms, many with fireplaces. Other highlights include refrigerators, coffeemakers, complimentary continen-tal breakfast, a heated pool, and a spa. Excellent value along the beach. Families welcome. $$$

Cambria Pines Lodge, *2705 Burton Drive; (800) 445–6868 or (805) 927–4200; www.cambriapines.lodge.com.* A wonderful place for families to stay. Located on a hilltop overlooking the village, the lodge has 125 units, including nice two-room family suites with connecting baths, fireplaces, microwaves, fridges, and coffeemakers. You'll also enjoy an indoor heated pool, spa, game room, lawn sports, and a restaurant serving California cuisine for breakfast, lunch, and dinner. Hearty breakfasts here will give you a good start on tour day. $$

Extra Special Tip

Moonstone Beach, just north of Cambria, is the place to find those smooth, milky-white stones and gnarled pieces of driftwood. Don't think about swimming here, because the water is really too cold, but beachcombing is the best! You can often see migrating whales passing by in January and February and hear the cries of sea otters and sea lions year-round. There are several bed-and-breakfast inns, motels, and restaurants along Moonstone Beach Drive if you want to savor the crashing surf.

For More Information

Cambria Chamber of Commerce. *767 Main Street, 93428; (805) 927–3624; www.cambriachamber.org.*

Lake Nacimiento

Just over the mountains from Hearst Castle lies Nacimiento, arguably the Central Coast's most beautiful human-made lake. Damming the Nacimiento River created 165 miles of gorgeous shoreline. Fishing, boating, water sports galore, and outstanding hiking make this one of the most popular family recreation destinations in the county.

LAKE NACIMIENTO RESORT

From U.S. Highway 101, take County Road G-14 out of Paso Robles, drive 16 miles northwest; mailing address: Star Route, Box 2770, Bradley, 93426; (805) 238–3256 or (800) 323–3839; www.nacimientoresort.com. $$$

Owned and operated by the Heath family since 1962, the resort is a safe, clean, fun environment, with everything you could possibly want for a great outdoors vacation. There is a full-service marina and dock where you can rent Jet Skis, Wave Runners, canoes, boats (power, paddle, and pontoon), sport-fishing tackle, and equipment for diving and windsurfing.

The lake is famous for its plentiful white bass, water-skiing, and salt-free swimming. Forgot your bathing suit or gear? The fully stocked general store has everything, including provisions for a barbecue or picnic. Lakeshore Cafe serves breakfast, lunch, and dinner. Open-air patio dining is available; great views!

Facilities include the boat launch, picnic grounds, playground, volleyball and basketball courts, swimming pool, and hiking trails around the meandering shoreline. Overnight accommodations include nineteen lodge units, one-, two-, and three-bedroom town houses (complete with mini-kitchens and decks) right on the lakeshore; plus forty RV hookups and 270 campsites. Extremely popular April to October, but winter season has mild weather, fewer crowds, and, of course, the same gorgeous scenery.

Paso Robles and Atascadero

Paso Robles (Spanish for "pass of the oaks") is located at the junction of U.S. Highway 101 and State Route 46. Atascadero (Spanish for "place of much water") is just south of Paso Robles at the crossroads of State Route 41. This area is famous for its stately trees, agriculture, and award-winning wineries and vineyards. Perhaps a taste of the grape for mom and dad before hitting the dusty trail again? (Phone the Vintners and Growers Association at 805-239-8463 for current maps and tasting rooms or access the Web site at www.pasowine.com.) Meanwhile, be sure to explore these area attractions with the entire family.

CALIFORNIA MID-STATE FAIR

Riverside Avenue between 21st and 24th Streets, just off U.S. Highway 101, Paso Robles; (805) 239–0655.

Call for annual lineup of musical and rodeo events. For two weeks in August, the annual fair turns Paso Robles into a rockin' and thumpin' western town. Kids will enjoy the 4-H animal exhibits, crafts, art, food booths, carnival rides, and world-class live entertainment (in years past, Kenny Rogers, Diana Ross, Julio Iglesias, and the Beach Boys have appeared).

PIONEER MUSEUM

Riverside Avenue between 19th and 20th Streets, Paso Robles; (805) 239–4556. Open year-round on Saturday and Sunday. Free admission; donations welcome.

Young cowpokes can amble over to see the farm equipment from the turn of the last century, while their folks check out home furnishings.

LAKE ATASCADERO PARK AND CHARLES PADDOCK ZOO

South of Paso Robles, Morro Bay/State Route 41, exit off U.S. Highway 101, west 1.5 miles; (805) 461–5080. Open 10:00 A.M. to 4:00 P.M.; hours extended in summer and vary by season. $

Thirty-five acres of water and wonder. This very intimate site allows close proximity to some one hundred rare and wonderful species. Among the selection: gleaming black brother-and-sister jaguars from Brazil, a pair of Bengal tigers, furry lemurs, sinewy pythons and boas, strutting pink flamingos, golden-bellied Mangabey chimps (three of only twenty-nine in the entire United States are here), and crested porcupines (can you make them strut their stuff?). Lake Atascadero is next to the zoo. Walk around the 2-mile perimeter of the lake and picnic on benches or dockside at the Lakeside Pavilion's snack bar. Strollers, a gift shop, refreshments, and rest rooms all make a visit easier for families.

For More Information

Atascadero Chamber of Commerce. *6550 El Camino Real, 93422; (805) 466–2044; www.atascaderochamber.org.*

Paso Robles Chamber of Commerce. *1225 Park Street, 93446; (805) 238–0506; www.pasorobleschamber.com.*

Morro Bay

Noted for two landmarks—nature's awesome Morro Rock and the human-made trio of smokestacks at the Pacific Gas and Electric power plant—bustling Morro Bay has a busy commercial fishing fleet and is a prized recreational and tourist town. You can't miss the magnificent 578-foot, dome-shaped Morro Rock, a long-extinct volcano, which marks the oceanfront end of the Embarcadero—several miles of waterfront filled with shops, restaurants, motels, and sailing vessels for charter.

TIGERS FOLLY II HARBOR CRUISES

1205 Embarcadero, near the Harbor Hut restaurant, across the street from the power plant; (805) 772–2257 or (800) 958–4437. $$

This 64-foot stern-wheeler paddleboat offers one-hour bay cruises—a gentle seafaring trip back into yesteryear. Sunday brunches are available seasonally. The bearded captain will delight the kids, especially when he lets them take the helm!

SUB/SEA TOURS

699 Embarcadero #9; (805) 772–9463. Call for reservations and current rates.

The company offers forty-five-minute trips in a semi-submersible vessel daily, generally on the hour depending on the tides. Kids love "diving" and seeing kelp forests and marine life. All trips narrated by a naturalist.

MORRO BAY STATE PARK

At the south end of town, off State Park Road; (805) 772–2560 or (800) 444–7275. Open daily year-round.

Nearly 2,000 acres along the Pacific shore contain many picnic and camping areas, an eighteen-hole golf course, a marina, a cafe, a primitive natural area, an estuary (great for bird-watching), and boat rentals.

MUSEUM OF NATURAL HISTORY

Perched on White Point, overlooking the bay and Morro Rock inside the Morro Bay State Park; (805) 772–2694. Open daily 10:00 A.M. to 5:00 P.M. except New Year's Day, Thanksgiving, and Christmas. $

Traditional and educational interpretive displays of local marine life, geology, and the history and culture of native peoples predominate. Video presentations in the auditorium. This is the last remaining blue heron rookery reserve between San Francisco and Mexico. These rare birds can be observed from hiking trails on the museum grounds.

MONTANA DE ORO STATE PARK

U.S. Highway 101 at Los Osos Valley Road, just south of Morro Bay in the tiny town of Los Osos; (805) 528–0513. Open year-round. Free day use, camping fees vary.

It is considered the Central Coast's premier park for hiking, nature walks, tide-pooling, horseback riding, camping, and shore fishing. The Spanish name means "mountain of gold," referring to the golden fields of poppies, mustard grass, and wildflowers enveloping the hillsides every spring. You can easily spend a day at this incredibly beautiful, 8,000-acre paradise.

Where to Eat

Harbor Hut Restaurant, *1205 Embar-cadero; (805) 772–2255.* It's right in the heart of the waterfront action. The seafood is fresh from the trawlers docked in front, making the Hut popular with locals and visitors alike. Lunch and dinner served daily from 11:00 A.M. $$

Where to Stay

The Inn at Morro Bay, *One mile south on Main Street, right before the entrance to Morro Bay State Park; (805) 772–5651 or (800) 321–9566; www.innatmorrobay.com.* Located on the bay, this comfortable ninety-eight-room, full-service hotel has both water- and garden-view rooms. Be sure to ask for a bay view with a balcony or patio to really relax. The dining room offers unobstructed views of the estuary and bay frontage while you are enjoying California cuisine for breakfast, lunch, and dinner. $$$

For More Information

Morro Bay Chamber of Commerce. *895 Napa Street, Suite A1, 93442; (805) 772–4467; www.morrobay.org.*

City of San Luis Obispo

This county seat sits in an inland valley ringed by pretty hills. A remarkably friendly municipality of 42,000 that is also home to California Polytechnic State University (known as Cal Poly), San Luis Obispo has a vibrant downtown area filled with historic sites, shopping, and restaurants. The **Free** downtown trolley runs a circuit that will give you and the kids a chance to take in the sights and sounds.

MISSION SAN LUIS OBISPO DE TOLOSA
Chorro and Monterey Streets, in the heart of Mission Plaza; (805) 543–6850. Open daily 9:00 A.M. to 5:00 P.M. except major holidays. **Free** *admission; donations welcome.*

Founded in 1772 and still in operation, the mission is the fifth in the twenty-one-mission chain of parishes founded by Father Junipero Serra. Take a self-guided tour through the *Life at the Mission* history exhibits and pause in the adobe-brick chapel constructed by the native Chumash people. The mission is named for a thirteenth-century saint, the bishop of Toulouse, often called "Prince of the Missions."

COUNTY HISTORICAL MUSEUM

696 Monterey Street, opposite the mission; (805) 543–0638. Open Wednesday to Sunday 10:00 A.M. to 4:00 P.M. Closed holidays and December 24. **Free** *admission; donations appreciated.*

Another trip down memory lane with old photographs and artifacts, all housed in a Romanesque granite, sandstone, and brick building that used to be the city library.

SAN LUIS OBISPO CHILDREN'S MUSEUM (ages 2 to 12, accompanied by an adult)

1010 Nipomo Street, corner of Monterey Street, downtown (same side of the creek as the Mission); (805) 544–6212 for times and admission fees. $

True to its motto of "education through exploration," this is a super, hands-on environment. It gives kids the chance to explore such future careers as news reporter, astronaut, postmaster, or bank teller. Kids can put on their own play, make giant bubbles (way cool!), or run a diner. The creek-side play zone works well for an outdoor picnic break.

GUM ALLEY

Higuera Street, between Garden and Broad Streets.

Before leaving downtown, you must seek out a relic you'll probably hate and your kids will undoubtedly love. Since the late 1950s, locals (mostly collegians) and visitors alike have been depositing their used gum on the narrow alley walls. Folk art or disgusting nuisance, who's to say, for this representation (it's the one and only) has been featured in *Smithsonian* magazine and on the *Ripley's Believe It or Not* TV show. Care to leave your sticky imprint? Let your taste decide.

FARMER'S MARKET

Downtown, Higuera Street. Every Thursday evening from 6:30 to 9:00 year-round.

Not to be missed is this world-famous farmer's market (a 7-block-long street fair). Kids will love the excitement of musicians, puppeteers, face painters, skate dancers, fire eaters, and, obviously, loads of fresh fruit, veggies, and mouth-watering barbecue. Don't be shy—join thousands of curbside dining families downing tasty ribs, chicken, or beef tritip sandwiches. Fantastic people-watching, too!

CALIFORNIA POLYTECHNIC STATE UNIVERSITY (CAL POLY)

About 2 miles north of downtown via Santa Rosa Street and Highland Drive; (805) 756–1111. Call for general information and to ask about guided inner-campus tours.

Located on more than 6,000 acres at the base of the Santa Lucia Mountain range, Cal Poly is renowned for its agribusiness department and the West's largest schools of engineering and architecture. Visitors and families are always welcome. For older children, see the Shakespeare Press Museum, or hike into Poly Canyon to see experimental architecture and construction. Kids of all ages will want to check out the Dairy Unit, where you can buy fresh-made ice cream and other dairy products at the campus store. Yum!

Where to Eat and Stay

Apple Farm Mill House, Restaurant and Inn, *2015 Monterey Street at U.S. Highway 101, just outside downtown San Luis Obispo; (805) 544–2040 or (800) 374–3705 for reservations and* **Free** *video tour; www.applefarm.com.* An authentic working gristmill set among gardens and waterfalls. The kids will love watching, and then eating, the results of an intricate series of pulleys, shafts, gears, and water producing fresh apple cider and even ice cream! A family restaurant here serves American favorites. The sixty-nine-unit motor inn is a fun place to stay, too, with rooms that feature early American decor and furnishings. Children under 18 **Free**. $$$

Embassy Suites Hotel, *333 Madonna Road, across from the Madonna Inn at U.S. Highway 101, San Luis Obispo; (805) 549–0800.* It has 195 two-room family suites, great rate specials, and a restaurant featuring American fare. More,

shall we say, traditional family lodgings than the neighboring Madonna Inn! $$$

Madonna Inn, *Roadside just south of downtown at U.S. Highway 101 and Madonna Road, San Luis Obispo; (805) 543–3000 or (800) 543–9666.* Not named after the provocative entertainer, this nonetheless hard-to-miss pink-and-white inn was built in 1959 by Alex and Phyllis Madonna. Each of the 109 guest rooms is wackily different. The Caveman Room was carved out of solid rock, for heaven's sake. The men's rest room is world famous for its imaginative waterfalls. The kids will definitely want to check this out! (Everyone does, for however strange, it's a Central Coast landmark. Trust us.) The restaurant is over the top in its pink decor (and its prices, too) for basic American fare. Stay if you dare but eat elsewhere. $$$

Pismo Beach Area

The Pismo Beach coastal resort area is actually comprised of the neighboring communities of Oceano, Grover Beach, Pismo Beach, Shell Beach, Avila Beach, and Port San Luis. The area stretches along U.S. Highway 101 and is only ten minutes south of the city of San Luis Obispo. Don't miss the Pismo Monarch Butterfly Grove, where these beautiful creatures congregate each winter. Tide-pooling is a great family activity at low tide; you never know what marine life or artifact you may find.

PISMO DUNES STATE BEACH VEHICULAR RECREATION AREA

Call (805) 473–7220 for complete details and entrance fees.

Rent all-terrain vehicles (ATVs) and cruise the sand dunes at the only place in California where it is still legal. Children under 18 must be accompanied by an adult or take a two-hour state certification safety test to pilot their own buggy.

B.J.'S ATV RENTALS

197 Grand Avenue, Grover Beach; (805) 481–5411 (reservations), (805) 481–0701 (fax). Cost per ATV approximately $42 per hour for adults. Children's machines also available.

The best place to rent your dream machine, with more than 200 to choose from. The staff is really helpful and concerned with your safety.

PISMO PIER

In the heart of downtown.

This 1,200-foot pier reopened in 1986. Great for strolling or fishing, but beware of nippy winter winds. Or rent some poles and try to catch your family dinner of red snapper or lingcod.

PORT SAN LUIS

At the very end of Avila Beach Road; (805) 595–5400.

This is a bustling fishing pier and commercial marina. Don't miss the chance to stroll down Harford Pier to find the **Free** marine touch tank and look into a fish-processing plant. You'll be amazed how fast sea creatures are transformed into seafood. Tons of salmon, crab, alba-core, halibut, cod, shark, and swordfish are brought in here every year by approximately seventy commercial fishing vessels.

*E*xtra *S*pecial *T*ip

Clamming Many families come to Pismo in search of the clams that made it famous around the turn of the last century. It is still known as the Clam Capital of the World. Minus tides are the best for clam digging; the limit is ten, each at least 4 inches in diameter. A California state fishing license is required to "catch" this bounty, however. Contact the Chamber of Commerce for current license vendors and more information.

GREAT AMERICAN MELODRAMA AND VAUDEVILLE THEATRE

1863 Front Street (State Route 1), Oceano; (805) 489–2499 for schedule and ticket prices.

Enjoy side-splitting comedy and family entertainment. Don't be put off by the industrial surroundings. Once inside this 260-seat old-fashioned cabaret-style hall, complete with sawdust on the floor, you'll feel completely at home. The theater is owned and operated by Lynn Schlenker and her family. The actors and actresses do triple duty—they serve you food and drinks before they perform, then act on stage, and finally they fraternize with you and other audience members after the show. The best time to attend is definitely during the December holiday season for *A Christmas Carol and Vaudeville Revue.*

Where to Eat

F. Mclintock's Saloon & Dining House, *750 Mattie Road, off U.S. Highway 101 between Spyglass Drive and Price Street exits, Pismo Beach; (805) 773–1892; www.mclintocks.com.* No visit to this area would be complete without enjoying dinner at this joint. It's easy to avoid the saloon and slip right into the dining rooms (voted as having the best kids menu in SLO County), where servers will amaze you with their fun attitudes and ability to pour water.

(Don't ask, just go and experience this!) The onion rings are a personal favorite, especially dipped in homemade salsa. Open for dinner daily and earlier on Sunday for brunch. $$$

Olde Port Inn, *Harford Pier, Port San Luis; (805) 595–2515.* Try some of the bounty from the sea at this historic dining spot. Downstairs is a very casual restaurant more suited for families. But upstairs offers a finer dining experience and an award-winning wine list. $$$

Where to Stay

Cottage Inn by the Sea, 2351 Price Street, Pismo Beach, 93449; (805) 773–4617 or (888) 440–8400; www.cottage-inn.com. The inn has seventy-nine units, all with gas fireplaces, many with ocean views and kitchenettes. You'll also enjoy charming English thatched-roof architecture with all modern amenities, plus free deluxe continental breakfast. There's an ocean-view pool and spa, plus beachside access down the cliff stairs. The inn is very friendly to families, with a welcoming staff. Call for specials and package plans. $$$

Spyglass Inn & Restaurant, 2705 Spyglass Drive, Pismo Beach, adjacent to U.S. Highway 101-Pacific Coast Highway 1, between Spyglass and Price Street exits. (800) 824–2612 or (805) 773–1892; www.spyglassinn.com. Located on the cliffs overlooking the Pacific Ocean, this nautical-themed eighty-two-room property is a super family value. Be sure to inquire about seasonal packages and specials. Guest rooms are spacious and many have ocean views. The heated pool and whirlpool make a relaxing destination after a day of "doing the coast." The Spyglass Restaurant, with its outdoor terraced decks, provides stunning ocean views and serves traditional American breakfast, lunch, and dinner daily—at prices that won't shock your wallet. Highly recommended. $$

For More Information

Pismo Beach Chamber of Commerce. 581 Dolliver Street, 93449; (805) 773–4382 or (800) 443–7778; www.pismochamber.com.

Arroyo Grande

"Wide gulch or streambed" is an English translation of this village's Spanish moniker. Founded in 1862, "A-roy-o Grahn-day" was settled in a wide fertile valley on either side of a creek that flows from the Santa Lucia Mountains to the Pacific Ocean. Branch Street is the main thoroughfare, one-quarter mile east off Highway 101. Many of the nineteenth-century buildings, like the Methodist Church, have been restored, and several have been turned into bed-and-breakfast inns.

 ### BURNARDOZ ICE CREAM
114 West Branch Street, downtown; (805) 481–2041. Open daily. $
Famous countywide. Yum! Plus, the trains and toys alone in this old-fashioned ice-cream parlor are worthy of a stop.

MUSTANG WATER SLIDES AND LOPEZ LAKE RECREATIONAL AREA

Outside Arroyo Grande, only 15 minutes off U.S. Highway 101 via Branch Street; (805) 489–8898 for directions and operating hours. Open daily.

There is camping, fishing, picnicking, water-skiing, and windsurfing (this is the favorite local place) year-round at Lopez Lake. The water slide is open from May to October. A refreshing good time!

Santa Barbara County

What do space shuttles, lemons, avocados, Danish pastries, and tri-tip barbecue have in common? They all are produced in the richly varied domain known as Santa Barbara County, named after the patron saint of mariners and travelers. With such a blessing, no wonder people from around the world are drawn here to visit and experience the joys of life. Santa Barbara County's Pacific sea breezes mean warm days and cooler nights both along the coast and in the interior valleys. The average annual temperature in Santa Barbara County is a mild sixty-two degrees. Very seldom do temperatures drop below forty in the winter or climb above ninety in the summer. Such great weather makes visitors as well as plants and produce happy.

The region's colonial history began when Portuguese explorer Juan Rodriguez Cabrillo sailed along the California coast in 1542 and claimed everything he saw for the Spanish crown. Sixty years later, another Portuguese seafarer, Sebastian Viscaino, dropped anchor in the bay. The day was December 4, the feast day of Saint Barbara, which explains the name given to the area. Both explorers were greeted warmly by the native Chumash Indians, who for 10,000 years or so had thrived in the area's gorgeous climate and year-round growing season. Viscaino's diary records the first evidence of the vaunted and legendary Santa Barbara hospitality. Today you can still experience the same warm welcome here with your family. Start at the Santa Maria River. Here's what you will discover.

Santa Maria

Heading south from San Luis Obispo County on U.S. Highway 101, you will cross into the Santa Maria Valley and find gentle foothills that descend toward the city of Santa Maria. It is surrounded by well-tended farms, where yummy you-can-pick-them strawberries and lots of produce are cultivated. Many award-winning vineyards and wineries are also located here; growers have discovered a micro-climate very similar to France. The town's roots are very deep in agriculture and ranching.

SANTA MARIA VALLEY DISCOVERY MUSEUM

321 Town Center West (located in Mervyn's Shopping Center); Santa Maria; (805) 928–8414, fax (805) 928–6634; www.discoverymuseumsantamaria.org; open Tuesday 11:00 A.M. to 4:00 P.M., Wednesday 10:00 A.M. to 5:00 P.M., Thursday and Friday 1:00 to 4:00 P.M., Saturday 11:00 A.M. to 4:00 P.M., and Sunday 1:00 to 4:00 P.M. $

More than thirty-five activities with eleven permanent exhibits and many rotating displays means you'll always find something fun for kids of all ages. Baby Space stimulates ages eight months to two years with colors, textures, shapes, mirrors, and sounds. In Toddler Territory, ages three to five pretend to be camping, enjoying the faux swimming hole, campfire, lean-to with picnic table, felt storyboard, and puppet theater. Check out the largest exhibit, SEA IT aboard the SS *Discovery;* straddle a life-sized John Deere tractor at Ag in the Valley; take a gander at the exotic arthropods in the Bug Zoo; the giant drawing table might beckon or perhaps Water in Your World or the Duck Under Kaleidoscope.

SANTA MARIA VALLEY HISTORICAL MUSEUM AND BARBECUE HALL OF FAME

616 South Broadway; (805) 922–3130. Open noon to 5:00 P.M., Tuesday to Saturday; closed major holidays. **Free** *admission; donations welcome.*

Have your kids "attend" the turn-of-the-last-century one-room schoolhouse, re-created here to help visitors appreciate how good things are today. The newly launched display of barbecue history and trivia is a hoot.

SANTA MARIA MUSEUM OF FLIGHT

3015 Airpark Drive; (805) 922–8758. Open Friday to Sunday, 10:00 A.M. to 4:00 P.M., April to November; 10:00 A.M. to 4:00 P.M. the rest of the year. **Free***, but donations appreciated.*

Aviators and wannabe pilots need to gear up for a visit to this exhibit, located next to the town airport within two dusty hangars. You can see the Fleet Model 2 and Stinson V77-Reliant airplanes, an extensive collection of model planes, and the once-secret Norden bombsight and its accessories.

Extra Special Tip

The History of Santa Maria–Style Barbecue The region's ranching heritage is most evident in the continuing tradition of Santa Maria–style barbecue. This cooking style dates back to the Spanish vaquero (cowboy) days, when a special cut of beef was butchered, marinated, and slow cooked over red-hot oak wood. This triangular cut of sirloin, the "tri-tip," is served with special Santa Maria Valley–grown pinquito beans, garden fresh tossed salad, toasted sourdough bread, and spicy salsa. You can find tri-tips sizzling most every weekend in barbecue pits on downtown street corners or marketplaces, presided over by cooks who are generally raising money for local service clubs.

WALLER COUNTY PARK
300 Goodwin Road, Orcutt Expressway and Waller Lane; (805) 934–6211 or (805) 937–1302. Open daily.
One hundred-acre park with lake, fountains, a waterfall, fishing, playgrounds, baseball diamonds, and most important for kids, pony rides. Call for schedule and fees.

Extra Special Tip

Guadalupe Dunes Head 9 miles west out of Santa Maria to the end of State Route 166, and your kids will think you've landed in the Sahara Desert by the Sea—officially known as the **Guadalupe-Nipomo Dunes Preserve.** Up to 500-foot sand dunes stretch for 18 miles along the Pacific Ocean here. More than 1,400 species of animals including 200 kinds of birds, and 244 species of plants migrate or live in this undisturbed, windswept landscape. To fully appreciate this magnificent work of nature, make your first stop at the **Dunes Visitor Center,** located in a restored Victorian house in downtown Guadalupe at 1055 Guadalupe Street; (805) 343–2455 or www.dunescenter.org. This wonderful, family-oriented facility provides entertaining interactive exhibits on dune mammals, birds, plants, and history. (Did you know that Cecile B. DeMille's 1923 film set of *The Ten Commandments* is buried underneath these dunes?) Free maps and tour programs are provided. If hunger strikes, mosey into the **Far Western,** a family-owned and -operated dining hall serving families lunch and dinner daily at 899 Guadalupe Street; (805) 343–2211. Your kids will groove on the rawhide booths and ranching artifacts while you savor the excellent steaks.

YMCA SKATEBOARD PARK

3400 Skyway Drive, Santa Maria; (805) 937–8521. Call for fees and operating hours.

Located adjacent to the YMCA facility, this 15,000-square-foot park contains numerous ramps, including quarter pipes, half pipes, boxes, rails, jumps, hills, and a vertical ramp. A special area for beginners is available.

Where to Eat

Klondike Pizza, *2059 South Broadway, Santa Maria; (805) 348–3667. Open daily from 11:00 A.M.* Total family-fun food—pizza, burgers, salads—and free roasted peanuts in shells that you're encouraged to throw on the floor. $

Maya Restaurant, *110 South Lincoln, Santa Maria; (805) 925–2841. Open daily from 8:00 A.M. to 9:00 P.M.* Family-owned establishment serving breakfast, lunch, and dinner, featuring Mexican specialties including homemade tortillas and fresh salsa. $

Where to Stay

Historic Santa Maria Inn, *801 South Broadway, exit Main Street west off U.S. Highway 101, then south on Broadway, Santa Maria; (805) 928–7777.* Near Santa Maria Town Center Mall shopping and area attractions, this English-style country inn was built in 1917 and has expanded over the years to include a restaurant serving lunch and dinner, a wine cellar, a gift shop, and newer tower suites for a total of 166 units. Be sure to inquire for current family package plans and special deals. A good choice for value in the area. $$$

For More Information

Santa Maria Valley Chamber of Commerce and Visitor & Convention Bureau. *614 South Broadway, 93454; (800) 331–3779 or (805) 925–2403; www.santamaria.com.*

Lompoc Valley

Say Lompoc (Lahm-poke) with me now, and then your entire family can start saying "oooh" and "aahhh" if you visit during the summer, when awesome fields of flowers bloom practically everywhere you gaze. Lompoc is a Chumash Indian word meaning "little lake" or "lagoon." More than 58,000 people call this beautiful Valley home now, including the military personnel at Vandenberg

Air Force Base. Don't miss more than 60 murals throughout the city. (Contact the Chamber of Commerce for a map.)

LOMPOC FLOWER FIELDS

Downtown Lompoc at the corner of Ocean Avenue and C Street; as well as along State Route 246, State Route 1 and Sweeney Road.

This valley produces a good part of the world's flower seeds. Over 1,000 acres are covered with more than 200 varieties of flowers, including marigolds, asters, larkspur, calendula, lavender, and cornflowers. To help "blooming idiots" identify these gems, there is a helpful, fully labeled display garden. The Lompoc Flower Festival is held every June to celebrate this incredible presentation of nature.

LA PURISIMA MISSION STATE HISTORIC PARK

Three miles northeast of State Route 246 at 2295 Purisima Road; (805) 773–3713. $

See the Americanos' complete and authentic restoration of this important mission back to the way it was in the 1800s. The primitive but effective water system has also been restored and will give kids a fresh appreciation for running *agua*. There are gardens, hiking trails, and picnic facilities.

Extra Special Tip

Lasso-ed into Los Alamos As you travel U.S. Highway 101, midway between San Luis Obispo and Santa Barbara, you'll discover a genuine Western town worth your family's visit. Now inhabited by about 1,200 friendly folks, Los Alamos (Spanish for "the cottonwoods") was founded by ranchers in 1876 and became a popular stagecoach and railroad stop—its appearance hasn't changed much since. (Yes, the town still sports two saloons and a wine tasting room!) For accommodations, check into the hillside **Skyview Motel,** with stunning 360-degree valley views, (805) 344–3770, or the quaint **Alamo Motel** (805-344-2852). The historic 1880 Union Hotel is open only for special events. For foodstuffs, check out the Quakenbush Cafe and Art Gallery, the Twin Oaks Restaurant, or Javy's Mexican Cafe, all on the main drag, Bell Street. Don't miss the antiques stores and the Depot Mall Antique Center in the old railroad station. The town honors its heritage during the last weekend of September with an annual Old Days Celebration. Here's to living history! See www.LosAlamosInfo.com.

VANDENBERG AIR FORCE BASE (ages 10 and up)

Public Affairs Office, 747 Nebraska Avenue, Room #A103, VAFB, 93437; (805) 606–3595; www.vandenberg.af.mil.

This base, begun in 1941, is located on the outskirts of Lompoc on 99,000 acres of incredibly beautiful Pacific oceanfront property that also includes an ecological preserve. This is the home of the U.S. military's West Coast Space Operations, including research and development. Fully guided base tours may be available. Call for current schedule and details.

For More Information

Lompoc Valley Chamber of Commerce and Visitors Bureau. *111 South I ("Eye") Street, 93436; (805) 736–4567 or (800) 240–0999; www.lompoc.com.*

The Santa Ynez Valley

South of Santa Maria on U.S. Highway 101, bordered by the Santa Ynez and San Rafael mountains, lies the Santa Ynez Valley. Many families bypass this magnificent triangle bisected by State Routes 154 and 246, home of more than fifty award-winning wineries and vineyards. Don't you dare miss these five towns that are only forty-five minutes inland from the coastal city of Santa Barbara yet feel like a world away: **Buellton**—home of the original Pea Soup Anderson's Restaurant, the commercial gateway to the valley; **Ballard**—with its continuously operating one-room school; **Los Olivos**—where the movie *Return to Mayberry* was filmed and many artists and galleries reside; **Santa Ynez** itself—a thoroughly western burg; and the largest town of **Solvang**—truly another world, it is Southern California's little bit of Denmark. As the locals say, "Velkommen!"

Solvang means "sunny fields" in Danish. You and your family will find plenty of sunny hospitality in this beautiful village, where the spirit of the founding Danes lives on. Visualize windmills, thatched-roof cottages with dormers and gables, fresh Danish pastries, groaning smorgasbords, kitschy trinket shops, friendly folks, comfortable lodging, and lots of sunshine. More than 300 stores in downtown Solvang will tempt you to open your wallet. You may become laden with goodies, including porcelain figurines, handmade lace, music boxes, jewelry, sweaters, candies, and western wear.

THE HONEN

Copenhagen Drive near First Street; (805) 686–0022. Daily operations in summer, seasonally on weekends and holidays. $.

Turn-of-the-last-century Copenhagen streetcar is pulled by two Belgian draft horses. Twenty-minute ride around town originates from the Solvang Visitor Center.

 HANS CHRISTIAN ANDERSEN MUSEUM

1680 Mission Drive in the Book Loft building; (805) 688–2052. **Free**.
Andersen was the Danish father of the modern fairy tale. See his books, sketches, paper cutouts, and collages.

 ELVERHOJ DANISH HERITAGE AND FINE ARTS MUSEUM

1624 Elverhoj Way; (805) 686–1211. Open Wednesday to Sunday. **Free**.
Located on a residential street, this attraction lets you discover the origins of Solvang's fascinating history and Danish legacy.

MISSION SANTA INES

1760 Mission Drive; (805) 688–4815, right near the village center. $
Number nineteen in the chain of twenty-one missions along the coast. Dedicated in 1804, Mission Santa Ines continues to hold services as well as to provide a museum for original Indian paintings, seventeenth-century European artworks, and religious vestments. The mission also houses a serene meditation garden in a quadrangle inside the walls. A perfect escape if your family is overdosing on Danish.

PACIFIC CONSERVATORY OF THE PERFORMING ARTS (PCPA)

In Solvang's outdoor Festival Theater at 420 Second Street; (805) 922–8313 or (800) 549–7272 for tickets and schedules. June to October; www.pcpa.org.
Stages world-class Theater Under the Stars, a Santa Barbara County family tradition. Don't miss out on the experience during your visit!

Extra Special Tip

Danish Food No visit to Solvang would be complete without tasting *aebleskivers*—the raspberry-jam-draped, powdered-sugar-coated Danish pancake balls sold throughout the village. This Danish version of the donut is made with a special flour in a unique round cast-iron pan and is definitely delicious. Be on the lookout for *frikadeller* (meat balls), *medisterpoise* (sausages), and *rodkaal* (red cabbage).

WINDHAVEN GLIDER RIDES

Santa Ynez Valley Airport, off State Route 246, near intersection of State Route 154; (805) 688–2517; www.gliderrides.com. Daily glider plane flights, weather permitting. Reservations highly recommended. Call for fares.

Two-seater planes flown by FAA-certified commercial pilots at approximately 2,500 feet and, pardon the pun, up from there! An incredible experience for older children to share with the folks.

NOJOQUI FALLS COUNTY PARK

Seven miles southwest of Solvang on Alisal Road. Open daily dawn to dusk. **Free.**

This 182-acre site is worth a visit to see the 164-foot waterfall (after a rainy season, of course). Rent a mountain bike and head for the waterfall or take the non-strenuous walking trail. Plenty of picnic spots and places to savor your Danish treats.

QUICKSILVER MINIATURE HORSE RANCH

Just east of Solvang on Alamo Pintado Road; (805) 686–4002. Open daily except Thanksgiving and Christmas from 10:00 A.M. to 3:00 P.M. **Free.**

Has everything from 18-inch newborns to 34-inch mature animals that will be sure to amaze and delight everyone.

OSTRICH LAND

610 East Highway 246 between Buellton and Solvang; (805) 686–9696. Open every day. **Free** *tours.*

This ranch is home to hundreds of the biggest birds in the world, reaching 8.5 feet in height and weighing up to 350 pounds when mature. Impress your children with the fun fact that ostriches run faster than any two-legged animal. How fast? Up to 45 miles per hour!

SANTA YNEZ VALLEY HISTORICAL MUSEUM AND PARKS–JANEWAY CARRIAGE HOUSE

3596 Sagunto Street, downtown Santa Ynez; (805) 688–7889. Open Tuesday to Sunday, closed most major holidays. **Free.** *Donations welcome.*

You can relive the valley's Old West origins with vehicles, including a full-size, outfitted covered wagon, phaetons, donkey carts, and a stagecoach. Don't miss the farm machinery, implements, saddle collection, and works by famed silversmith Edward Bohlin.

Extra Special Tip

Wining and Picnicking The Santa Ynez Valley is the premier, award-winning wine region of Southern California and home to more than fifty wineries, vineyards, and tasting rooms that include such household names as Fess Parker and Firestone. Older children may be fascinated by the rituals of grape growing, harvesting, and wine making, but they will have to wait until they are twenty-one to do more than sniff the bouquet. Many vineyards and wineries have lovely picnic areas that make delightful lunch spots for the entire family year-round. Contact the Santa Barbara County Vintners Association at (800) 218-0881 or www.sbcountywines.com for a free map and more information.

LAKE CACHUMA COUNTY PARK

20 minutes outside Solvang, 18 miles northwest along Scenic State Route 154 over the San Marcos Pass from Santa Barbara; (805) 688–4658. Two-hour guided eagle cruises available seasonally. Call for schedule. $$

This human-made lake (pronounced Ka-choo-ma) takes its name from a nearby Chumash village. The reservoir has a dual purpose as Santa Barbara's water supply, but is more famous as the winter home of hundreds of bald eagles. The eagle cruises, aboard comfortable pontoon (patio) boats, bring you and your "eagle-eyed" children within 200 yards of the birds' roosting sites. More than 275 other species of birds have been identified on the lake, plus plenty of fish, other wildlife, trees, and plants.

Forty-two miles of shoreline offer 500 regular campsites and ninety EWS hookups on a first-come, first-served basis. There are **hiking, fishing, boating,** and other facilities galore, including a general store, Laundromat, snack bar, marina, picnic areas, and barbecues for daytime use year-round.

Where to Eat

Cold Spring Tavern, *5995 Stagecoach Road, one-half mile off State Route 154, approximately thirty minutes from Solvang and twenty minutes from Santa Barbara; (805) 967–0066.* Make a detour as you go over the San Marcos Pass upon leaving the Santa Ynez Valley and wet your whistle like horse-drawn passengers on the stagecoaches of yesteryear did.

Since the 1880s, this historic spot has been serving lunch and dinner and libations daily. Hearty country breakfast on Saturday and Sunday. Kids will love the rustic walls, stone floors, and chance to eat buffalo burgers and venison stew. Family owned and operated. $$$

Pea Soup Andersen's Restaurant and Motor Inn, *One block west of junc-*

tion U.S. Highway 101 and Highway 246 in Buellton; (805) 688–5581. Open from 6:30 A.M. to 10:30 P.M. every day. Home of the original (1924) restaurant serving hearty, bottomless bowls of split pea soup and other family favorites. This is one of our family's traditional stopovers, no matter what the occasion. The inn has ninety-seven rooms around an attractive central courtyard with a pool, spa, and putting green. Good value for a roadside stopover. $$

Where to Stay

Alisal Guest Ranch and Resort, *Two minutes outside the village of Solvang at 1054 Alisal Road; (805) 688–6411 or (800) 4A–ALISAL; www.alisal.com. Rates include dinner and full American breakfast served in the homey Ranch Room.* This is a truly one-of-a-kind family-owned and -operated haven after "doing Danish" all day. The resort boasts seventy-three family bungalows with wood-burning fireplaces and no television or telephones in your room. The peace of this 10,000-acre working ranch envelops you immediately upon driving up the tree-lined lane.

Organized family activities and supervised play are featured all summer long. Year-round, you and yours can swim, spa, take in a movie, read in the library, play on one of the Alisal's two golf courses, try your hand at tennis, go horseback riding, or spend a day at Alisal's private 90-acre spring-fed lake for fishing, swimming, canoeing, and sailing.

A two-night minimum stay is required—and worth every moment! Be sure to call for special seasonal packages. Since 1946 the Alisal has been welcoming generations of families with its western hospitality and charm. We recommend you consider starting a family tradition of your own here. $$$$

Rancho Santa Barbara Marriott Hotel, *555 McMurray Road, Buellton, 93427; (805) 688–1000. www.santaynez hotels.com.* Conveniently located at the intersection of U.S. Highway 101 and State Route 246, the gateway to the Santa Ynez Valley. You'll find 149 well-appointed rooms and suites, most with a balcony or patio. There's a large outdoor pool, spa, game room, fitness center, and family-friendly dining on-premises and within walking distance. Excellent value. Ask about promotional packages. $$$

For More Information

Buellton Visitors Bureau & Chamber of Commerce. *376 Avenue of the Flags, 93427; (805) 688–STAY or (800) 324–3800; www.buellton.org.*

Los Olivos Business Organization. *Box 280, Los Olivos, 93441; (805) 688–1222; www.losolivosca.com.*

Santa Ynez Valley Visitors Association. *Box 1918, Santa Ynez, 93460; (800) 742–2843; www.santaynezvalleyvisit.com.*

Solvang Conference & Visitors Bureau. *1511 Mission Drive, 93464; (800) 468–6765 or (805) 688–6144; www.solvangusa.com.*

Santa Barbara

If you and the kids want outdoor recreation, nature, scenery, stars, shopping, history lessons, museums, art, culture, great restaurants, and trendy places to hang out, just make your plans for the destination resort of Santa Barbara. The city was first hailed as a prime tourist stop in 1872 by East Coast travel writer Charles Nordhoff, who said, "Santa Barbara certainly is the most pleasant place throughout the state." The blend of Chumash, Spanish, Mexican, and American cultures has given Santa Barbara an extremely rich heritage— which is visible in the city's lovely buildings with red-tiled roofs and whitewashed adobe walls. Devastated by an earthquake in 1925, downtown Santa Barbara was rebuilt in a Spanish-Moorish colonial motif that is strictly regulated by law.

Along with architecture, locals are proud of their area's well-preserved natural beauty, bounded by the Santa Ynez Mountains and Pacific Ocean to the south. Yes, that's right. All the beaches face south along the Pacific (the only place in the United States where this happens), so when you want to check out the magnificent sunsets, you must look over the mountains behind you, not over the water. This takes some getting used to, so you just might have to stay an extra night to see it again!

MISSION SANTA BARBARA

2201 Laguna Street, at the corner of Laguna and East Los Olivos Streets, approximately five minutes from downtown; (805) 682–4149. Open daily from 9:00 A.M. to 5:00 P.M.; except Easter, Thanksgiving, and Christmas. $

You will definitely want to tour "the Queen of the Missions" and still the longest continuously operating parish among California's renowned chain of twenty-one missions. Founded on December 4, 1786, the feast day of Saint Barbara, and finally completed in 1820, it is one of the best-preserved missions. A fascinating self-guided walking tour that includes artworks, fountains, a courtyard, and a cemetery is available.

SANTA BARBARA MUSEUM OF NATURAL HISTORY AND PLANETARIUM

2559 Puesta del Sol Road (just around the corner from the Santa Barbara Mission), (805) 682–4711; www.sbnature.org. Hours Monday to Saturday 9:00 A.M. to 5:00 P.M., Sunday and holidays 10:00 A.M. to 5:00 P.M. $$. Free *to all on the last Sunday of every month.*

Extra Special Tip

Special Santa Barbara Festivals
Festivals and celebrations abound in the city of Santa Barbara year-round. Oak Park, on the city's north side, hosts ethnic and cultural festivals in the spring and summer. However, the following two events are worth a special visit for your entire family, from toddler to grandparent.

Summer Solstice Celebration. This is a fantasy fun romp celebrating the arrival of summer on the Saturday closest to the first day of summer. The parade features no motorized floats or amplified music, but almost one hundred "non-floats," including **bands, clowns, dancers,** and perhaps a **rubber sea of sharks, rolling bubble machines,** or even a **briefcase brigade of lawyers.** A different theme is carried out each year. After the parade up State Street from the waterfront, the participants and spectators all congregate at Alameda Park at the corner of Sola and Anacapa Streets. You will love the energy, color, food booths, and vendors at this afternoon, post-parade party. The day concludes with a musical and dramatic program on a stage set up at the Courthouse Sunken Gardens at nightfall. For more information and a detailed schedule of events, call (805) 965-3396.

Old Spanish Days (Fiesta). If you visit during the first weekend of August, experience the sights, sounds, and foods of California's early settlers during Old Spanish Days. Commonly known as Fiesta, the celebrations begin with the padre's blessing on the steps on the historic mission on Wednesday evening, followed by performances by the junior (under twelve) and senior (under eighteen) Spirit of Fiesta Dancers. Your family will shout "Viva la Fiesta!" along with the natives during Friday's **Annual El Desfile Historico**—one of the world's most colorful parades, attracting the most horses and riders in America along with 100,000 enthusiastic spectators.

Your kids can participate in **El Desfile de Los Ninos** (the **Children's Parade**) on Saturday morning. During the five-day festival, the entire family can enjoy the *mercados* (marketplaces with traditional foods), **carnival rides at the beach,** and the family entertainment spectacular, **Noches de Ronda,** each evening under the stars in the gardens of the courthouse. Call (805) 962-8101 year-round for free brochures and schedules; www.oldspanishdays-fiesta.org.

The museum has exhibits on early Native American tribes as well as animals, birds, insects, plants, minerals, marine science, and geology. The planetarium hosts impressive star shows. Call (805) 682–3224 for a schedule.

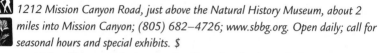

SANTA BARBARA BOTANIC GARDEN
1212 Mission Canyon Road, just above the Natural History Museum, about 2 miles into Mission Canyon; (805) 682–4726; www.sbbg.org. Open daily; call for seasonal hours and special exhibits. $

Kids will love exploring the 5 miles of trails through forests and plant life on 65 exquisite acres devoted only to California species. Guided tours available.

SANTA BARBARA HISTORICAL MUSEUM AND COVARRUBIAS ADOBE
136 East de la Guerra Street, downtown; (805) 966–1601. Tuesday to Saturday, 10:00 A.M. to 5:00 P.M., Sunday, noon to 5:00 P.M. **Free**. *Donations appreciated.*

The Santa Barbara Historical Museum's permanent exhibits include documents, furniture, decorative and fine arts, and costumes from all periods of the area's history. Covarrubias Adobe, circa 1817, may have served briefly as the headquarters of Pio Pico, the last Mexican governor of California. Guided tours available.

EL PRESIDIO DE SANTA BARBARA STATE HISTORIC PARK
100–200 blocks of East Canon Perdido Street, downtown; (805) 965–0093. Open daily 10:30 A.M. to 4:30 P.M. except for major holidays. **Free**.

This was the last military outpost built by Spain in the New World, dedicated in 1782. A continuous project restores the actual structures including El Cuartel, padre's quarters; the chapel, and the commandant's office. A slide show and guided tours are offered upon request. This is a piece of living history you just can't ignore. Our kids really liked the story of the lost cannon. Ask a docent for the details.

SANTA BARBARA MUSEUM OF ART
1130 State Street; (805) 963–4364. Open Tuesday to Saturday 11:00 A.M. to 5:00 P.M., Friday to 9:00 P.M., and Sunday noon to 5:00 P.M. $. **Free** *admission on the first Sunday of every month and every Thursday.*

The museum has important works by American and European artists, including Monet and other impressionists. Displays include American, Asian, and nineteenth-century French art, plus Greek and Roman antiquities and major photographic works. Special exhibits rotate throughout the year. Narrated tours available, usually at 1:00 P.M. The Children's Gallery is outstanding. And don't miss the lovely Cafe and Museum Store.

KARPELES MANUSCRIPT LIBRARY MUSEUM

21 West Anapamu Street (one-half block off State); (805) 962–5322. Open daily 10:00 A.M. to 4:00 P.M. **Free**.

Houses original manuscripts of great authors, scientists, and leaders from all periods of history. Rotating exhibits show fascinating glimpses into antiquity.

*E*xtra *S*pecial *T*ip

Book Row Located along Anapamu Street on opposite sides of State Street, this area is affectionately called "book row." It is anchored by the impressive 225,000-volume **Santa Barbara Public Library** at 40 East Anapamu, (805) 962-7653. You and your family will discover the joy of finding every type of literature imaginable in the following unique, independent Santa Barbara bookstores. Special events with authors and storytellers abound, so be sure to contact each shop for schedules and hours of operation.

- **Pacific Travellers Supply,** *12 West Anapamu, (805) 963–4438*—guidebooks, maps, and luggage
- **Metro Comics & Entertainment,** *6 West Anapamu, (805) 963–2168.*
- **The Book Den,** *11 East Anapamu, (805) 962–3321*—used, rare and out-of-print books
- **Paradise Found,** *17 East Anapamu, (805) 564–3573*—metaphysical books
- **Sullivan Goss Books & Prints,** *7 East Anapamu (805) 730–1460*—art books
- **Valley Book & Bible,** *1200 State Street at Anapamu, (805) 884–5166.*

On the Waterfront

STEARNS WHARF. *At the foot of State Street on the waterfront; (805) 564–5518. Parking is $2.00 per hour or* Free *with a wharf merchant purchase validation.* Built in 1872 to serve cargo and passenger ships, this Santa Barbara historic landmark is now the site of specialty shops, family-friendly restaurants, a small museum, a boat charter dock, and a fishing spot. You can actually drive as well as walk onto the wharf. The kids think it sounds like rumbling thunder when you drive across the wooden planks. Don't worry, it really is quite safe.

THE NATURE CONSERVANCY. *213 Stearns Wharf; (805) 962–9111. Open daily, except major holidays,* Free. A visitor center dispenses information about the conservancy's Santa Cruz Island Preserve at the Channel Islands some 24 miles off the coast.

CAPTAIN DON'S HARBOR TOURS. *219 Stearns Wharf; (805) 969–5217. Call for current schedule and fares.* Offers a variety of sunset cruises, coastal excursions year-round, and whale-watching trips in winter.

SANTA BARBARA MARITIME MUSEUM. *In the Marina, 113 Harbor Way, (805) 962–8404; www.sbmm.org. Open daily 10:00 A.M. to 4:00 P.M. Call for hours and admission fees.* Located in the former Naval Reserve Building in the heart of the harbor, the museum illustrates the evolution of nautical technology, starting with local origins in the Chumash culture up to modern-day boats and submarines. Highly interactive exhibits are kid-friendly.

SANTA BARBARA YACHT HARBOR, MARINA, AND BREAKWATER. *West of Stearns Wharf, motor entrance along Cabrillo Boulevard just past Castillo Street intersection. Harbor Master's office phone, (805) 564–5520.* More than 1,000 work and pleasure craft rest at Santa Barbara's fascinating yacht harbor and breakwater, home to the city's commercial fishing fleet, which rakes in a catch of more than $6 million annually. Where else can you get "up close and personal" with a spiny sea urchin heading off to market or purchase shrimp, rock cod, and crab fresh from the fisherfolk themselves? Take the older children for a walk along the half-mile breakwater and dodge the incoming surf. Not for the water-timid during high winds or rough seas! Your family's ticket to floating fun can be found right here at the following vendors.

SEA LANDING. *In the marina; (805) 882–0088; www.condorcruises. com. Call (888) 77–WHALE for current schedules and fares.* Hook your own seafood on a fishing expedition charter boat that docks here, or sign up for a dive trip. This is also the home dock of the new *Condor Express,* a 75-foot, 149-passenger high-speed jet-powered catamaran, custom designed and launched in 2002 specifically for naturalist-led whale-watching trips, sunset cruises, and group charters.

TRUTH AQUATICS. *In the marina; (805) 962–1127. Call for seasonal times, schedules, and fares.* Arranges popular scuba and diving charters and also acts as official concessionaire for boat trips to the **Channel Islands National Park,** some 20 miles offshore. (See listing in Ventura section for more details on the park.)

SANTA BARBARA SAILING CENTER. *In the marina; (805) 962– 2826 or (800) 350–9090; www.sbsailctr.com.* Rent a sailboat (with or without a skipper) or even a Jet Ski or Wave Runner. This is the home dock of the *Double Dolphin* catamaran, a forty-nine-passenger sailboat that runs whale-watching trips, sunset cruises, and private charters. The sailing school here offers beginning through advanced instructions. Call about family learn-to-sail packages, including accommodations. How would you like to live aboard a sailboat while learning the ropes and sheets?

Extra Special Tip

"Take a Vacation from your Car!" It's easy to do by accessing a new Web site, www.santabaracarfree.org, or calling (805) 696–1100. Discover walking tours, bike maps, bus routes, AMTRAK schedules, free maps, and vacation packages/hotel discounts. Plus, there is a 25-cent electric shuttle that runs along State Street and the waterfront. State Street, Santa Barbara's most famous thoroughfare, leads into the heart of downtown. It is extremely pedestrian- and family-friendly, with benches, outdoor dining, and plenty of greenery.

KIDS WORLD

In Alameda Park, at the corner of Micheltorena and Garden Streets, downtown.
Free.

Designed by city children and built by them, as well as community volunteers, this two-story wooden play land is truly a kid's dream come to life. A tot lot and sandbox are available for the very young, while older sibs can cruise through tunnels and stride over bridges or clamber up the tree house. Way cool fun!

SANTA BARBARA COUNTY COURTHOUSE

1100 Anacapa Street, downtown; (805) 962–6464. Open Monday to Friday 8:00 A.M. to 5:00 P.M., Saturday and Sunday 10:00 A.M. to 5:00 P.M. **Free.**

Most kids would not want to tour a courthouse, except in Santa Barbara, where you can climb the 80-foot clock tower stairs (or take the elevator, for us fogeys) for a stunning panoramic view over the city, all the way to the ocean. The courthouse was built in 1929. You cannot miss the award-winning Spanish-Moorish design from anywhere in the city. Its sunken gardens are perfect for picnicking.

SANTA BARBARA ZOOLOGICAL GARDENS

500 Ninos Drive, 2 blocks from East Beach off Cabrillo Boulevard; (805) 962–5339. Open daily 9:00 A.M. to 6:00 P.M. during the summer months and 10:00 A.M. to 5:00 P.M. the rest of the year. $$

This is as wild as Santa Barbara gets! The zoo is renowned for its easy accessibility and more than eighty exhibits with 700 child-friendly animals, including big cats, roaring elephants, and gangly giraffes. The huge aviary is a favorite. The zoo, on a former estate overlooking the glittering Pacific, is a must-see. Take a picnic lunch to eat after your morning visit or savor a tasty snack in the **Ridley-Tree House Cafe.** The miniature train that circumnavigates the zoo's beautiful garden setting is a big plus, and so are the dedicated playground and all the services (easy access bathrooms, strollers, guided tours, zoo-camp programs for children, just to name a few).

CHASE PALM PARK & CAROUSEL

Stretching east from Stearns Wharf along the waterfront on both sides of beachfront Cabrillo Boulevard.

In May 1998, the ten-acre north side of the park opened with a totally festive antique carousel (enclosed in its own pavilion, nominal fee, open daily); a kids-only (toddler to twelve years) Shipwreck Playground with a rubberized deck; grassy knolls and picnic tables, rest rooms, a snack bar, and an entertainment zone. "Way cool" characterizes this area—don't miss this park on your tour of the beach area.

Extra Special Tip

Whale-Watching The Santa Barbara Channel is becoming well-known not only for the traditional California gray whale migration that occurs annually here between late January and mid-April but also as a year-round whale viewing and research destination. More than twenty-seven different types of whales inhabit the waters offshore. Blue whales, the largest animals ever to live on earth, have been seen here for the past few summers, apparently feeding on the abundant krill. Humpback whales, minke whales, and orcas or killer whales are also often sighted on channel excursions, not to mention porpoises, dolphins, sea lions, and harbor seals. Contact any of the charter boat operators at the harbor or marina for current whale-watching schedules and fees.

THE UNIVERSITY OF CALIFORNIA AT SANTA BARBARA (UCSB)

In the neighboring town of Isla Vista, 2 miles south of U.S. Highway 101 via Ward Memorial Boulevard (State Route 217). Free *campus tours; (805) 893–2485. The UCSB Family Vacation Center; (805) 893–3123; www.instadv. ucsb.edu/vacation.*

The gorgeous 815-acre, oceanfront campus features the landmark Storke Tower, University Center, and renowned Marine Sciences Institute. During July and August, the UCSB Alumni Association offers eight weeklong sessions, providing a fully programmed family resort. Rates include three meals daily, residential hall living, recreational and social activities, all-day child care, and theme programs. This incredible Santa Barbara family vacation bargain sells out each summer.

SOUTH COAST RAILROAD MUSEUM

300 North Los Carneros Road in adjacent town of Goleta; (805) 964–3540 for track times for the miniature train. Generally open Wednesday through Sunday. Free.

Budding conductors and engineers will want to explore the wooden Goleta depot. Built in 1901, the depot was in use until 1973, when it was dismantled and moved to its current site. Restoration began in 1981, and the collection of railroad memorabilia continues to grow.

Where to Eat

Sambo's on the Beach, *216 West Cabrillo Boulevard, two blocks from Stearns Wharf; (805) 965–3269.* This is the original and only remaining Sambo's restaurant founded here in 1957 by two Santa Barbara friends (Sam Battistone and Newall "Bo" Bohnett). Owned and operated by Sam's grandson Chad Stevens, Sambo's dishes up hearty breakfasts featuring their famous pancakes and syrup, and all-American lunches, served seven days a week. $$

Santa Barbara County Certified Farmer's Markets, *(805) 962–5354 for seasonal times.* The freshest fruits and veggies available. The most popular site is in downtown Santa Barbara every Saturday, at the corner of Cota and Santa Barbara Streets (2 blocks off State) from 8:30 A.M. to 12:30 P.M. Kids will love the musicians, jugglers, and clowns, plus the free samples available from generous vendors. Also in Goleta, Carpinteria, and Montecito. $

Woody's Barbecue, *5112 Hollister Avenue, Goleta; (805) 967–3775.* Dishing up Santa Barbara's favorite BBQ ribs and chicken. Kids' meals start at $2.95, making this a great family value. Don't worry about getting messy—just throw the peanut shells on the floor, slather on the sauce, and clean off in the old bathtub washbasin provided. $

Where to Stay

El Capitan Canyon, *11560 Calle Real, Goleta, CA 93117; (805) 685–3887 or (866) 352–2729; www.elcapitancanyon. com.* An ocean-side retreat only 17 miles from downtown Santa Barbara; private, family-owned property on 300 acres featuring cozy cabins and safari-canvas tents. A kids camp, botanical hikes, massages, swimming pool, campfires, and outdoor summer concerts are highlights, along with bicycling and it's only a half-mile from the beach for watersports. A grocery store, gift shop, and deli are here too. Absolutely ideal for families. $$$

Fess Parker's Doubletree Resort, *633 East Cabrillo Boulevard; (805) 564–4333 or (800) 879–2929; www.fpdtr.com.* Owned in part by local resident Fess Parker (famous for his *Davy Crockett* acting role), this Spanish Mission–style property has all the requirements of a headquarters for your family oceanfront vacation. Located on twenty-three acres across from East Beach, this 360-room resort (Santa Barbara County's largest) has a heated outdoor swimming pool, whirlpool, fitness center, spa, beauty salon, gift shop, putting green, tennis and basketball courts, bicycle and skate rental shop, game room, and full concierge services. Two restaurants and a lounge at the resort include the casual, California cuisine of **Cafe Los Arcos** for breakfast, lunch, and dinner (best for kids); **Rodney's Steakhouse** for dinner; and Barra Los Arcos, hosting happy hours and live entertainment (best for adults). Roomy accommodations feature ocean, mountain, or courtyard views—many with patios or decks—great for enjoying the fresh sea breezes. Call for seasonal specials and package plans. $$$$

San Ysidro Ranch Resort, *900 San Ysidro Lane, Montecito; (800) 368–6788 or (805) 969–5046; www.sanysidroranch. com.* A legendary luxury resort catering to families since 1893. It's located on 500 rolling acres overlooking the Pacific, only 2 miles from the beach. Accommodations are in forty-four cottages with names like Creek, Rose, Jasmine, and Pine and feature deluxe furnishings, fireplaces, and decks or patios. Many have private whirlpool spas and wet bars. The award-winning Stonehouse Restaurant and Plow & Angel Bistro on premises serve regional American cuisine. Camp SYR is the summertime and holiday seasonal children's program that wins rave reviews from kids and parents alike. Highlights include nature hikes, arts and crafts in the Treehouse—the official headquarters—and trained staff to take care of kids ages two to twelve. This is one of the finest properties for families who want (and can afford) only the very best. $$$$

Upham Hotel & Garden Cottages, *1404 De La Vina Street, just 2 blocks off State Street, downtown; (805) 962–0058 or (800) 727–0876; www.uphamhotel.com.* Built in 1871, the Upham is Santa Barbara County's oldest continuously operating hotel. It is located on an acre of eye-catching gardens. You can choose from fifty different Victorian-style rooms or cottages, filled with comfortable, not stuffy antiques. Kids like to play in the garden courtyard with the resident cat, while the older folks enjoy complimentary afternoon wine and cheese. All rates include a deluxe continental all-you-can-eat breakfast buffet, plus Oreo cookies and milk in the evening—a big child pleaser! You can leave your car and walk to all the downtown attractions, or take the 25 cent shuttle bus 14 blocks down to the waterfront. The hotel has always been independently owned and operated and feels like a family home. Call and inquire for special rates and packages. **Louie's Restaurant** on premises serves lunch weekdays and dinner every night on the veranda. $$$

For More Information

Goleta Valley Chamber of Commerce. *5582 Calle Real, Suite A, Box 781, Goleta, 93116; (805) 967–4618; www.goletavalley.com.*

Santa Barbara Conference and Visitors Bureau. *1601 Anacapa Street, 93101; (800) 927–4688 or (800) 676–1266 or (805) 966–9222; www.SantabarbaraCa.com.*

Summerland

About 5 miles southeast of Santa Barbara is the neighboring antiques, artists', and writers' haven of Summerland. Traveling in either direction along U.S. Highway 101, just exit at the ramp called Summerland and head toward the oceanfront Lookout Park with its rest rooms, volleyball courts, playground, and easy access to a lovely 2-mile stretch of beach. This is the quintessential California beach town, where the 900 or so residents enjoy the views from their hillside homes. You and your traveling family can kick back here, too.

Where to Eat

Big Yellow House Family Restaurant, *108 Pierpont Avenue; (805) 969–4140.* Easily visible from U.S. Highway 101, this restored 110-year-old Victorian home has been a roadside landmark since opening as a restaurant in the 1970s. Serving reasonably priced, American fare for breakfast, lunch, and dinner daily, it's popular with locals and visitors for a neighborly, casual atmosphere. Dine in the parlor next to the fireplace or the library upstairs that overlooks the ocean. Don't miss the crispy fried chicken, fresh clam chowder, or a piece of double-chocolate fudge cake. You might be haunted by the house's legendary ghost unless you indulge! $$

Summerland Beach Cafe, *2294 Lillie Avenue; (805) 969–1019.* Located in a rambling white clapboard house with a big veranda, this is the place for the best omelets and breakfast fare, as well as lunch, served daily from 7:00 A.M. to 3:00 P.M. The decor is eclectic and sure to hold the family's interest, including some old booths with their own phones. $

Carpinteria

The small seaside community of Carpinteria, about 12 miles southeast of Santa Barbara, down the coast along U.S. Highway 101, was originally a Chumash fishing village and canoe-building spot. It boasts the **Carpinteria State Beach,** a.k.a. the "world's safest beach"—a claim justified, perhaps, by a natural reef breakwater that prevents nasty riptides. There are outstanding recreational opportunities and a variety of camping facilities around and inland from the beach. Many flower firms are based here, growing roses, orchids, and mums. Another of Carpinteria's blossoms, a hardy perennial fruit if you will, is celebrated with the popular **Avocado Festival,** held the first weekend of October downtown on Linden Avenue.

CARPINTERIA VALLEY MUSEUM OF HISTORY
956 Maple Avenue, 93013; (805) 684–3112. Open Tuesday through Saturday from 1:00 to 4:00 P.M.; closed holidays. **Free**; *donations welcome.*

Check out the valley's heritage from Chumash Indian settlement to today with charming exhibits and knowledgeable docents.

RINCON POINT

Just south of Carpinteria along U.S. Highway 101.

At Rincon Point, surfing's legendary mecca, known worldwide as "Queen of the Coast," waves come down the Santa Barbara Channel, hit the corner, and wrap around the shore, creating awesomely "radical" surf, dude! If your kids aren't surfers, they will still enjoy watching the sets and playing along the shore

Where to Stay

Comfort Suites, *5606 Carpinteria Avenue, 93013; (805) 566–9499.* Opened in 2000, this 108-unit property has easy access to U.S. Highway 101, beaches, and local attractions. A nice outdoor pool, spa, and complimentary continental breakfast buffet are other highlights. Ask about special package rates. $$$

For More Information

Carpinteria Valley Chamber of Commerce. *5285 Carpinteria Avenue, Box 956, Carpinteria, 93014; (805) 684–5479 or (800) 563–6900; www.carpchamber.org.*

Ventura County

The mighty U.S. Highway 101, known hereabouts as the Ventura Highway (and popularized in the '70s hit song by America), winds south from Santa Barbara County. It is the major artery through such rapidly growing communities as San Buenaventura (Ventura for short), Oxnard, Port Hueneme, Camarillo, Westlake Village, and Thousand Oaks. Exiting this concrete thoroughfare into the interior of Ventura County will reveal such treasures as the artistic and spiritual town of Ojai, rugged Santa Paula, and burgeoning Simi Valley. Embracing its cultural and geographic diversity is a key to enjoying Ventura County. With its mild climate and proximity to Los Angeles, the county offers an affordable getaway less than an hour from the big city. If you have limited time to show your family some California beach living, you can quickly and easily do it in the place Los Angelenos call "up the coast."

Extra Special Tip

Our Fortieth National Park The Channel Islands National Park Visitor Center is located at 1901 Spinnaker Drive in Ventura Harbor Village, (805) 658-5730. It is open daily, except Thanksgiving and Christmas. Less than 20 miles off the coast of Ventura and Santa Barbara Counties, the **Channel Islands National Park** comprises five of the eight offshore Channel Islands: Santa Barbara, Anacapa, Santa Cruz, Santa Rosa, and San Miguel. These islands provide an unparalleled introduction for your family to the flora and fauna of the local marine environment. Nature, unspoiled and unsullied by humans, is the main attraction here; quite frankly, it's the only attraction! Because the balance of nature on these islands and their surrounding waters is so fragile, visitors' activities are strictly regulated. For instance, there are no snack bars or RV campgrounds, and when you tour the area, you must bring (and take back what remains of) your own food, water, and other supplies. Rangers conduct guided hikes on San Miguel and Santa Rosa. Private concessionaires' boats or charter craft provide transportation across the channel to specific embarkation points.

The harborside **visitor center** houses quality exhibits that graphically describe the entire park, including its ecosystem, mammals, and birds. Plus, the center has an indoor tide pool, great for learning about the sea creatures your kids will see en route. There is also a movie and video about the islands shown here. A stairway and elevator lead up to the observation tower that will give you a 360-degree view of the harbor and, on most clear days, all the way to the islands themselves. Taking a day to visit our fortieth national park is well worth the effort and will be a sea journey to another dimension your family won't forget.

Ventura

Wrapped around the east-west ribbons of U.S. Highway 101, the city of Ventura has a historic downtown area that includes the restored Mission San Buenaventura; the Ventura Pier and State Beach, approximately 6 blocks from downtown; and the Ventura Harbor Village, some 2 miles away. Ventura has a population of about 100,000 and is a major agricultural center for citrus and other fruits. Its warm, sunny climate and value-priced accommodations and restaurants make this a very affordable family vacation spot as well as a jumping off point for visiting the Channel Islands National Park.

VENTURA HARBOR VILLAGE

1559 Spinnaker Drive, about 1 mile west of the Harbor Boulevard/Seaward exit from U.S. Highway 101; (805) 644–0169; www.venturaharborvillage.com.

Sailing, fishing, scuba diving, and sightseeing trips can all be arranged at the village. Shops and restaurants abound here, too. Home of the Channel Islands National Park Visitor Center. (See description in this chapter for more information.)

ISLAND PACKERS COMPANY

1867 Spinnaker Drive, Ventura, adjacent to Channel Islands National Park Visitor Center; (805) 642–1393.

A tour operator based here since 1968 offers scheduled charters to all the islands, as well as whale-watching trips and cruises. Call for special packages and itineraries.

*E*xtra *S*pecial *T*ip

Digging into History These three nearby attractions all make for refreshing steps back into early California history. Each is located in downtown Ventura, within easy walking distance, and can be accomplished in a long morning. While you're in the downtown shopping and dining zone, catch some vintage stores.

VENTURA COUNTY MUSEUM OF HISTORY AND ART. *100 East Main Street; (805) 653–0323. Tuesday to Sunday 10:00 A.M. to 5:00 P.M. $.* Features attractive displays blending local chronicles and illustrations along with the popular George Stuart historical figures, changing exhibits, and a good research library.

ALBINGER ARCHAEOLOGICAL MUSEUM. *113 East Main Street; (805) 648–5823. Wednesday to Sunday 10:00 A.M. to 4:00 P.M. Free.* Museum contains artifacts spanning 3,500 years, all excavated from a single dig site next to the mission. Available on request: audiovisual programs describing the labor-intensive process of excavation.

MISSION SAN BUENAVENTURA. *225 East Main Street; (805) 648–4496. Monday to Friday 10:00 A.M. to 5:00 P.M., Saturday 9:00 A.M. to 5:00 P.M., and Sunday 10:00 A.M. to 4:00 P.M. $.* Founded in 1782 and completed in 1809. The present mission includes a small museum and a restored church that continues to be an active parish.

SKATE STREET (ages 6 and up)

1954 Goodyear Avenue, Ventura; (805) 650–1213. Open daily (closed major holidays), call for current schedules and special discounts. $$$

One of the newest and most popular indoor skating "theme parks" in Southern California, Skate Street is THE place for in-line, roller, and skateboard enthusiasts. Features include bowls, pipes, half pipes, ramps, and a 12,000-square-foot street course with curbs, benches, planters, and streetlights. (If you have to ask what these features are—you won't enjoy this attraction!) Rental skates, pads, and helmets are available.

GOLF N' STUFF

5555 Walker Street, Ventura. Just off U.S. Highway 101 at the Victoria exit; (805) 644–7131; www.golfnstuff.com. Open daily; Sunday to Thursday from 10:00 A.M. to 11:00 P.M., Friday and Saturday until 1:00 A.M. Certain height restrictions apply for every activity; please check in advance. $$

Choose from two miniature golf courses, bumper boats, Lil' Indy race cars, arcade games, snack bar, and much more fun stuff!

Where to Stay

Pierpont Inn & Restaurant, *550 Sanjon Road, adjacent to U.S. Highway 101, northbound exit Sanjon Road, southbound exit Seaward Avenue, Ventura; (805) 653–6144 or (800) 285–4667.* Children ages twelve and under stay **Free** at this attractive, seventy-two-unit property, established in 1928. Check out the two cottages! Some rooms have fireplaces, and most rooms have ocean views with balconies. Even through you are across the highway from the beach, this property has two heated pools (one indoor). It also has twelve lighted tennis courts and a very friendly, helpful staff. The ocean-view restaurant serves breakfast, lunch, and dinner daily. $$$$

For More Information

Ventura Visitors Bureau. *89–C South California Street, 93001; (800) 333–2989 or (805) 648–2075; www.ventura-usa.com.*

Ojai

From Ventura, you can take either State Route 150 or State Route 33 inland to reach Ojai, a warm, dry, spiritually inclined artists' colony nestled in a peaceful valley. Say "Oh-high," and you will have mastered the most difficult part of the area. The drive here alone is worth the trip, because of the scenic

Extra Special Tip

Eating Ojai Oranges One of our favorite things to do is buy fresh Ojai Valley oranges from a roadside stand. They are so juicy and so delicious, you just can't eat enough. But whatever you do, don't peel them out the car window (like someone did whose name we shall not mention), because the juice will run down the side of your car and make an ooey, gooey mess. (That took a lot of work to clean after it had dried in the sun!)

mountains and lakes. The quaint downtown features **Libbey Park**—home of the annual Bowl Full of Blues concert series and the Ojai Music Festival. The **Ojai Center for the Arts** has displays by California artists and a changing calendar of events. Call (805) 646-1107 for current happenings.

OJAI VALLEY MUSEUM

130 West Ojai Avenue, located downtown in the historic chapel; (805) 640–1390. Open Wednesday to Friday 1:00 to 4:00 P.M. and Saturday and Sunday 10:00 A.M. to 4:00 P.M. $

Changing exhibits of art, natural history, and local lore. Chumash garden and gift shop provide interesting diversions. **Free** admission, donations welcome.

LAKE CASITAS RECREATION AREA

Off State Route 150, approximately 3 miles west of junction of State Route 33, about fifteen minutes from downtown Ojai; (805) 649–2233. Open year-round for day use during daylight hours. Overnight campsites subject to availability, fees vary.

Set in a valley of its own, this 35-mile-long, irregularly shaped lake is actually a human-made reservoir that provides drinking water for Ventura County. Consequently, there is no swimming in the lake, but the fishing for trout, bass, crappie, and catfish is excellent. Powerboats, canoeing, and sailing are fun, here, too, year-round. There is a basic snack bar, small grocery store, boat rental, bait shop, and a large kid's playground. Our advice is to pack a picnic lunch and come kick back here for the day. We do as often as we can!

Where to Eat

Boccali's, *11675 Santa Paula–Ojai Road, at the corner of Reeves Road;* (805) 646–6116. Casual, fun dining inside or outside on the patio. Great pizzas and loads of pastas. Very family-oriented, take-out available. Serving dinner seven nights a week and lunch Wednesday through Sunday. $

41

Where to Stay

Ojai Valley Inn & Spa *905 Country Club Road, just west of town off State Route 150; (805) 646–5511 or (800) 422–6524; www.ojairesort.com.* This magnificent resort nestled in the foothills is a one-stop family fun destination. If you and yours can't find something to keep you happy here, go home! Situated on 220 landscaped acres, the resort offers 207 first-class rooms and suites overlooking gardens, pools, a golf course, and woods. This is the home of the Senior PGA Tour, and the 18-hole golf course is very challenging, yet forgiving. Warm up on the putting green, or perhaps try tennis (four courts), horseback riding, a jogging course, hiking, and biking (rentals available). Better yet, let the kids enjoy the petting zoo and incredible supervised children's programs that change with the season. Meanwhile, you can experience the 31,000-square-foot spa facility—featuring a full complement of deluxe services like hydrotherapy, massage, facials, manicures, beauty, toning, aromatherapies, and more. Maravilla Dining Room and Oak Cafe open daily for all meals, but feasting poolside is our favorite. Breakfast buffet ranks right up there, too. Be sure to call for special family packages and rates. A destination resort not to be missed! $$$$

Rose Garden Inn, *615 West Ojai Avenue, 93023; (805) 646–1434; www.rosegardeninn.com.* A conveniently located, very moderately priced eighteen-unit motel with two spacious cottages. Highlights include lovely gardens, a large swimming pool, a steam sauna room, a whirlpool, and a playground. You'll also enjoy **Free** continental breakfast plus **Free** popcorn in the evening. Neighborly welcoming staff. $$

For More Information

Ojai Valley Chamber of Commerce and Visitors Bureau. *150 West Ojai Avenue, 93023; (805) 646–8126; www.the-ojai.org.*

Santa Paula and Fillmore

Exiting Ventura Highway 101 onto State Route 126 leads you through citrus groves and ranches to the pretty villages of Santa Paula and Fillmore. The **Santa Paula Airport** at Santa Maria and Eighth Streets has an extensive collection of privately owned antique, classic, and homebuilt aircraft. Call the chamber of commerce for a current schedule of tours and air shows.

SANTA PAULA UNION OIL MUSEUM

1001 East Main Street; (805) 933–0076. **Free** *admission, donations appreciated. Open Wednesday to Sunday; closed holidays.*

The museum depicts the history of oil exploration in California through relics, photos, computer games, and videos. Thinking about a career in oil or gas? Drive in and fill 'er up!

 ## FILLMORE & WESTERN RAILWAY

Central Park Plaza, downtown Fillmore. (805) 525–2546 or (800) 773– TRAIN; www.fwry.com. Runs Saturday and Sunday, but not major holidays. Times change seasonally. $$$

This antique train offers one-hour scenic sightseeing trips between Fillmore and Santa Paula. Vintage cars include a 1920s Pullman and restored dining, sleeper, and parlor carriages. Train workers dress in period costume. Theme parties and dinners are popular, especially the Christmas tree trains. Call for a current schedule and fares.

For More Information

Santa Paula Chamber of Commerce. *Santa Barbara at 10th Street, 93060; (805) 525–5561; www.santapaulachamber.com.*

Oxnard

What could you possibly find to do, see, or enjoy in a place with the funny name of Oxnard? The town got its name from entrepreneur Henry T. Oxnard, a visionary who foresaw that the fertile plain just north of the Conejo Hills would be an excellent place to raise sugar beets. In 1899 he built the $2 million American Sugar Beet Company processing plant, which remained in operation until 1959. Legend has it that the all-powerful Henry wanted to name his company town Sakchar—the Greek word for "sugar." Fortunately or not, when the day came in 1903 to register the name with the clerk in the state capital of Sacramento, Henry had a bad phone connection and decided to settle for his surname, Oxnard. Sweet history aside, Oxnard has grown into a culturally and economically diverse community, with business parks, sandy beaches, and a fine marina, just 60 miles north of Los Angeles.

🏛 HERITAGE SQUARE

Downtown at 715 South A Street; (805) 483–7960. Open every day during day-light hours. **Free.**

The square reflects the area's past, with its faithful restoration of a late-1800s church, water tower, pump house, and eleven vintage homes. The buildings were moved from various parts of Oxnard to this single block. Be sure to call for guided tours and frequent special events.

📷 GULL WINGS CHILDREN'S MUSEUM (ages 2 to 12)

418 West Fourth Street, downtown, a bit off the beaten path in the old USO Hall; (805) 483–3005. Open Tuesday to Sunday from 10:00 A.M. to 5:00 P.M. $

Children will find plenty to do and dream about here. Indoor sports abound at this innovative museum, from a variety of hands-on exhibits (can you find the fossil?) to a medical room with cutaway models to a stage to do a rock-and-roll show on video and see yourself on the screen to a simulated campground and farmer's market. How about that apparatus for making giant soap bubbles? Can you do it?

📷 CARNEGIE CULTURAL ARTS CENTER

424 South C Street; (805) 385–8157. Open Thursday to Saturday 10:00 A.M. to 5:00 P.M.; Sunday 1:00 to 5:00 P.M. $

A dozen art galleries are scattered about like candy waiting to be unwrapped for the arty family unit. Carnegie Art Museum is housed in an imposing, two-story structure built in 1906 as a library. The museum's permanent collection focuses on twentieth-century California painters. Ever-changing exhibits highlight photography, sculpture, oils, watercolors, and some humorous displays.

⛵ CHANNEL ISLANDS HARBOR & VISITOR CENTER

3810 West Channel Islands Boulevard. (805) 985–4852.

Fisherman's Wharf Harbor Landing and the Marine Emporium have shopping, fine dining, and plenty of sailing and fishing options as well. Twenty-six hundred working and pleasure craft call this bustling port home. There are plenty of parks, a swimming beach, and the Maritime Museum. The Harbor Hopper Water Taxi, with its painted-on smiling face, is the best way to see the seafront. Call (805) 985–4677 for current schedule and fares.

VENTURA COUNTY MARITIME MUSEUM

2731 South Victoria Avenue, just past Channel Islands Boulevard; (805) 984–6260. Open Thursday to Monday. Closed major holidays. **Free**.

You and your mates will find a collection of ship models, made with materials ranging from bone to wood to metals, that reflect maritime history from ancient to modern times. Changing exhibits deal with maritime commerce, Channel Islands history, whaling, and shipwrecks.

OXNARD STATE BEACH AND MCGRATH STATE BEACH

3.5 miles south of Ventura off U.S. Highway 101 via the Harbor Boulevard exit.

Perfect for kicking off your shoes and letting go on miles of white sand. Delight in sunbathing, barbecuing, playing volleyball, swimming, snorkeling, and surfing in an uncrowded, peaceful environment. Camping facilities are available for the tent-inclined. A nearby bird sanctuary is home to egrets and great blue herons.

OXNARD FARMER'S MARKET

At the corner of B and Fifth Streets, downtown; (805) 483–7960. Open Thursday from 9:00 A.M. to 1:00 P.M. year-round.

This market is a sure hit for fresh fruit and veggies—perfect ingredients for a picnic lunch at the beach.

Where to Eat and Stay

Casa Sirena Marina Resort & Lobster Trap Restaurant, *3605 Peninsula Road, at Channel Islands Harbor, exit Victoria Avenue off Highway 101, to Channel Islands Boulevard; (805) 985–6311 or (800) 447–3529.* This is a value-priced family-fun place to stay right at the marina, with 273 rooms including 26 two-bedroom units. There is so much to see and do right from your patio overlooking the marina or gardens. Try to stay in the main hotel instead of the nondescript north wing. Some rooms may be a bit tired, but focus on the view and the feeling of being in the heart of the marina activity. There is a pool, whirlpool spa, tennis court, exercise room, sauna, gift shop, coffee shop, and the Lobster Trap Restaurant for luncheon, dinner, and Sunday brunch. Select the children's menu; casual attire is fine. $$$

Embassy Suites Mandalay Beach Resort & Capistrano's Restaurant, *2101 Mandalay Beach Road; (805) 984–2500, on the beach, just off Channel Islands Boulevard.* All 250 units here are two-room, two-bath suites, just perfect for family accommodations. You will love the deluxe amenities in every suite—fridge, microwave, coffeemaker, two TVs; plus a **Free** cooked-to-order hot breakfast every morning and **Free** beverages and refreshments every evening in the garden courtyard. This resort is right on the sand, with its own beach, and you can rent boogie boards, bicycles, beach chairs, snorkeling gear, and the like. Or just kick back in the serpentine pool. Dine at Capistrano's on fresh seafood and pasta. $$$$

For More Information

Oxnard Convention & Visitors Bureau. *200 West Seventh Street, 93030. (800) 2–OXNARD or (805) 385–7545; www.oxnardtourism.com.*

Port Hueneme

In 1941 the U.S. Navy took advantage of the only natural deepwater harbor between Los Angeles and San Francisco to build its Construction Battalion (known as CB or Seabee) in Port Hueneme (pronounced Why-nee-me). Named after a Chumash settlement, Weneme, that occupied the site, this town of 20,000 actually was plotted in 1869, but its prominence today is its military importance as the home base of the U.S. Navy Civil Engineer Corps (CEC). These skilled construction experts have actively fought in military engagements around the world.

CEC/SEABEE MUSEUM

U.S. Naval Construction Battalion at Ventura Road and Sunkist Avenue. Call ahead to confirm hours and current accessibility to civilians at (805) 982–5163. Under 16 must be accompanied by an adult. **Free**.

You can see models of equipment, actual weapons, and uniforms of the Civil Engineer Corps and U.S. Navy Seabees.

Simi Valley

The Simi Valley lies on a plateau at around 800 feet above sea level, about twenty minutes inland from Oxnard. State Route 118 (also known as the Ronald Reagan Freeway) bisects the valley, connecting it to State Route 23 with access to U.S. Highway 101 along the coast. With a population of over 100,000, this area is a popular bedroom community for adjacent Los Angeles County. It is worth a visit to see Ronald Reagan's legacy at his presidential library.

RONALD REAGAN PRESIDENTIAL LIBRARY & MUSEUM

40 Presidential Drive. Five miles inland from U.S. Highway 101 at Simi Valley off State Highway 118 (follow the signs); (805) 522–8444. Open daily 10:00 A.M. to 5:00 P.M., closed New Year's Day, Thanksgiving, and Christmas. $$

Located in a Spanish Mission–style building constructed around a courtyard and set on a hilltop, this site provides you with an incredible view of the rolling hills leading down to the Pacific Ocean. Within the library's museum are photographs and memorabilia of President Reagan's entire life, gifts of state he received during his administration, and a replica of the Oval Office. Perhaps most impressive to the younger generation is a piece of the crumbled Berlin Wall. This facility provides all generations with a compelling look at "The Great Communicator" and his legacy.

Where to Eat and Stay

Grand Vista Hotel, *999 Enchanted Way, exit First Street off State Route 118, only 2 miles from Reagan Library, Simi Valley; (805) 583–2000 or (800) 455–7464; www.grandvistasimi.com.* Offers family value packages including the Presidential, which features lodging, passes to the library, and **Free** shuttle transportation. Very spacious 195-room, full-service hotel with two swimming pools (one heated) and the **Vistas Restaurant** ($$$). Complimentary continental breakfast will get your family off to a good start. $$$$

Thousand Oaks and Westlake Village

The adjoining communities of Thousand Oaks and Westlake Village are located just off U.S. Highway 101 in the southernmost section of Ventura County. Originally part of a Spanish land grant called Rancho El Conejo (co-nay-ho), today this lovely residential area still has plenty of open rangeland, parks, and things for your family to take pleasure from.

STAGECOACH INN MUSEUM

51 South Ventu Park Road, off U.S. Highway 101, Thousand Oaks; (805) 498–9441. Open Wednesday to Sunday, 1:00 to 4:00 P.M., closed holidays. $

First opened in 1876, this Monterey-style structure, now faithfully restored, was a major stopover on the stage route between Los Angeles and Santa Barbara. The carriage house, pioneer house, adobe, and ever-changing exhibits will give the kids a great taste of western life in the 1800s.

THOUSAND OAKS CIVIC ARTS PLAZA

2100 East Thousand Oaks Boulevard, Thousand Oaks; (805) 449–2787.
Performance art in every shape and form takes place here year-round. This complex has beautiful sculpture, fountains, an 1,800-seat auditorium, a 400-seat theater, and a seven-acre park. Be sure to call for a current schedule of events. There is always something happening here for families.

Where to Eat and Stay

Westlake Village Inn, *31943 Agoura Road, Westlake Village, exit Westlake Boulevard South off U.S. Highway 101; (800) 535–9978 or (805) 496–1667; www.wvinn.com.* This beautifully landscaped, full-service property has 140 rooms and eighteen suites to house your family in luxury. Relax from your travels in the pool/whirlpool spa area or play golf (eighteen holes), practice on the putting green, play tennis (ten courts), or merely stroll around the pretty lake. Package plans and special rates for families abound at this deluxe oasis in the toney community of Westlake. **Provence** ($$$$), the restaurant on the property, is perhaps a bit too formal for youngsters, but let your taste decide. $$$$

Annual Events

The Central Coast covers a lot of wonderful territory, but your Southern California family fun has only just begun!

The following list of events planned in the Central Coast area is made available thanks to the California Trade and Commerce Agency.

JANUARY

Winter Bird Festival—Morro Bay. *(800) 231–0592 or (805) 772–4467.* Guided tours of estuary and surrounding areas; plentiful bird-watching.

FEBRUARY

Whale Celebration—Ventura. *(805) 644–0169.* Celebrate the annual gray whale migration with music and entertainment, environmental booths, and touch tanks in Ventura Harbor Village.

Celebration of The Whales—Oxnard. *(800) 269–6273 or (805) 385–7545, fax (805) 385–7571.* Weekend celebration highlights gray whale migration; full-day trips, arts and crafts, and photo exhibit. **Free.**

MARCH

International Film Festival—Santa Barbara. *(805) 963–0023.* Premieres and screenings of independent U.S. and international films; gala opening, workshops and seminars by film professionals. Admission fees vary.

Taste of Solvang—Solvang. *(800) 458–6765 or (805) 688–6144, fax (805) 688–8620.* Food festival features dessert showcase, walking smorgasbords, world's largest Danish pastry, and entertainment. Fees vary.

APRIL

Ventura County Food and Wine Festival—Oxnard. *(805) 985–4852, fax (805) 994–4852.* Waterfront festival featuring fine foods from local restaurants accompanied by musical entertainment. Fees vary.

I Madonnari Italian Street Painting Festival—San Luis Obispo. *(805) 781–2777, fax (805) 543–1255.* Event features sidewalk and street pastel creations. **Free.**

Children's Day in the Plaza—San Luis Obispo. *(805) 781–2777, fax (805) 543–1255.* More than forty booths featuring spin art, water toys, face painting, and a petting zoo; singers, dancers, clowns, and jugglers. **Free.**

Presidio Day—Santa Barbara. *(805) 966–1279.* Celebration of early California arts, crafts, and music at historic 1782 Presidio Park. **Free.**

MAY

Garden Festival—San Luis Obispo. *(805) 781–2777, fax (805) 543–1255.* Floral displays and sale at a judges' show with speakers, exhibits, demonstrations, children's activities, music, and commercial and gardening booths. **Free.**

Annual California Strawberry Festival—Oxnard. *(805) 385–7578, fax (805) 486–2553.* Strawberry foods, contests, music, and arts and crafts.

I Madonnari Street Painting Festival—Santa Barbara. *(805) 569–3873.* More than 200 local artists and children create chalk paintings in front of the Old Mission; Italian market and entertainment. **Free.**

JUNE

Summer Solstice Celebration—Santa Barbara. *(805) 965–3396.* (See complete description on page 27.) **Free.**

Seafest—Ventura. *(805) 644–0169.* Celebrate the beginnings of summer with entertainment booths, environmental instruction, a chowder cook-off, and a children's harbor land and show.

Elks Rodeo and Parade—Santa Maria. *(805) 922–6006.* Calf roping, bull riding, bronco riding, steer wrestling, and barrel racing.

JULY

Fireworks by the Sea—Oxnard. *(800) 269–6273 or (805) 385–7545, fax (805) 385–7571.* Family-oriented daytime activities (arts and crafts, entertainment, and more), concluding with a fireworks display over the water. **Free.**

Fourth of July Celebration—Ventura. *(800) 333–2989, fax (805) 698–2150.* Parade, street fair with eight blocks of arts and crafts, food and entertainment; fireworks in the evening. **Free.**

Santa Barbara County Fair—Santa Maria. *(805) 925–8824.* Country fair includes carnival, produce, livestock, and western music.

AUGUST

Olde Towne Fair—Lompoc. *(800) 240–0999 or (805) 736–4567.* Celebrate Lompoc's 107-year history with children's events, live music and entertainment, and an arts and crafts fair. **Free.**

California Mid-State Fair—Paso Robles. *(800) 909–FAIR or (805) 239–0655, fax (805) 238–5308.* The Central Coast fair includes five stages of entertainment featuring top names daily, PRCA rodeo, Destruction Derby, animal exhibits, arts and crafts, a working farm, wine tasting, pig races, and nightly dancing. Admission fees vary.

Annual Salsa Festival—Oxnard. *(805) 483–4542.* Salsa-making contest, 5k run, arts and crafts, dancing, music, and a carnival for children. **Free.**

Old Spanish Days Fiesta—Santa Barbara. *(805) 962–8108.* (See complete description on page 27.) **Free.**

Ventura County Fair—Ventura. *(800) 333–2989 or (805) 648–3376, fax (805) 648–1012.* Traditional county fair features top-name entertainment, exhibits, livestock, motor sports, rodeo, food, and fireworks. Admission fees vary.

SEPTEMBER

Taste of the Town—Santa Barbara. *(805) 892–5556.* More than sixty local restaurants and wineries provide tastes of their best fare in the beautiful Riveria Research Park overlooking the city. Always held the first Sunday after Labor Day as a benefit for the local branch of the Arthritis Foundation. Ticket prices vary.

Simi Valley Days—Simi Valley. *(805) 581–4280.* Fair features a carnival, hoedown, barn dance, horse show, parade, 5k and 10k runs, food, and entertainment. Admission fees vary.

Danish Days—Solvang. *(800) 468–6765 or (805) 688–6636.* Celebration of Solvang's rich Danish heritage features Danish folk dancing, music, food, parade, and entertainment. **Free.**

California Beach Festival—Ventura. *(800) 333–2989 or (805) 654–7830, fax (805) 643–4555.* Three stages of entertainment, food, a surfing contest, and beach volleyball. **Free.**

OCTOBER

California Avocado Festival—Carpinteria. *(805) 684–0038.* Avocado celebration includes food, arts and crafts, music, and a flower show. **Free.**

Souper 101 Roundup—Buellton. *(805) 688–7829, fax (805) 688–5399.* All-day entertainment includes a parade, car show, animal exhibits, pea soup eating contest, food and beverages, activities for kids, and equestrian events. **Free.**

Lemon Festival—Goleta. *(805) 967–4618, fax (805) 967–4615.* Family event featuring a lemon pie eating contest, food, arts and crafts show, children's activities, farmer's market, and entertainment. **Free.**

Golden Oak Festival—Paso Robles. *(805) 238–4103, fax (805) 238–4029.* Arts and crafts, collectibles, food, music, and classic cars. **Free.**

Heritage Scare—Oxnard. *(805) 385–7545.* Halloween-time tours of decorated ghostly Heritage Square historic district.

NOVEMBER

Holiday Walk and Light the Downtown—Paso Robles. *(805) 238–4103, fax (805) 238–4103.* Lighted trees, candlelight caroling, farmer's market, and Santa and Mrs. Claus. **Free.**

DECEMBER

Winterfest—Solvang. *(805) 688–6144, fax (805) 688–8620.* Danish Village celebration features thousands of twinkling lights. **Free.**

Holiday Parade—San Luis Obispo. *(805) 541–0286, fax (805) 781–2647.* Holiday celebration includes floats, marching bands, youth organizations, and Santa Claus. **Free.**

Ventura Harbor Parade of Lights—Ventura. *(800) 333–2989 or (805) 644–0169.* Colorful parade of decorated lighted boats on Ventura Harbor. **Free.**

Christmas Lite Parade—Paso Robles. *(805) 238–4101, fax (805) 238–4029.* Christmas parade includes youth organization, merchant floats, bands, and Santa Claus. **Free.**

Holiday Boat Parade of Lights—Oxnard. *(800) 269–6273 or (805) 389–9495.* Lighted boat parade in the Channel Islands Harbor, holiday activities, and entertainment. **Free.**

Victorian House Tours—Oxnard. *(805) 483–7960.* Guided tours of turn-of-the-last-century homes, explaining the families who first settled here.

Greater Los Angeles

Say it like a native—L.A.—and you're already on the road (or freeway, as it were) unlocking the mystique of one of the most fascinating places on earth. For L.A. is many different things to many millions of ethnically diverse people. For some, the city is synonymous with Hollywood and the legends of glamour that go along with it. For others, it is the leading metropolis of the Pacific Rim, a cutting-edge capital of culture and industry where culture happens be a thriving industry unto itself. As the official *Destination LA* guidebook (published by the Los Angeles Convention and Visitor's Bureau) states, "the cultural wave that washes the nation and the world starts here."

Indeed. And for just about everyone, L.A. means paradise. Palm trees, beaches, and the best darned weather in the world. In recent years Los Angeles has suffered more than its fair share of problems, both sociological and geological. But more impressive than the scope of these setbacks is the furious pace at which the city rebounds. The vaunted laid-back mindset of Los Angelenos belies their determination to make L.A. as livable as it can possibly be. Creativity, hard work, and frequent trips to the beach help make civic aspirations come alive.

The size of the city provokes inspiration or consternation, depending on your point of view. On a clear day—of which, contrary to popular belief, there are many—one gets a sense of its general proportions. The core of Los Angeles, city and county, is a vast, level basin studded with palm trees and laced with freeways. (By the way, always remember the name and the number of the freeway you are on or looking for, as both locals and road signs use them interchangeably. Thus "the 5" is also the Golden State, "the 101" is also the Hollywood, which turns into the Ventura, etc. Radio traffic reports generally refer to freeways by their names.) The L.A. basin is flanked on all sides by foothills and mountains, many of which are snowcapped in winter. In the city

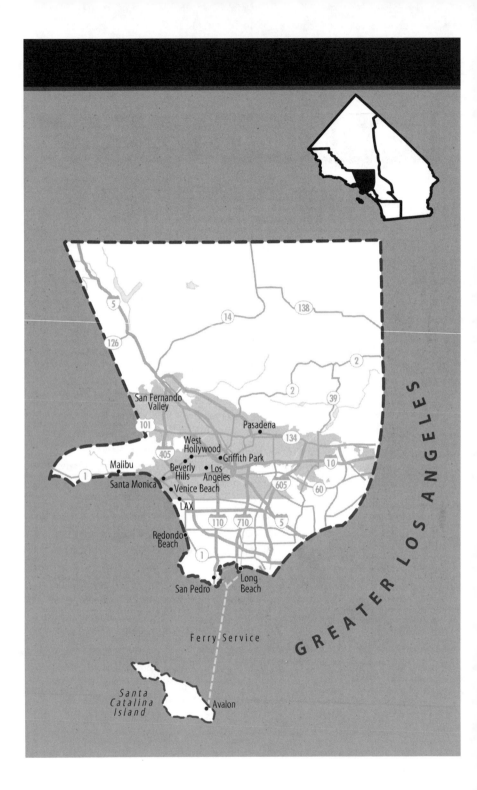

5

126

14

138

2

2

101

San Fernando
Valley

Pasadena

134

39

405

West
Hollywood

Griffith Park

Beverly
Hills

Los
Angeles

10

Malibu

605

60

Santa Monica

Venice Beach

LAX

Redondo
Beach

110

710

5

1

San Pedro

Long
Beach

1

Ferry Service

Santa
Catalina
Island

Avalon

GREATER LOS ANGELES

itself, the higher up in the hills you go, the bigger the mansions get. These are actually the Santa Monica Mountains, an enchanting urban oasis with miles of hiking trails, scenic drives, and, after a good rain, even a waterfall or two. Of course L.A. is prime beach country: In the land where Beach Blanket Bingo was born, there are 72 miles of county coastline, from Malibu in the north to Long Beach in the south. Oldies radio stations have an unabashed bias for Beach Boys hits. But despite its reputation for sunshine and stars, L.A. County also boasts a vast array of stellar cultural attractions.

Over the years, a patchwork of quite separate cities and towns in the L.A. basin was incorporated into the City of Los Angeles, creating a sprawling urban tapestry of contrasting colors and textures. Even if you're superparents, you won't be able to explore all 4,083 square miles of Los Angeles County, or even the City of Los Angeles's 467 square miles. No matter, because the most interesting things to see and do are relatively concentrated in five or six areas, distinctive places where the civic personality truly sparkles. By East Coast standards, things are still very spread out, but that merely adds to the adventure, even for natives. Equipped with a reliable car—an absolute necessity—a full tank of gas, and the stamina to tackle the world's most extensive network of freeways, you and your family are prepared for experiencing a great deal of the excitement this pocket of the world has to offer.

Downtown Los Angeles

Start at the center. That's as good a rule as any for those unfamiliar with the greater L.A. area. Even though it is not as trendy as the Westside, downtown Los Angeles has been the commercial and cultural core of this sprawling city since it was merely a pueblo. Downtown gives the city a focus, and many central district attractions are perennial favorites among Southern Californian youths—people truly spoiled with choices. You will instantly recognize downtown by its cluster of skyscrapers.

LOS ANGELES CITY HALL

200 North Spring Street; (213) 485–4424; www.ci.la.ca.us/. Tours take place Monday through Friday from 10:00 to 11:00 A.M. Reservations are required.

Free tours of City Hall feature the central rotunda, ceiling decorations, the press room, and the council chamber of this 27-story art deco building, which (although your kids doubtless are too young to be aware of it) was the *Daily Planet*'s home in the original *Superman* TV series. This site will work for your family best if you plan a day touring the downtown area. We don't recommend this as a special trip.

THE LOS ANGELES TIMES (ages 10 and older for tours)

202 West First Street, right across the street from City Hall; (213) 237–5757; www.latimes.com/ (or 800–528–4637 and ask for tour info). **Free** *parking at 213 South Spring Street.*

The *Los Angeles Times* is the nation's biggest newspaper. Kids love to see the newsroom and printing facility, with its mesmerizing, rapid-fire machinery that churns out over a million newspapers each day. **Free** 35-minute "editorial" tours of the original plant are given Monday through Friday at 11:15 A.M. No reservations necessary. But reservations are a must for the Olympic production plant (Monday through Friday 10:00 A.M. and 1:15 P.M.; tour participants must be at least ten years old).

MUSIC CENTER

135 North Grand Avenue; (213) 972–7211; fax (213) 972–7339; www.music center.org/index.html.

Tours are **Free** and include the Dorothy Chandler Pavilion, the Mark Taper Forum, and the Ahmanson Theatre.

Pause to sip lemonade while you watch the festive central fountain, with its dancing, mist-spraying columns of water. Kids also love the 128-foot-tall purple tower and circular pool with the mini-waterfall at this futuristic spot. Don't let them jump in, though, for ample opportunities for refreshment await at downtown's famous and historic indoor bazaar.

GRAND CENTRAL MARKET

317 South Broadway; (213) 624–2378; fax (213) 624–9496; www. grandcentralsquare.com/. Open Monday through Sunday 9:00 A.M. to 6:00 P.M.

Opened in 1917, Grand Central Market is L.A.'s oldest and largest food market. Here you can sample not just a cross-section of L.A.'s ethnic diversity but some of the country's best Mexican and Asian food as well. Locals come here to bargain for bananas, try authentic burritos, or indulge in raspberry guava smoothies at the all-natural exotic juice bar. You may hear more Spanish than English, but that's half the fun, and *gracias* is really all the Spanish you need to know anywhere in Los Angeles.

MUSEUM OF CONTEMPORARY ART (MOCA)

250 South Grand Avenue, in California Plaza; (213) 626–6222; fax (213) 620–8674; www.moca.org. Open Tuesday through Sunday 11:00 A.M. to 5:00 P.M.; Thursday 11:00 A.M. to 8:00 P.M. $$

Kids will find the often outrageous and totally unexplainable artwork here to be, well, mysterious. Many people do! The eclectic, always changing, never boring collections range from the cute to the controversial. Kids can roam at will through the museum to see an artistic show, including enormous multimedia sculptures, unpredictable creations of various shapes and sizes, and monochromatic paintings of nothing much at all. **Free** on-site children's workshops are offered. And stop by the museum's cafe, operated by the owners of Pinot, one of L.A.'s trendy restaurants, for an imaginative California-style salad or pasta. After placing your order, you can sit inside or on the patio. It's a perfect spot to relax, sip a tropical iced tea, and savor an L.A.-ish dessert—like raspberry crème brûlée or apple crumble—while the kids explore the traffic-free areas.

THE MUSEUM OF NEON ART

501 West Olympic Boulevard; (213) 489–9918; www.neonmona.org. Open Wednesday through Saturday 11:00 A.M. to 5:00 P.M.; Sunday 12:00 to 5:00 P.M. Second Thursday of the month: 11:00 A.M. to 8:00 P.M. Closed Mondays, Tuesdays, and major holidays. **Free** *parking available underground in Renaissance Tower. $. Children 12 and younger,* **Free**.

Here's the place to gaze upon a glowing collection of electronic-media neon signs. Nostalgia lovers will enjoy the exhibits of the neon signs their grandparents grew up with.

WELLS FARGO MUSEUM

333 South Grand Avenue, two blocks south of the Music Center; (213) 253–7166; fax (213) 686–2269; www.wellsfargo.com. Open Monday through Friday 9:00 A.M. to 5:00 P.M. **Free**.

Chronicles 130 years of western history. **Free** concerts are frequently held at noon and in the evening on the plaza; call (213) 687–2159 for schedule information.

Extra Special Tip

DASH around downtown L.A. Hop on one of the 25-cent Dash shuttle buses and visit the Flower Market and Fashion District without having to hassle with expensive parking. Customer Service: *(213) 808–2273.*

EXPOSITION PARK

Located adjacent to the Los Angeles Memorial Coliseum and close to L.A.'s biggest private university, the University of Southern California.

Admire the coliseum, stroll through the campus, then make time to visit.

THE L.A. COUNTY MUSEUM OF NATURAL HISTORY

900 Exposition Boulevard; (213) 763–DINO (3466); fax (213) 763–4843; www.nhm.org. Open Monday through Friday 9:30 A.M. to 5:00 P.M.; Saturday and Sunday 10:00 A.M. to 5:00 P.M. Closed major holidays. $. Children under five, **Free**.

Kids love the museum because of its lifelike dinosaur replicas, animal habitat dioramas, and insect zoo.

THE CALIFORNIA SCIENCE CENTER

700 State Drive, west of the 110 Freeway; (213) 744–2019; fax (213) 744–2934; www.casciencectr.org. Open 10:00 A.M. to 5:00 P.M. daily. Closed Thanksgiving, New Year's, and Christmas. **Free**.

Popular for its fun, innovative, and interactive exhibits. There is also a wide-screen IMAX theater here. For current IMAX production schedule and admission fees, call (213) 744-2019. Don't leave the Science Center until you meet Tess, the 50-foot animatronic woman. She is the star of a show that uses videos, sound effects, and pulsating strobe lights to explain how the body works. Wonder Woman, watch out! Parking is available at 39th Street and Figueroa.

ROSE GARDEN

Meander through the ever-fragrant home of 150 varieties of roses (blooms peak April through May and September through October) in this gorgeous 114-acre garden.

Extra Special Tip

Up All Night? Try the **Pacific Dining Car**, 1310 West Sixth downtown; (213) 483-6000; open twenty-four hours. Just look for the revolving cow. If the kids want a big breakfast, L.A.-style, this is the place. Dinner is expensive, but the lunch menu is good family fare. Kids will like the railway car ambience reminiscent of the good old Union Pacific days.

While you could easily spend a day exploring this area, if you're pressed for time you can cover the highlights in a half day. Save the other half for exploring L.A.'s celebrated downtown ethnic districts. Though the city is a melting pot of many peoples, certain sections are strikingly similar to the places immigrants left behind.

LITTLE TOKYO

Bounded by Fourth, Second, San Pedro, and Los Angeles Streets.

With its carefully landscaped gardens and plazas, Little Tokyo now has a commemorative timeline, Omoide No Shotokyo ("Remembering Little Tokyo") and a 1,000-foot Japanese Walk that traces six decades of Japanese American culture, including the tragic wartime internment period.

JAPANESE VILLAGE PLAZA

327 East Second Street.

Resembles a rural native village in Japan. In the mood for some rice-paste candy?

JAPANESE AMERICAN NATIONAL MUSEUM

369 East First Street; (213) 625–0414 or (800) 461–5266; fax (213) 625–1770; www.janm.org/main.htm. Open Tuesday through Sunday 10:00 A.M. to 5:00 P.M.; Thursday 10:00 A.M. to 8:00 P.M. $$

The museum chronicles the history of Japanese immigration to and life in the United States.

CHINATOWN

Nestled between Bernard, North Broadway, College, and Hill Streets.

The architecture here is more lavish than Little Tokyo. Not surprisingly, Chinese restaurants abound in this compact neighborhood. Go on Sunday morning for dim sum (Chinese brunch). Many cultural festivals are held throughout the year here and in Little Tokyo.

OLVERA STREET

At the heart of El Pueblo de Los Angeles Historic Park, 125 Paseo de la Plaza; (213) 628–1274; www.olvera-street.com. Open Monday through Saturday 10:00 A.M. to 3:00 P.M. (to 8:00 P.M. in the summer). Shops open 10:00 A.M. to 7:00 P.M.

This is an authentic L.A. experience that is ideal for the family. Kids will love the wide variety of brightly colored piñatas—splendid, reasonably priced souvenirs. Don't ask us how you'll get one on the plane or in your trunk. This 44-acre cluster of shops and landmark buildings is the birth-place of Los Angeles. Every day seems to be Cinco de Mayo at El Pueblo, located at the site of a Spanish farming village founded in 1781. Kids and adults alike may be surprised to learn Los Angeles was actually a Mexican city from 1835 (when Spain ceded it to Mexico) until 1847, when it became American. Nowhere in the city is the proud Spanish her-itage kept alive to the extent it is here.

The effect is like making a detour to Mexico without a passport. More than twenty historic buildings line the colorful streets of El Pueblo. One is the Avila Adobe, built in 1818, today the oldest house still stand-ing in Los Angeles. At the center of El Pueblo is La Placita (the Plaza), where the rich Spanish influence is visible in art and architecture. Kids love the old-fashioned candy shops and the sound of mariachi music in the Mexican marketplace. Everyone loves the aroma of Mexican food and the unparalleled sombrero-buying opportunities. Not even Disney-land has atmosphere like this.

Extra Special Tip

Thomas Bros.—A Good Travel Companion Welcome! You'll be joining thousands of travelers taking to the roads to explore the scenic highways and byways (and freeways) of Southern California. Get off on the right foot by investing in the 336-page full-color *Thomas Bros. Califor-nia Road Atlas and Driver's Guide.* Your family will benefit from the useful mileage charts, the index of cities, state highway maps, street details, metropolitan area maps, and a separate foldout map. We especially liked the driving tours and points of interest for the Greater Los Ange-les area, the deserts, Orange County, the Inland Empire, and the Central Coast—all part and parcel of the *Fun with the Family in Southern California* guide. To obtain your copy, try any bookstore or visit **Thomas Brothers Maps and Books,** 521 West Sixth Street, downtown Los Angeles; (800) 899–6277. The soft-bound, wire-ringed book (the bible to Southern Cal-ifornians) costs $24.95. And it's worth every penny.

After all, in 2002 alone, there were hundreds of new streets in Los Angeles and Orange Counties! You'll find the guide to be indispensable, with its foldout maps and easy-to-read index. With your trusty Thomas Guide in hand, you can navigate L.A. like a native—from "the 5" to "the 10" and beyond!

STAPLES CENTER

1111 South Figueroa Street; (213) 742–7340; fax (213) 624–3054; www. staplescenter.com.

This is L.A.'s new state-of-the-art sports and entertainment center and the home of the L.A. Lakers, L.A. Clippers, and L.A. Kings. They say they can seat 20,000 just for basketball. Other events will be scheduled year-round.

Where to Eat

Ciudad, *445 South Figueroa Street, Suite 100; (213) 486–5171; fax (213) 486-5172; www.millikenandfeniger.com.* As long as you are downtown, make it a point to visit this colorful (yellow interior!), noisy, and always busy restaurant. It has an exciting Latin-inspired menu for adults and a pretty good one for the kids created by MarySue Millikan and Susan Feniger, known around these parts as the Two Hot Tamales. Among the seven choices for the little ones (para los ninos) are el Cubanao Wedges with roasted pork, ham, Swiss cheese, and pickles, served with fries at $4.50. The desserts, such as cookies and flan, made in-house, have charmed the most jaded L.A. restaurant critics. You can make reservations via their Web site.

The Original Pantry, *877 South Figueroa Street, Downtown Los Angeles; (213) 972-9279.* This historic institution in Los Angeles is owned by a former mayor of Los Angeles, Richard Riordan. His slogan is "Never closed. Never without a customer!" The restaurant has an incredibly diverse menu. Cash only—no credit cards. $-$$

Philippe The Original, *1001 North Alameda Street; (213) 628–3781; www. philippes.com.* If the kids' tastebuds don't blossom over the prospect of a platter of sushi or a bowl of bird's nest soup, you might stroll over to Philippe's, the city's best-known place for roast beef sandwiches. Arrive early (before noon) to secure one of the roomy booths (we old-timers called them "booths") and dig into a classic Philippe's roast beef sandwich, a heaping portion of coleslaw, and a juicy baked apple. Yum! Remember that there are no hamburgers served here. An added perk: Free parking adjacent to the restaurant and across the street. $-$$

Where to Stay

New Hotel Otani & Garden, *120 South Los Angeles Street; (800) 273–2294; fax (213) 622–0980; www.newotani.com.* This 434-room hotel is ideal for families interested in exploring the downtown neighborhood. There are Western and Japanese suites, and best of all you are near the Japanese American National Museum. $$$

Extra Special Tip

AMTRAK (800) 872–7245 or www.amtrak.com. Extend your trip to Southern California and beyond by taking an AMTRAK ride. Their new bilevel Pacific Parlour Cars recapture the golden era of rail travel. Family friendly, these lounge cars have it all, from onboard entertainers to a mini-theater with theater-style seating and surround sound! The Kiddy-Kar has children's books and games. And you'll discover that Union Station, the departure point for this fab train, is a trip in itself. The depot, a lovingly renovated landmark, has been captured on film in dozens of movies over the years.

Hollywood

Movie stars, glamour, palm tree–lined streets, and excitement in the air— hooray for Hollywood! If downtown is the city's historic center, Hollywood is its heart. For millions around the world, Hollywood *is* Los Angeles, an illusion promoted by movie studios that remain (fortunately or not, depending on your viewpoint) very much alive in these quarters. Although the Golden Age of Hollywood is long gone, the 50-foot-high HOLLYWOOD sign still proclaims it to be the entertainment capital of the world. With the exception of the beaches, Hollywood is probably where your kids will have the most fun in Los Angeles. For that reason we suggest you spend at least two full days here.

WALK OF FAME

Hollywood Boulevard from Gower Street to La Brea Avenue and along Vine Street from Yucca to Sunset Boulevard.

In Hollywood even the sidewalks have stories to tell. This is most visibly apparent on the Walk of Fame. There is no admission charge to stroll along sidewalks with more than 1,900 terrazzo-and-brass stars etched into them. Some stars' famous sidewalk addresses are: 1644 Hollywood Boulevard (Marilyn Monroe), 1719 Vine Street (James Dean), 1750 Vine Street (John Lennon), and 6777 Hollywood Boulevard (Elvis Presley).

EL CAPITAN THEATER

6838 Hollywood Boulevard, (800) DISNEY–6.

Disney and Pacific Theaters restored this historic theater, now on the National Register of Historic Places. Originally built in 1925, it is now where Disney previews all of its movies. It is across the street from Mann's Chinese Theatre.

🏛 MANN'S CHINESE THEATRE

Adjacent to the Hollywood Entertainment Museum at 6925 Hollywood Boulevard; (323) 461–3331; http://mann.moviefone.com. $$

Hollywood doesn't get any more Hollywood than at the unofficial emperor of Hollywood Boulevard. Both the young and young at heart revel at the sight of what looks like the entrance to a Chinese imperial palace. But the main attractions here are in the theater's forecourt, where the handprints, footprints, and signatures of Hollywood celebrities dating from 1927 are quite literally cast in stone. "Gee, Mom, did Rita Hayworth really have such tiny feet?" The proof is in the pavement.

On busy street corners along Hollywood Boulevard and particularly in front of Mann's Chinese Theatre, you might spot tanned young men and women wearing sun visors and holding clipboards. If they don't approach you, make a point of approaching them: They have passes for movie previews at area studios, and sometimes you are paid to see them. It's a way the studios get audience feedback before films are released and a way for you to learn about an important, if little known, aspect of the entertainment industry.

MUSEUMS ON HOLLYWOOD BOULEVARD

📷 HOLLYWOOD GUINNESS WORLD OF RECORDS MUSEUM

6764 Hollywood Boulevard; (323) 463–6433. Monday through Friday, 10:00 A.M. to midnight; weekends 10:00 A.M. to 1:00 A.M. $$

The museum showcases offbeat testimonials to a wide variety of facts, feats, and incredible achievements. It is located in Hollywood's first movie house, The Hollywood, which is now a national historic landmark.

📷 HOLLYWOOD WAX MUSEUM

6767 Hollywood Boulevard; (323) 462–8860, fax (323) 462–3953. Open Sunday through Thursday, 10:00 A.M. to midnight; Friday and Saturday until 1:00 A.M. $$

The wax museum has 220 life-size renditions of celebrated film stars, political leaders, and sports greats. Park at the rear of the building and visit all the museums at one stop. For a discount, purchase one ticket for both the wax museum and the Guinness museum.

Extra Special Tip

Hollywood Celeb Homes If you want a guided tour past Hollywood celeb homes, here are some choices:

- **L.A. Tours** (323-469-3361). A two-hour tour by minivan through Beverly Hills and Bel-Air.
- **Starline Tours** (323-463-3333 or 800-959-3131; www.starlinetours. com). Has two-hour tours in Beverly Hills and Bel Air. The company promises fifty to sixty stars' homes.

HOLLYWOOD ENTERTAINMENT MUSEUM

7021 Hollywood Boulevard; (323) 960–4833, fax (323) 469–9576; www. hollywoodmuseum.com. Open Tuesday through Sunday, 10:00 A.M. to 6:00 P.M. $$

This museum, which opened in 1996, is the Smithsonian of the film and television world, à la L.A. gaudy, brassy, and neon-lit. It's a monument to Hollywood's glitzy and glamorous past and provides a behind-the-set look at the nuts-and-bolts mechanics of the movie and TV industry, from sound effects to scenery. There are high-tech and multimedia exhibits, too. Small-group tours are available with savvy guides. *Star Trek* lovers will go ballistic over the props and sets from that series.

RIPLEY'S BELIEVE IT OR NOT! ODDITORIUM

6780 Hollywood Boulevard; (323) 466–6335; www.ripleys.com/odditorium. Open 10:00 A.M. to 10:00 P.M. daily. $$

No problem finding the place; there's a giant Tyrannosaurus rex poking his mighty head and substantial torso out of the rooftop. The Odditorium claims to have the world's most outstanding collection of the bizarre and unusual, and it probably does. Kids love the innovative special effects, which actually help them learn some quirky facts of history they'd really have to dig for in schoolbooks.

As you stroll down Vine Street, you will stumble across another Hollywood landmark: the **Capitol Records Tower**. Resembling a stack of albums, the tower gives kids a graphic lesson that buildings can be circular, too. At night, you can see the light on top of the roof flashing "Hollywood" in Morse code.

Walking along Hollywood Boulevard any time of year, day or night, tends be an electrifying experience and one that works up hearty appetites.

HOLLYWOOD TOYS AND COSTUMES

6600 Hollywood Boulevard; (323) 464–4444; fax (323) 464–4644.
　　Here's where kids can find that monster mask they won't find back home or that conversation starter costume perfect for next Halloween. There are tiaras in all shapes and sizes and novelties too numerous to describe. This has to be the biggest supermarket of Hollywood-inspired memorabilia and trinkets in town.

MUSSO AND FRANK

6667 Hollywood Boulevard; (323) 467–3360. Closed Sunday and Monday. $$.
　　A Hollywood institution where movers and shakers have "done deals" over chicken pot pie since 1919. Whether you go for the atmosphere or the food, you simply must go.

CINEMA COLLECTORS

1507 Wilcox Avenue; (323) 461–6516. Open 10:00 A.M. to 6:00 P.M. Monday through Friday; Saturday 10:00 A.M. to 5:00 P.M.; closed Sunday.
　　What better souvenir of a visit to historic downtown Hollywood than an authentic screenplay or advertisement of your favorite movie? Pop in and treat yourself and/or your tykes to the kind of movie poster you normally find only in theaters. Because you can usually buy these posters only in Hollywood, they are often highly sought-after collectors' items. As a rule, the more vintage the movie, the more expensive the poster. Posters for newer movies typically cost about $15. There are also collectible glossy photos. Black and white reprints cost $3.50; color $5.00.

*E*xtra *S*pecial *T*ip

Hollywood & Highland This shopping and entertainment complex is an ideal venue for families to explore, from Nestlé's toll house cookies to Hollywood souvenirs in all shapes and sizes, making this modern mall "eye candy" at its best. Located at the intersection of Highland Avenue and Hollywood Boulevard, it's open daily. Validated underground parking is $2.00 for four hours. For more information, call (323) 467–6412 or go to www.Hollywood-Highland.com.

Extra Special Tip

Hollywood on Location Kids will find it fascinating to visit locations where actual filming has taken place. Hollywood on Location, a joint effort of the California Film Commission and CalTour gives movie-lovers a chance to check out these spots. To obtain their map call CalTour at (916) 322-3429 or get it faster on-line: gocalif.ca.gov, click the "movie" icon.

SAMUEL FRENCH INC.

7623 Sunset Boulevard; (323) 876–0570. Open Monday through Friday 10:00 A.M. to 6:00 P.M., Saturday 10:00 A.M. to 5:00 P.M. Parking on Stanley behind the building.

This is the ultimate bookstore for entertainment-industry-related publications. It has a wide selection of books for kids—along with an extensive selection of works on the theater, movies, television, and the other performing arts. This is your chance to add a serious and educational dimension to the pomp and puffery purveyed by Hollywood's ubiquitous PR spin doctors.

Extra Special Tip

Hollywood's Rockwalk Hollywood's Rockwalk 7435 Sunset Boulevard, in the outer lobby of Hollywood's Guitar Center. Open Monday through Friday 10:00 A.M. to 9:00 P.M., Saturday 10:00 A.M. to 6:00 P.M., Sunday 11:00 A.M. to 6:00 P.M. Inductees include Black Sabbath, Elvis Presley, Johnny Cash, Bo Diddley, the Doobie Brothers, Jimi Hendrix, and Eddie Van Halen, just to name a few.

Where to Eat

Hamburger Hamlet, *Across the street from Mann's (a.k.a. Grauman's) Chinese Theatre, 6914 Hollywood Boulevard; (323) 467–6106.* C. C. Brown's (noted for its mega-delicious hot fudge sundaes) closed a few years back after a half century of operation to become just another T-shirt outlet along Hollywood Boulevard. Since then, we now recommend that you satisfy your family's sweet teeth here. The Hamlet serves up generous, sloppy, and always scrumptious desserts. Great burgers and salads too!

For More Information

The Hollywood Visitor Information Center. *Janes House Square, 6541 Hollywood Boulevard, 90028; (213) 689–8822; www.visitLAnow.com. Open Monday to Friday, 8:30 A.M. to 5:00 P.M.* Pick up the free handy pocket guides on dining, shopping, and entertainment in Los Angeles.

Griffith Park

With its 4,000-plus acres, this park has some of L.A.'s most renowned attractions.

LOS ANGELES ZOO

Griffith Park, Golden State Freeway at Ventura Freeway, downtown; (323) 644–6400; fax (323) 662–9786; www.lazoo.org. Open daily from 10:00 A.M. to 5:00 P.M. $$

Let your kids run wild in this parklike setting where wildlife from around the world now resides. Be sure to spend at least two hours here before proceeding to other area attractions, such as the inimitable Autry Museum.

GENE AUTRY WESTERN HERITAGE MUSEUM

4700 Western Heritage Way; (323) 667–2000; fax (323) 660–5721; www.autry-museum.org. Open Tuesday through Sunday 10:00 A.M. to 5:00 P.M. Open Thursday until 8:00 P.M. $$ Second Tuesday of the month **Free**.

More than 4,000 Old West artifacts and hands-on exhibits are here, including many designed with children in mind. Special exhibits explore America's western heritage such as Native American culture, early tourism, and weaving.

TRAVEL TOWN

Griffith Park, 5200 Zoo Drive; (323) 662–5874, fax (818) 247–4740. Weekdays 10:00 A.M. to 4:00 P.M.; weekends 10:00 A.M. to 5:00 P.M. **Free** *parking.*

Kids love this outdoor transportation museum with steam locomotives to scramble over and Live Steamers, a large collection of miniature trains.

HOLLYWOOD BOWL AND HOLLYWOOD BOWL MUSEUM

2301 North Highland; (323) 850–2000; fax (323) 617–2017. Visit the museum (it's **Free***!) October through June, Tuesday through Saturday 10:00*

A.M. to 4:30 P.M. and July through September, Tuesday through Saturday 10:30 A.M. to 8:30 P.M.

The summer home of the Los Angeles Philharmonic Orchestra, the bowl is a terrific place to take in a concert. Pack a picnic to get the most out of an outdoor performance at this gleaming Los Angeles landmark.

UNIVERSAL STUDIOS HOLLYWOOD

100 Universal City Plaza (Universal Center Drive or Lankershim Boulevard from the Hollywood Freeway); (818) 622–3801; fax (818) 622–6444. Open weekdays 10:00 A.M. to 6:00 P.M. and weekends 9:00 A.M. to 6:00 P.M. $$$$

An integral part of L.A.'s history, Universal Studios is considered part of Hollywood all the same. And while another version is now in Florida, for Southern Californians there is but one Universal Studios. The movie theme links all rides and attractions, making this the quintessential L.A. theme park. And like many legends, it just gets better with age. Recent additions include **Back to the Future—the Ride, The Flintstones Show,** and the latest **Jurassic Park ride.**

But it's the classics that make Universal a genuine hoot for both kids and adults. The staple is the forty-five-minute, California-corny tram ride (catch one every five to ten minutes until 4:15 P.M.), during which Hollywood history and special effects cast their magical spell. You're whisked past the Norman Bates House (from the movie *Psycho*), over a collapsing bridge, into a Mexican village that falls prey to a flash flood, and through a Red Sea that parts just for you. Then there's a landslide and a simulated fishing village where the naughty shark from the movie *Jaws* surfaces with a vengeance. Adults fidget nervously when this happens; kids go wild. The tram ride also takes visitors past enormous studio back lots, reminding you that this is the world's biggest film and television studio. Something is almost always in production, and chances are you'll catch a bit of the action. Once you disembark, make time for the Wild West Stunt Show and Animal Actors Stage, where kids can see their favorite on-screen animal stars perform an amazing array of tricks. Those sitting in the front rows may even be asked participate on stage.

UNIVERSAL CITYWALK

1000 Universal Center Drive, Universal City. (818) 622–4455; fax (818) 622–0427. Open 11:00 A.M. to 9:00 P.M. Monday through Thursday; 11:00 A.M. to 12:00 A.M. Friday through Saturday; 11:00 A.M. to 10:00 P.M. Sunday.

Extra Special Tip

Filmed Before a Live Studio Audience . . . If the anatomy of

Tinsel Town provided by the Universal Studios experience whets your appetite to see some real lights, camera, and action, you're in the right place. People the world over watch television shows created, scripted, produced, and finally taped in and around Hollywood—and live audiences are always in demand.

TICKET TIPS

Most tickets are Free, but most shows have a minimum age requirement of fourteen. You can pick up tickets in person at Mann's Chinese Theatre and Universal Studios.

For *The Tonight Show* at **NBC Studios** in Burbank, get tickets by showing up early in the morning, then returning to wait in queue at a predesignated time the same day. And:

- **Paramount Studios Hollywood Lot** (323) 956–5000. Don't miss the studio's famed arched entrance on Melrose Avenue.

- **Warner Brothers' VIP Tour** (818) 954–1744. This is the most comprehensive tour available. It's well worth the steep $30 price. Tour guides provide a candid view of the filmmaking process. Tours leave on the hour, from 9:00 A.M. to 3:00 P.M. Tour size limited to twelve people. Children under eight not allowed. Free parking available. Tickets available up to five working days in advance.

- **Paramount Television Audience Shows** (323) 956–5575. Phone number provides latest taping schedules via touch-tone prompting (don't give up, sooner or later the taped info begins). Shows change seasonally. Keep in mind most shows, such as *Frasier*, admit kids eighteen or older. Others, such as the *Amanda Show*, admit kids seven and older. Parking for programs taped on the lot can be found on Melrose and Bronson. Some programs are taped off-lot at 5555 Melrose Avenue. Note: You must reconfirm your reservation from 9:00 A.M. to noon on taping day; it takes up to three hours to wrap a twenty-two-minute episode, so kids can get antsy. Parents must accompany children.

- **Audiences Unlimited** at Fox Television Center; (818) 753–3483 or try NBC (818) 840–3537 or CBS (323) 575–2624.

Tickets are also available outside Mann's Chinese Theatre in Hollywood, Universal Studios in Hollywood, and the Glendale Galleria. The Los Angeles Convention and Visitors Bureau's Information Centers in Hollywood and downtown L.A. also have tickets to tapings.

An eclectic outdoor pedestrian promenade with an atmosphere made to resemble a studio back lot. There are actually two streets lined with palms and joined by a central courtyard area with fountains. But all is not so sedate: A mammoth King Kong clings to the facade of one building, and a huge photographic likeness of Wayne Gretzsky adorns a sports memorabilia emporium. Get the picture? There are several theme restaurants here, including **Gladstones, B.B. King's Blues Club,** and a new **Hard Rock Cafe.** CityWalk is adjacent to the **Cineplex Odeon,** which houses—count 'em—eighteen movie theaters. Only in L.A.!

LARCHMONT VILLAGE

Los Angeles can be a *very* loud place, so if you'd like to give your ears a reprieve before heading out toward West Hollywood and the Westside communities, make a detour to Larchmont Village. This vintage neighborhood, tucked between Third Street and Beverly Boulevard, is reminiscent of the Los Angeles of decades ago. Angelenos wonder how it happened, but this nook, in full view of the HOLLYWOOD sign, has somehow escaped the onslaught of overcommercialization that has seeped into much of the city. So if you've seen one Benetton too many or have wearied of having to get your parking stubs validated, pull into one of the numerous metered spots along calm, tree-lined Larchmont Boulevard and unwind for the afternoon.

Extra Special Tip

Getty Package Check out Luxe Summit Hotel Bel Air (11461 Sunset Boulevard, Los Angeles; 800–HOTEL–44 or 310–476–6571), centrally located near the Getty Center and only 12 miles from Los Angeles International Airport. The 119-room, 52-suite hotel affords privacy and elegance. Families will appreciate the seven-acre garden setting with easy access to the 405 Freeway. Kids will like the outdoor heated pool and complimentary tennis. Parents can slip into the Bungalow Spa, which offers a variety of facials and massages. Ask about the value-packed "Getty Package." $$$$

Extra Special Tip

Gayot's L.A. Restaurant Guide This guide demystifies the restaurant scene in this sprawling city. The 2001 edition cost $14 (www.gayot. com; info@gayot.com). Twenty contributing editors descended upon restaurants from Arcadia to Zuma Beach, and you can reap the benefits of their reviews. For example, in the Larchmont area, you're directed to Chan Dara, 310 North Larchmont, one of L.A.'s first hip Thai restaurants, still serving that inimitable barbecued chicken. There are special sections for "Fun and Unusual Ways to Dine." How else would you know to pick up a picnic lunch at Rosti in Brentwood for a taste of Tuscany you can transport to the beach?

L.A. is one of the country's most fashion-savvy cities, so don't be too surprised if your kids want to get in on the act. Indulge them at **Flicka,** a children's clothing store at 204 Larchmont Boulevard, and they won't be disappointed.

CHEVALIER'S BOOKS

126 North Larchmont Boulevard; (323) 465–1334.
Check out the abundant collection of children's books.

Where to Stay

Sheraton Universal, *333 Universal Terrace Park; reservations (800) 325–3535.* This family-friendly Sheraton offers discounted rates using the Entertainment Guide. Children seventeen and under stay **Free** sharing a guest room with parents. You'll appreciate the shuttle service to Universal Studios. $$$$

Sportsmen's Lodge Hotel, *12825 Ventura Boulevard, Studio City; (818) 769–4700 or (800) 821–8511; www. slhotel.com.* This triple-A-rated hotel, with 193 country–style rooms and three restaurants, offers **Free** Universal Studios shuttle services and discount tickets for guests.

West Hollywood

Pop culture types regard West Hollywood, while small by Los Angeles standards (just 1.9 square miles), as the center of the city. This enclave, bordered by Beverly Hills on the west, is a trendy one that will appeal to older, more "cool conscious" kids. Unpredictable and irreverent, West Hollywood-ites work and play by their own rules (of which there aren't many), but for the young and the young at heart, it simply spells F-U-N.

ELLIOTT KATT

8568 Melrose; (310) 652–5178; fax (310) 652–2778; www.abebooks.com/home/filmbook.

Katt's stocks vintage and rare books—nothing new here—on the performing arts, dance, cinema, and music. This is the largest bookstore on performing arts in Los Angeles.

Extra Special Tip

A Truly L.A. Experience West Hollywood is truly a world unto itself. To really explore the countless shops along Sunset, Melrose, and Santa Monica Boulevard, consider staying at one of the tucked-away suite-type hotels. We recommend **Le Montrose Suite Hotel**, 900 Hammond Street; (310) 855–1115 or (800) 776–0666 (www.Lemontrose.com). Located in a quiet residential area only a block east of Beverly Hills and two blocks from "the Strip," the Montrose has stylish, spacious suites, many with kitchenettes, plus a rooftop pool and tennis court. Under the same ownership is Le Parc Suite Hotel, 733 West knoll Drive; (310) 855–8888 or (800) 578–4837. www.Leparcsuites.com. Hop on a complimentary bike to tour the neighborhood. Le Parc has similarly comfortable, roomy, and quiet accommodations that are perfect for families. A great respite from traffic, street noise, crowds—yet moments from the action. Ask for special rates.

SUNSET BOULEVARD

Few drives in Los Angeles are as exhilarating. Originating downtown, Sunset winds up at the Pacific Ocean. Zipping along its famous curves in Beverly Hills, you'll see stunning mansions and gorgeous gardens at every turn. But the most famous stretch, hands down, is the **Sunset Strip**, directly after Beverly Hills in

West Hollywood. The heart of the action, the 1.2-mile portion between numbers 8221 and 9255, is the mecca of L.A. nightlife. Celebrities are sighted so often here that they hardly raise eyebrows. After cruising Sunset (preferably in a convertible), park your car 𝓕𝓻𝓮𝓮 at number 8600, **Sunset Plaza,** an open-air mall. From here, you can see the entire city of L.A. teeming and (if it's nighttime) twinkling below.

Where to Eat

House of Blues, *8430 Sunset Boulevard; (323) 848–5100; www.hob.com.* Take the kids to dinner at the ultimate Sunset hot spot. Great southern cooking, a wild decor, and daily live blues performances will make for an unforgettable evening. Try the popular Sunday Gospel Brunch (served at 9:30 A.M., noon, and 2:30 P.M.) or, to save the whopping $10 valet parking fee, stop for lunch Monday through Saturday. The menu features "eclectic southern fare" such as barbecue chicken and ribs.

The House of Blues is the best compromise if you wish to steer the kids clear of the area's irresponsibly loud and obscenely crowded evening concerts. To enjoy the decor (recycled bottle caps, auto license tags, etc.), take your time. Don't leave without pigging out on a hefty slab of banana cream pie laced with chocolate fudge and caramel. Afterwards, work off those calories by simply strolling along the boulevard's trendy boutiques, sidewalk cafes, and record stores—all aglow under a sea of neon lights.

Tail O' The Pup, *329 San Vicente Boulevard; (310) 652–4517.* A Los Angeles landmark. Predating drive-ins, this giant hot-dog stand is actually shaped like a hot dog, bringing smiles to kids' faces even before they order. For those who don't mind dining in the midst of the traffic, take your place in line. Dogs range from $2.30 to $3.10, depending on what you find to stuff the bun. Look for this landmark across the street from the Hard Rock Cafe between Melrose and Beverly. $

Westside and Beverly Hills

In this immense, loosely defined swath of the city, punctuated by estates and eateries, museums and boutiques, trendiness reigns supreme. Here you may quite acceptably judge your neighbors according where they "do lunch." You're more apt to bump into a celebrity in the Westside than in Hollywood, and if you spend only five minutes driving around tony Beverly Hills, you'll find out why. There is one (perhaps only one) rule in these parts: If you've got it, flaunt it—and preferably in style. And the sheer amount of wealth people have here simply must be seen to be believed.

MELROSE AVENUE

But not all of the Westside is given over to ostentation and glitz. Here it must be said that, to an Angeleno, certain areas of L.A. defy easy geographical classification. One of these is Melrose Avenue, which is neither part of the Westside nor quite part of anything else, either.

Melrose, now immortalized by the hit TV series *Melrose Place*, actually begins (or ends, depending on your point of view) in Hollywood. The hippest sections begin at La Brea and branch out toward the west. But the street is as much a state of mind as it is a chunk of asphalt. This is a place with a carnival-like atmosphere, where anything goes. Find a parking spot (keep looking, you'll find one) and simply drift. Whatever boutique, gallery, or cafe you settle into is not as important, though, as the simple act of "doing" Melrose, which affords a close-up look at what makes Los Angeles tick. An hour or two or three here, and you'll begin to understand the triple L.A. creed: creativity, individuality, and sunshine. You'll love it.

BEVERLY CENTER

A mega-mall where Beverly Boulevard meets La Cienega. Here you will find the original **Hard Rock Cafe,** easily recognizable by the automobile projecting from the rooftop. For an upscale Italian lunch where kids are welcome (and where Al Pacino has been seen feasting on pasta), venture across the street to tiny **Locanda Veneta,** 8638 West Third Street; (310) 274–1893.

MUSEUM ROW

Stretching along the "Miracle Mile" of busy Wilshire Boulevard, this is the home of a singularly fun and educational selection of museums.

GEORGE C. PAGE MUSEUM OF LA BREA DISCOVERIES

5801 Wilshire Boulevard; (323) 934–7243, fax (323) 783–4843; www.tarpits.org. Open Tuesday through Sunday 10:00 A.M. to 5:00 P.M. $$

The Page Museum can be found at the **La Brea Tar Pits,** a black and slightly malodorous lake of ancient goo that trapped thousands of Ice Age creatures. More than 100 tons worth of their fossilized remains have been extracted from the pits, and new discoveries are always being made. Dozens of saber-toothed tiger and wolf skulls, woolly mammoth skeletons, and other specimens are on display. This is educational, unadulterated magic for adults and the under-twelve crowd.

LOS ANGELES COUNTY MUSEUM OF ART

5905 Wilshire Boulevard; (323) 857–6000, fax (323) 931–7347; www.lacma.org. Open Monday, Tuesday, Thursday: 12:00 to 8:00 P.M.; Friday: 12:00 to 9:00 P.M. (except for the Japanese Pavilion); Saturday, Sunday: 11:00 A.M. to 8:00 P.M.; closed Wednesday. $$

The anchor museum for Museum Row, it now spans the world from prehistory to the present. If you manage your time right, you can sweep through in two hours or less and still be able to visit other museums in the neighborhood. Music, film, and educational events happen year-round, and there's a good chance something is happening during your stay. The information desk is accommodating, so just ask. While you're here, be sure to step over to the legendary La Brea Tar Pits. Your kids might recall the pits erupting in the film *Volcano*. Don't worry, the site is perfectly benign. The only thing you have to fear around these parts is the horrific traffic on Wilshire Boulevard.

 ## PETERSON AUTOMOTIVE MUSEUM

6060 Wilshire Boulevard; (323) 930–2277. Open Tuesday through Sunday 10:00 A.M. to 6:00 P.M. $$. Children five and younger, **Free**.

This new museum, already a landmark by virtue of its striking, futuristic design, celebrates L.A.'s icon, the automobile—its history and role in the development of Southern California. In its 80,000 square feet of exhibition space, you'll find more than 200 cars and motorcycles, plus loads of fascinating automotive memorabilia.

FARMER'S MARKET

6230 West Third Street, a few footsteps north of Museum Row; (323) 933–9211. Open Monday through Saturday 9:00 A.M. to 7:00 P.M. and Sunday 10:00 A.M. to 6:00 P.M. **Free** *entrance.*

This is the Westside's answer to downtown's Grand Central Market, with 120 restaurants, produce stands, and retail stores.

Where to Eat

Johnny Rockets, *7507 Melrose Avenue; (323) 651–3361.* A 1950s-style chain that imparts the past with panache. Kids will get a kick out of tabletop jukeboxes, singing wait staff, and chrome counters. $

Beverly Hills

If you continue west on Wilshire Boulevard, you will enter the heart of Beverly Hills. The chief appeal of this city (population 33,000) for many families will be strolling up and down **Rodeo** (row-DAY-oh) **Drive**, a scaled-down version of New York's Fifth Avenue—with palm trees. It's fun to do a little window shopping at the most exclusive boutiques in Los Angeles. This is the center of the Golden Triangle district, framed by Crescent Drive and Wilshire and Little Santa Monica Boulevards, which represents the crème de la crème of Beverly Hills shopping. **Via Rodeo,** a new addition to Rodeo Drive, is a cobblestoned cache of shops and eateries at the Wilshire Boulevard end that resembles a charming European village.

After the price tags make you wonder who in the world can afford all of this stuff, hop in your car and find out. The gracefully curving palm- and jacaranda-lined streets between Santa Monica and Sunset Boulevards are home to affluent Mediterranean-style villas and many an elegant English Tudor-style manse. North of Sunset, however, especially in the exclusive **Bel Air** neighborhood farther west on the boulevard, is where the real estate truly boggles the mind. If you feel like a Peeping Tom, don't worry—every Angeleno worthy of the name has looky-looked at least once at these estates.

Extra Special Tip

Museum of Tolerance AT THE SIMON WIESENTHAL CENTER. *Simon Wiesenthal Plaza, 9786 West Pico Boulevard, between Century City and Beverly Hills; (310) 553–8403; www.wiesenthal.com. Open Monday through Thursday 10:00 A.M. to 4:00 P.M., Friday 10:00 A.M. to 3:00 P.M.; Sunday 10:30 A.M. to 5:00 P.M. Closed Jewish holidays, January, July, Labor day, and December 25. Recommended for kids age ten and older.* $$

Inside a shimmering $50 million building are a series of high-tech exhibits dedicated to the promotion of understanding among people from all backgrounds and walks of life. Interactive exhibits chronicle the history of racism in American history and the events and consequences of the Holocaust. The presentations have been crafted with historical precision and much sensitivity. Both children and adults will leave the museum enlightened and moved by history and the dangers of forgetting it. Allow two and a half hours for a docent-guided tour.

BEVERLY HILLS TROLLEY

Leaves from the corner of Dayton Way and Rodeo Drive, in front of the Chanel boutique, every half hour Tuesday through Saturday, beginning at 10:30 A.M. $.

If you'd rather leave the driving to someone else for a while, park your car at one of Beverly Hills's numerous two-hour Free parking lots and head for the **Beverly Hills Trolley**, a San Francisco–style cable car that takes visitors on thirty-minute guided tours of the area's historical landmarks and residential areas. In a city where Rolls Royce Silver Clouds seem to outnumber Toyotas, the trolley is a welcome bargain.

No tour of the Westside would be complete without visiting **Westwood Village**, a vibrant neighborhood just west of Beverly Hills bounded by Wilshire Boulevard, the 405 (San Diego Freeway), and the UCLA (University of California, Los Angeles) campus. UCLA's presence imbues Westwood with a youthful air. It is an ideal area for walking around, browsing in record stores, or simply "hanging out" at a cafe or ice cream parlor. College students aside, it's movies that really make Westwood tick. Movie theaters are everywhere, and these are not your ordinary theaters. Screens are enormous. Seats are plush and tilt back. Popcorn is fresh and usually made with real butter. We're talking cinematic heaven here.

CORINTH CERAMICS STUDIO

2237 Corinth Avenue; (310) 444–0901.

When the kids are getting antsy and they feel like throwing things, take them to the Corinth Ceramics Studio. Children five and older can get their hands dirty while learning how to make wild and wonderful things with clay.

KID'S UNIVERSE

15327 Sunset Boulevard, Pacific Palisades; (310) 454–6867.

A toy store for parents who prefer to invest in educational toys. This means no toy guns or violent games. Art projects, chemistry labs, and computer classes fascinate the kids, who don't seem to miss Barbie Dolls and tea sets.

WESTSIDE PAVILION

Where Westwood Boulevard meets Pico.

This is a *very* Los Angeles mall, with more than 180 shops and the **Samuel Goldwyn Movie Theater**, which usually shows foreign and artsy films. But of course, children, there are plenty of places to eat at the mall.

Extra Special Tip

Getty Center, *1200 Getty Center Drive; (310) 440–7300; www.getty.edu. Open Sunday 10:00 A.M. to 6:00 P.M.; Tuesday through Thursday 10:00 A.M. to 6:00 P.M.; Friday and Saturday 10:00 A.M. to 9:00 P.M. Closed Monday and major holidays. Admission is* Free. *Parking $5.00. It is essential that you call ahead for a parking pass.*

This landmark complex on a dramatic hilltop location commands breathtaking views of Los Angeles, the Santa Monica Mountains, and the Pacific. Its vast collection of art defies imagination. The 110-acre complex, designed by Richard Meier, is designed as a nexus for families and neighbors, as well as scholars and students. It all begins with a tram ride to the summit, where your family will be awed by panoramic views of the L.A. area. The center will fascinate every family member, even the two-year-olds in strollers with microscopic attention spans. At the central plaza, you'll find gardens, terraces, and dramatic architecture.

Start your exploration by viewing the film at the 450-seat auditorium, so you can best decide how to spend the next few hours. There are five two-story pavilions around an open courtyard. Each gallery pavilion has an information room: Stop here to watch an artist carve a block of marble or have your kids handle a piece of wood. These hands-on experiences are accentuated by ongoing films, concerts, and demonstrations. Try to visit on the weekends when family festivals give you and your kids "new ideas about the cultures and people behind the art."

Just to give you a hint of the magnitude of the collection, there are fourteen galleries of French furniture and decorative arts, including four eighteenth-century paneled rooms. After an hour or so of visiting the galleries, we suggest stopping off the courtyard at the Museum Cafe for a snack. The center houses such masterpieces as *Adoration of the Magi*, by Andrea Mantegna, *Irises* by van Gogh, *Spring* by Sir Lawrence Alma-Tadema, and Middle Ages miniatures by various painters. Plus there are sculptures, manuscripts, and photographs. After all this, you'll be ready for time in the Family Room for a look at activity guides and game boxes for children and adults. Arrive when the center opens (10:00 A.M.). The "Getty experience" should generate enthusiasm to ignite your children's appreciation of art—they may just want to return again!

THE SKIRBALL CULTURAL CENTER AND MUSEUM

2701 North Sepulveda Boulevard; (310) 440–4600, fax (310) 440–4595; open Tuesday, Wednesday, and Friday 10:00 A.M. to 4:00 P.M.; Thursday 10:00 A.M. to 9:00 P.M.; Saturday and Sunday noon to 5:00 P.M. Closed Monday. $$

This museum highlights the experiences of American Jews as they transitioned from the Old World to the New World. The goal of the Skirball Center is to bring people of all backgrounds together. The museum enjoys a tranquil setting along the Sepulveda Pass near the **Getty Center,** so you can plan a full day of museum touring while in this vicinity. Children will enjoy the Skirball's hands-on **Discovery Center,** which will give them a more realistic perspective of archaeology and history.

Exhibits here follow the ebb and flow of Jewish immigration; displays include fragments of original Ellis Island wooden benches and a sectional reconstruction of an archaeological dig. For lunch, **Zeidlers** at the museum entrance can't be beat. Cuisine is light, fresh, and imaginative. Salads, sandwiches, and desserts are reasonably priced, and the ambience is family-friendly. The gift shop has an impressive range of books covering the Jewish experience, with an excellent selection of books for children. Count on two hours, including lunch.

Brentwood is a posh enclave that spreads on either side of Sunset Boulevard west of the 405. Here you begin to feel the Pacific breezes, but they are best enjoyed while experiencing perhaps the finest ice cream L.A. has offer. You'll find it at:

 ### EIGER ICE CREAM
124 East Barrington Place; (310) 471–6955. Hours vary.

The decor is minimalist. The ice cream is not. With an 18 percent butterfat content, we're talking ice crème de la crème here. Most flavors, including the ever-popular dark chocolate and raspberry combo, taste surprisingly light because of the purity of the ingredients. No wonder Eiger is a favorite snack spot for quality-conscious Westside families. A calorie cone costs $2.85; we loved their chocolate chip ice cream in one.

Where to Eat

Apple Pan, *10801 West Pico Boulevard; (310) 475–3585. Closed Monday.* Here's a diner of sorts that has been feeding hungry Angelenos since the 1940s. The layout is simple: a long, three-sided countertop with a kitchen in the center. Wait for a vacant stool (there are no tables) then move in for the kill: The burgers served here are so divine they have been known to reconvert vegetarians. Many visit for the apple pie (it's the Apple Pan, after all), but the banana cream is really luscious.

California Pizza Kitchen, *121 North La Cienega Boulevard, between Beverly Boulevard and Third Street; (310) 854–6555.* Kids of all ages flock to this haven of "designer" pizzas. When all else fails to win a majority vote, try a

delicious bacon, lettuce, and tomato pizza. $$

Where to Stay

Hotel Oceana, *849 Ocean Avenue, Santa Monica, 90403; (310) 393– 0486 or (800) 777-0758; fax (310) 469–1182; beachsuite@aol. com; www.hoteloceana.com.* The designers had families in mind when they put the finishing touches on this sixty-three-room suite-style hotel. Super stylish, splashed with kid-friendly colors and designs, every suite over-looks the pool—and the ocean is across the street. Kids will love exploring the nearby Third Street Promenade. Suites average around 860 square feet and have kitchens. Continental breakfast, included in the room rate, is delivered to you at the time you specify. Rates for suites are $195, and you're about fifteen minutes by car from the Getty Center. $$$

L'Ermitage Hotel, *9291 Burton Way; (800) 800–2113 or (310) 278-3344;*

www.lermitagehotel.com; Member of Preferred Hotels. L'Ermitage epitomizes the Beverly Hills "90210" lifestyle. If you want to splurge just once on your Southern California tour, this is the hotel, in a lovely residential area, where you can make it happen! Spacious rooms with two dreamy queen-size beds start at $335. One-bedroom suites with lots of space to spread out are one option for families. Tell the kids not to roller-skate on the gorgeous marble bathroom floors! $$$$

Le Meridien, *465 South La Cienega Boulevard, Beverly Hills; (800) 543–4300 or (310) 247–0400.* Le Meridien is situated in the middle of Restaurant Row and 2 blocks from one of the region's twenty most visited attractions, the Beverly Center. The four-star deluxe hotel has 297 rooms. $$$$

The Valleys

Did you think a trip to L.A. would be, like, complete without a visit to the valleys? Think again, dude (or dudette). The valleys are worlds unto themselves.

When you hear people talk about "the Valley," they are referring the **San Fernando Valley**, home of over a million people and bigger than metropolitan Chicago. You can get an overview of the valley from serpentine **Mulholland Drive**, which bisects the Santa Monica Mountains, the natural topographical separator of the Los Angeles Basin from the vast valley floor.

If you have time for an outdoor interlude, by all means explore the **Santa Monica Mountains National Recreation Area**. These chaparral-covered slopes, which stretch 55 miles from Griffith Park all the way to Point Mugu in Ventura County, have provided the backdrop for many a Hollywood movie. For instance,

M*A*S*H (movie and TV show) was filmed at **Malibu Creek State Park** (alongside Las Virgenes Road/Malibu Canyon) and at **Paramount Ranch**, Agoura Hills, 1813 Cornell Road; (805) 370–2301. The latter, once owned by Paramount Studios, still has the fabricated western town used in dozens of films and TV shows. Horseback riding and nature walks through the canyons covering 2,400 acres also make for refreshing mini-escapes from the city's bustle.

Coldwater Canyon (which connects Beverly Hills to Studio City) and, about 10 miles to the west, **Topanga Canyon** (connecting Malibu to Woodland Hills) are sights to see. *Topanga* is a Chumash Indian word meaning "mountains that crash down to the sea." You'll see what the Chumash meant if you drive the length of the canyon. If you park your car along any of the turnouts along the road and look closely at the exposed mountain sides, you may well see fossils of ancient sea creatures—proof positive the whole area was once under water.

The intersection of Topanga and Old Topanga Canyon Roads is marked by the village of—no surprise here—Topanga, with its health food stores, hippie feel, and more, including:

WILL GEER THEATRICUM BOTANICUM

1419 North Topanga Canyon Boulevard, 5 miles from U.S.–101; (310) 455–2322, fax (310) 455–3724; for schedule, (310) 455–3723; www. theatricum.com.

An open-air ancient Greek-style amphitheater that features first-rate performances of Shakespearean works and other classics. Open in May, this outdoor theater offers more than culture. It occupies a natural setting with a youth drama camp, youth classes, and a variety of plays. Call ahead for schedule.

TOPANGA DAYS

See how Californians celebrate the "mountains that crash down to the sea" each May during a three-day funfest of food, music, and arts and crafts. Special events such as Best Dressed Live Fowl and Best Weed Arrangement are sure to tickle kids' funny bones.

If you have more time, explore the stretch of miles-long **Ventura Boulevard,** which bisects Encino and Sherman Oaks. Together with U.S. Highway 101 (the Ventura Freeway), "the Boulevard" is the valley's main artery. Of the two, Encino has the more upmarket sections, whereas Sherman Oaks (along Ventura Boulevard) has a myriad of Melrose-like establishments.

WARNER BROS. STUDIOS

4301 West Olive; (818) 954–1669. Monday through Friday, every hour on the hour, 9:00 A.M. to 3:00 P.M. Children under eight not allowed. $$$$

This two-hour tour is an eye-opening experience for the family. Tour guides give educational, inside information on popular TV shows. You will see a lot of action on the back lots if you are fortunate enough to be on the tour while filming is in progress.

Santa Clarita Valley, which lies just north of the San Fernando Valley, means one thing:

SIX FLAGS CALIFORNIA

26101 Magic Mountain Parkway (just northeast of downtown Los Angeles on Interstate 210); (661) 255–4100 or (661) 255–4849; accommodations, (800) 718–TOUR, ext. 123; www.sixflags.com. $$$$

The foothills here house legendary roller coasters: Colossus, the Revolution, Viper, Ninja, and the Riddler's Revenge. There's also Batman—the Ride, Tidal Wave, Goliath, and Roaring Rapids. **Six Flags Hurricane Harbor,** a new fantasy-theme water park, adjoins Magic Mountain. The two-park complex is now officially known as **Six Flags California**. Though this is the place for thrill seekers, there are plenty of "soft adventure" activities for the less daring.

Extra Special Tip

Time Out for Mom! While the family is reeling on the roller coaster, mom can slip off to the L'Espirit day spa and salon (661–284-3633) for a well-deserved Raindrop Therapy massage or Ultimate Pampering facial. And when the kids are munching on chips and cookies, mom can have a spa-style lunch while waiting for her next appointment! Located in a shopping center at 25832½ McBean Parkway, in Santa Clarita, the spa offers an ideal place for mom to relax before the next leg of the journey.

Pasadena

Pasadena is the shining star of the San Gabriel Valley, just northeast of downtown L.A. While the annual **Tournament of Roses Parade** and **Rose Bowl** football game have made the city famous, the charm is in Old Pasadena with its Spanish Mission–style buildings, many of which are listed on the National Register of Historic Places.

RAGING WATERS

111 Raging Waters Drive (take the Raging Waters Drive exit off Interstate 210), San Dimas (east of Pasadena) where the 10, 210, and 57 freeways meet; (909) 592–1457, 24-hour information line (909) 802–2200, fax (909) 592–1457; www.ragingwaters.com. Daily June 1 to late September; weekends in May. It is essential you call in advance as hours and days of operation constantly change. $$$$

The fifty-acre park, the largest water theme park west of the Mississippi, houses fifty *million* gallons of water and more than twenty water attractions for aquatic thrillseekers, including the Vortex, a four-story tower with two enclosed, 270-foot-long, spiral body flumes; and the world's highest headfirst water ride, the High EXtreme. For those not inclined to plunge from such heights or velocities, there are tamer options, including a children's activity pool and play area. The Wedge is the latest daunting water experience.

HUNTINGTON LIBRARY ART COLLECTION AND BOTANICAL GARDENS

1151 Oxford Road, San Marino (2 miles from Pasadena); (626) 405–2100; fax (626) 405–0225; webmaster@huntington.org; www.huntington.org. Open noon to 4:00 P.M. Tuesday through Friday and weekends 10:30 A.M. to 4:30 P.M. $$

At the 150-acre Huntington, you can walk through perfectly manicured gardens on your way to view a precious scrap of Emily Dickinson poetry or other historical documents and manuscripts. The library is home to many first-edition books, including a Gutenberg Bible. The wonderful exhibits bring history into perspective, reminding us how people managed to communicate before computers and faxes. The oil paintings, furniture, and decorative accessories are elegantly displayed. There's a restaurant, the **Rose Garden Cafe** (enjoy an English tea) (626) 683-8131, and an excellent bookshop.

SANTA ANITA PARK

285 West Huntington Drive, Arcadia, (626) 574–7223.

Located just a few miles east of Pasadena, Santa Anita Park is more than just a racetrack. The architecture is art deco and the cuisine is outstanding. Thoroughbred racing is the main event at the track, but this park is relaxing, exquisitely landscaped, and worth the trip.

Extra Special Tip

Driving Excitement While you're driving around this sprawling city, you might just run into the Irwindale Speedway, a 6,500-seat motor sports and entertainment mecca in the heart of the Los Angeles Basin. Families can share the excitement (and noise, we recommend ear plugs!) of this $5 million facility that has twin, integrated one-half- and one-third-mile paved oval tracks and close-to-the-action spectator grandstands. It's the Irwindale Speedway, 13300 East Live Oak Avenue, Irwindale; (626) 358-1100; fax (626) 357-4227 or call (888) 954-2500 (California, Nevada, and Oregon only); www.irwindalespeedway.com for events and driving directions. Your kids can even get autographs by visiting "the pits." VROOM!!!!

Where to Stay

The Ritz-Carlton, Huntington Hotel and Spa, *1401 South Oak Knoll Avenue, (626) 568-3900 or (800) 241-3333; www.ritzcarlton.com.* Located in Pasadena, fifteen minutes from downtown Los Angeles, this lovingly restored historic landmark first opened in 1907 and recalls the grace and elegance of a past era. The hotel has two restaurants, a full-service spa, twenty-three acres of gardens and grounds, and eight guest bungalows with working fireplaces. Special packages are available. $$$$

Coastal Los Angeles

After a few days spent driving, museum hopping, driving, stargazing, driving, shopping, and driving some more, you and the kids may begin to feel a little antsy. If you're starting to think "L.A.'s great, but . . ." then it's high time you hit the beach. Whereas in cities like Boston or New York there are only gradations of stress—it never totally dissipates—in L.A., stress can be lowered to tolerable levels thanks to the proximity of a long and stunning coastline and the beach. And when it comes to beaches, you're truly spoiled with choices in Southern California. Three areas are absolute must-sees for families on vacation: Venice Beach, Santa Monica, and Malibu. While there are other beaches, none bear the singular L.A. signature as indelibly as these. (The Long Beach area is discussed separately.)

Venice Beach

Venice Beach lies due south of Santa Monica and just up the sand from **Marina del Rey**, which has the world's largest human-made harbor, plus a re-created New England fishing village. Venice is sort of like Melrose Avenue (see Westside, above) meeting the sea: Anything goes, but with copious amounts of suntan oil.

While L.A. beaches are endowed with over 22 miles of bicycle paths, the most colorful swath is **Oceanfront Walk** in Venice, where bikers, roller skaters, and zany in-line skaters all compete with pedestrians for maximum mobility. Add street performers—from jugglers and mimes to musicians and comedians—and you'll get an idea of the carnival-like atmosphere permeating the place. People come to Venice Beach not so much for the beach, which is actually quite nice, but to watch other people. A serious amount of body spotting goes on at **Muscle Beach**, a section of the sand where bodybuilders work out in the sun and flex their Schwarzenegger deltoids, pectorals, and biceps. If your kids are needling you for souvenirs, this is the place (and remember that when buying trinkets on the beach, tackiness is a virtue).

There are many colorful little cafes and restaurants practically on the beach; you have only to choose. Otherwise, we recommend:

JODY MARONI'S SAUSAGE KINGDOM
2011 Ocean Front Walk; (310) 822–5639. Open, thankfully, every day.
This zany beach is the perfect place for this eclectic stand that brings sausage to a new level. Just try the Mexican Jalapeno and you'll understand why! Open for breakfast, too. Check out the Family Special: four hot dogs, four soft drinks, and fries for $10.99!

Marina del Rey

C & C TRATTORIA
31 Washington Boulevard; (310) 823–9491. Serves breakfast, lunch, and dinner.
This restaurant has been around since the 1960s, a record by L.A. standards. Those $6.95 plates of spaghetti, large enough for two, come with garlic rolls you can't stop eating. Kids will like the casual ambience.

Santa Monica

One beach up from Venice is Santa Monica, perhaps more fun for kids on account of the famous **Santa Monica Pier**, which takes L.A.'s seaside fun quite literally into the Pacific. Built in 1909, the pier houses a boardwalk complete with shops, snack stops, bumper cars, and a colorful turn-of-the-century carousel. You can even try your hand at fishing from the pier. Santa Monica's wide, sandy beach might be ideal for families with younger children, because even on windy days there is very little surf.

BERGAMOT STATION ARTS CENTER

2525 Michigan Avenue, Santa Monica, CA 90404. Take Olympic Boulevard to Cloverfield and a right to Michigan Avenue, where you will find the gated entrance.

Check your street map because this enclave of forty eclectic art galleries exhibits a range of art, some of which kids might like. This is a light industrial area, so galleries have metallic roofs, high ceilings, and lots of wall space. From sculpture and wearable art to paintings, photography, and prints, this is a wonderland of creativity. Recent artists seen here include Frank Stella, Robert Motherwell, and David Hockney. There is a schedule listing each gallery, openings, and current exhibits. The Gallery Cafe is a good place to stop first and take a moment to plan your gallery stops. The **Santa Monica Museum of Art** has changing exhibits as well, and kids will find it a friendly place to start their art exploration. Plan to spend about an hour. Parking is free. For information on the Santa Monica Museum of Art, call (310) 586-6488 or fax (310) 586-6487; www.smmoa.org. Hours are Tuesday through Saturday 11:00 A.M. to 6:00 P.M.; Sunday 12:00 to 5:00 P.M.

THIRD STREET PROMENADE

In Santa Monica, some of the best times await families just a few blocks from the sand. Here you can shop in the sunshine or at night until midnight at this ultra-lively spot that begins at Broadway (actually at the Santa Monica Place mall) and stretches north to Wilshire Boulevard along Third Street. Now one of the hippest areas in L.A., the promenade overflows with shops, restaurants, entertainment centers, and street performers. Wander and enjoy.

MAGICOPOLIS

1418 Fourth Street; (310) 451-2241; fax (310) 451-2341; www.magicopolis. com. $$$

This new 350-person, two-theater club welcomes all ages to ninety-minute magic shows Tuesday through Sunday. World-class magicians entertain at evening performances (8:00 P.M.) and weekend matinees (2:00 P.M. and 7:00 P.M).

MUSEUM OF FLYING

2772 Donald Douglas Loop North; (310) 392–8822; fax (310) 450–6956; www.museumofflying.com. Open Wednesday through Sunday, 10:00 A.M. to 5:00 P.M. with reservations. $$

Visitors often forget that, like Beverly Hills, Santa Monica is a separate municipality from L.A., even though L.A. surrounds it. So it should not be too surprising that Santa Monica has its own airport. But what makes it such a Southern California airport is that, in addition to the usual runways and airplanes, it has the **Museum of Flying**. The museum offers a new "Airventure" attraction. Here, aspiring aviators can tinker with exhibits detailing airplane maneuvers, pilot procedures, and aircraft design. Lest you think this is all straying too far from the beach, don't worry—there's always Malibu.

Where to Eat

Cora's Coffee Shop, *1802 Ocean Avenue; (310) 451–9562.* Located next door to Capo Restaurant, this great institution is a leftover from the 1930s. This tiny diner serves marvelous daily specials, a terrific steak salad, and fresh-baked pies, such as pear and peach. A real find. Limited free parking. $$

Drago, *2629 Wilshire Boulevard (26th Street), (310) 828–1586.* This new "family-style dining" concept is certain to spread like wildfire. At this popular Sicilian-style restaurant, you'll forget mundane pizza when pumpkin tortelloni and other specialties arrive. The family can share and explore the true tastes of Italy here. $$$$

Typhoon, *3221 Donald Douglas Loop South, Santa Monica 90405; (310) 390–6565 at the edge of the Santa Monica Airport.* This is the place kids will love on Sunday afternoons, thanks to a terrific brunch designed by Brian Vidor, the proprietor. Kids can watch the airplanes land between Vietnamese spring rolls, fried rice, and puffy *bao* buns. New on the menu are insects! Yes, there are crunchy crickets, stir-fry crickets, giant mountain ants, and Thai-style crispy scorpions. Now that's a mouthful! Celebrities such as John Travolta have been known to fly their private planes to Typhoon, so be prepared for a stellar dining experience. $$$

Where to Stay

Casa Del Mar, *1910 Ocean Front Walk; (800) 898–6999 (a member of the Leading Hotels of the World). Ask about rates and seasonal packages.* Another newcomer is the 129-room Casa Del Mar, built in 1926 and renovated to perfection, complete with two-tiered Venetian glass chandeliers. It's a splurge to stay here, but the location makes the choice irresistible. Kids will enjoy skating along the famous bike path and being near that inimitable Santa Monica Pier. $$$$

Le Merigot Beach Hotel, *1740 Ocean Avenue; (310) 395–9700 or (800) 926–9524; fax (310) 395–9200.* Le Merigot is a French-themed 175-room hotel. Families will appreciate the spacious guest rooms, 27-inch television and in-room movies, and the 24-hour room service. $$$$

Both hotels are minutes from the J. Paul Getty Museum and 9 miles north of the Los Angeles International Airport, Beverly Hills, and Century City. There are good views of Catalina.

Looking for rentals? At **Spokes and Stuff,** on the beach in front of the hotel, you'll find boogie boards, bikes, and in-line skates for rent.

The Fairmont Miramar Hotel, *101 Wilshire Boulevard, Santa Monica, (310) 576–7777.* Just minutes away from area attractions including the Getty Center, Beverly Hills, Malibu, and Venice Beach. The historical bi-level suites with one and two bedrooms are ideal for families. Kids' menus, CD players, babysitting services, and cribs are some of the amenities offered. $$$$

Malibu

Malibu is Beach Boys country, where a dozen or so beaches beckon alongside the Pacific Coast Highway (PCH) at the foot of the Santa Monica Mountains. Although part of Los Angeles County, Malibu is actually a separate city—and a funny-shaped one at that. Because of the area's geography, Malibu is barely 1.5 miles wide but some 27 miles long. PCH is the lifeline of this seaside community and the commuting route to Hollywood for the hundreds of celebrities who live in seaside villas and estates here. You might even bump into one or two on the beach—it happens all the time.

RAMIREZ CANYON PARK (ages 10 and above)

5750 Ramiriz Canyon Road, off Pacific Coast Highway; (310) 589–2850; fax (310) 589–2561; www.smmc.ca.gov. Garden tours are scheduled on Wednesday. Reservations should be made at least one month in advance. One-hour tours, followed by tea, fill one to two months in advance. $$$$

This is another celebrity retreat to marvel at. On nearly twenty-three acres of verdant, rolling hills, orchards, and meadows, the center was Barbra Streisand's gift to the Santa Monica Mountains Conservancy in 1993. It serves today as a think tank for environmental issues. That activity and the residential nature of the area limits parking and public access. But there are limited tours of the Center's botanical, historical, and architectural background. Just imagine the parties, the celebs, and the glamour of this fairy-tale estate.

One of the finest stretches of sand is **Malibu Beach**, on either side of the **Malibu Pier** (you can't miss it). White sand, pounding surf, sun-bronzed life-guards with fluorescent-colored zinc oxide on their noses—yes, this is Malibu. Even in summer, the beach is not as crowded as those in Santa Monica and Venice, and there is less emphasis on people-watching. Malibu-ites know what's really important in life: surfing.

Actually, the best surfing beach is **Zuma Beach**, 5 or 6 miles farther up PCH. If you head in that direction, we recommend:

Where to Eat

Dukes at Malibu, *21150 Pacific Coast Highway; (310) 317–0777. Lunch and dinner daily.* Named after Duke Kahanamoku, the "father of surfing," this is the ideal place for your family to get the feeling of the Malibu lifestyle, thanks to the magnificent stretch of windows overlooking the beach. The prices are reasonable, and the kids will like the exhibit of surfing memorabilia. You might remind them about the Beach Boys and all of those surfing movies from the 1960s. $$

Granita, *23725 Pacific Coast Highway; (310) 456–0488.* A nifty lunchtime stop, Granita is the brainchild of super-chef Wolfgang Puck (of Spago fame). It resembles a temple in Atlantis from the outside and a futuristic aquarium on the inside. Named for an Italian dessert of flavored, shaved ice (always available), Granita offers a California eclectic menu, and the desserts are deliciously inventive. Recommended for brunch Saturday or Sunday, Granita is located in a shopping center with a variety of trendy Malibu boutiques. Pick up a free copy of the local newspaper, the *Malibu Times,* for a look at what's happening around town. $$$$

Long Beach

As its name indicates, life in Long Beach centers around things of a coastal nature. From Los Angeles, take the San Diego Freeway to the Long Beach Freeway to Long Beach. With more than 50 miles of sandy beaches and shorelines, this seaside city in southern L.A. County makes an ideal setting for the TV show *Baywatch*, which began filming here several years back. Settled by the Spaniards in 1784, Long Beach has been a visitor-friendly place ever since. Real live guides are at visitors' disposal in the animated downtown area. Though close to downtown Los Angeles, Long Beach has a distinctly different, somewhat lower-key feel. If you have the time, give yourself two full days here.

In Long Beach, you will find an array of peaceful beaches that invite sunbathing and sand-castle building. Thanks to a human-made breakwater, the beaches of Long Beach do not experience high surf and are therefore ideal for families with small children.

MARINA BEACH

(a.k.a. Mother's Beach). (562) 570–3215 for directions; www.ci.long-beach. ca.us.

This half-park, half-beach site has an enclosed swimming area monitored by a lifeguard daily 8:30 A.M. to 7:00 P.M. If surfing is pretty much out of the question, these beaches have other assets. For example, they are the only ones in L.A. County where water enthusiasts can launch small boats, catamarans, and personal watercraft directly from the sand.

Extra Special Tip

All Aboard! There are many fun family attractions in Long Beach, but none so famous as the majestic *Queen Mary*. The world's largest luxury liner is permanently docked in the fifty-five-acre **Queen Mary Seaport**. There are many hotels in Long Beach, but if this is your first visit, try the **Hotel Queen Mary**, 1126 Queens Highway; (562) 435-3511, fax (562) 437-4531; www.queenmary.com. The ship has been converted into the 365-stateroom hotel. While aboard, you can take a Behind the Scenes guided tour or dine in one of the ship's restaurants. The **Chelsea** serves lunch and dinner. Here you'll also find the **Piccadilly Circus**, the boat's original shopping center. If you can't stay on the ship for a night or two, be sure to indulge in a tour. Add a tour of the Russian Foxtrot Submarine *Scorpion*. $$$

Long Beach is also L.A. County's foremost jumping off point for whale-watching excursions. From January to March every year, 15,000 Pacific gray whales migrate from Arctic feeding grounds to their Baja breeding grounds by way of the waters just off the L.A. County coast. Unlike their East Coast counterparts, excursions here are generally warm-weather affairs, even on the open sea.

CABRILLO MARINE AQUARIUM

3720 Steven White Drive, in nearby San Pedro; (310) 548–7562; (310) 548–2649; www.cabrilloaq.org. Open Tuesday through Friday 12:00 to 5:00 P.M.; Saturday and Sunday 10:00 A.M. to 5:00 P.M. Parking is $6.50 per car. **Free** *but a donation of $2.00 for adults and $1.00 for children appreciated.*

Featuring thirty-five aquaria, these innovative exhibits will teach kids about the plant and animal life of Southern California. The simulated "tide pool touch tank" is a good place to start this aquatic journey. In fact, there are whale trips organized from December through March focusing on the Pacific gray whale. This museum predated the Long Beach Aquarium by sixty-five years. Here's where it all started, and that's no fish story.

LONG BEACH AQUARIUM OF THE PACIFIC

Downtown Long Beach, 100 Aquarium Way; (562) 590–3100; www.aquariumofpacific.org. Open daily 9:00 A.M. to 6:00 P.M. $$$

When you see the full-scale model of a blue whale, you'll know you're at the Long Beach Aquarium, a 156,000-square-foot facility that covers five acres and includes 550 species and 12,000 specimens. After you've checked out the wonderful displays, head for **Kid's Cove.** A playground of the Pacific Ocean, Kid's Cove is a hands-on interactive aquarium experience for kids of all ages. The focus is on feeding habits, family structures, and the lives of the exhibit specimens.

ON THE WATER

- **Alfredo's Beach Rentals.** *(562) 434–6121.* Boogie boards? Skates? Bikes? All of the equipment you couldn't get on the plane and in your car can be rented from Alfredo! Also in Redondo Beach and Manhattan Beach.

- **Catalina Channel Express.** *(800) 481–3470.* These speedy boats take one hour; there are thirty departures daily.

- **Star Party Cruises.** *(562) 799–7000.* Offers a 300-passenger, 100-foot motor cruiser.

- **Long Beach Sport Fishing.** *(562) 432–8993.*

- **Spirit Cruises.** *(310) 548–8080.* Out of San Pedro.

- **Off Shore Water Sports.** *(562) 436–1996.* **Bay Boat Rentals.** *(562) 598–BOAT;* *(562) 433–9595.* **Gondola Getaway.** *(562) 433–9595.* Capture the romance of an Italian gondola ride by way of the canals that meander through Naples. Naples, California, that is!

- **Shoreline Village Cruises.** *(562) 495–5884.* Sail aboard a 90-foot motor yacht. All tours include narration, and Shoreline guarantees sightings or a second trip is **Free**.

- **Tall Ship *Californian*.** *(800) 432–2201; www.californian.org.* Located at the foot of the Pine Avenue Pier in the Rainbow Harbor area, halfway between Parker's Lighthouse and the Long Beach Aquarium of the Pacific. You can't miss this ship—it's 145 feet long and ready to hoist its sails. The main purpose is educational. Call in advance for sailing dates. Cruises are usually four hours around Long Beach Harbor. Guests are invited to participate in sailing the ship thanks to the friendly crew. $$$$

Of course, you don't have go whale-watching to take a cruise out of Long Beach Harbor. Most of the aforementioned companies offer charter cruises on a regular basis.

Where to Eat

The Chelsea, *located on the Queen Mary, the south end of the 710 Freeway.* *(562) 499–1685.* Winner of the 2001 Golden Scepter Award for excellence in cuisine, the Chelsea is located on what is considered to be one of the most luxurious ships in the world, the Queen Mary. The restaurant is noted for its fantastic fresh seafood specialties. Reservations are strongly suggested. $$$

King's Fish House/King Crab Lounge, *100 West Broadway at Pine Avenue;* *(323) 423–7463.* Here are the ingredients for a popular family restaurant: friendly service, comfortable wood booths, and fair prices. It all adds up to our favorite seafood restaurant in Long Beach. $$

Where to Stay

Dockside Boat & Bed, *Long Beach, Rainbow Harbor;* *(562) 436–3111;* *www.boatandbed.com.* Four private

moored yachts to stay aboard overnight. All boats fully furnished; continental breakfast basket provided.

Next to Aquarium of the Pacific and Shoreline Village. A highly recom- mended unique family lodging experi- ence. $$$$

For More Information

Long Beach Area Convention and Visitor's Bureau, *1 World Trade Center, Third Floor, 90831; (562) 570–3170; fax (562) 435–5653; www.golongbeach.org; staff@ longbeachcvb.org.*

Santa Catalina Island

Sail away to Mediterranean-like Santa Catalina Island, a relaxing 22-mile trip from Long Beach. You might want to spend a couple of days on this enchanted isle, where you won't need a car for a change. The best way to get to Santa Catalina is aboard **Catalina Channel Express,** *(310) 519–1212; fax (310) 548–8425; www.catalinaexpress.com.* See sun-splashed **Avalon**. With its restaurant- and boutique-filled streets and a population of around 3,000, it's Catalina's biggest town.

ART DECO CASINO BUILDING

You can't miss this red-roofed Avalon landmark as you approach the harbor. Never actually used for gambling, the casino is famed for its ballroom and the **Avalon Theatre**, the first theater designed for sound movies. Art deco murals of stylized underwater scenes grace the theater, which also has a full-scale pipe organ with 250 miles of wire.

Extra Special Tip

On the Wild Side Catalina now has a four-hour off-road tour that is ideal for familiies. Visiting the "wild side" of the island on the Cape Canyon Tour, passengers ride in a four-wheel-drive vehicle driven by a Catlina Island Conservancy-trained guide. The tour features a scenic drive along a ridgeline overlooking coves of west Avalon, a guided tour of the American Bald Eagle Habitat at Middle Ranch, and a ride in Cape Canyon for stunning views of the Catalina outback. Contact the Catalina Island Visitor's Bureau and Chamber of Commerce, P.O. Box 217, Avalon, CA 90704, (310) 510-1520, fax (310) 510-7607 or www. catalina.com.

But the real fun of Catalina is outside. Kids go bonkers over naturalist-guided **Jeep Eco-Tours** that permit off-road exploration of portions of the island's natural habitat not normally open the public. It's a great way to take in vast expanses of unspoiled scenery and look for herds of wild buffalo.

To really probe the depths of Catalina's natural beauty, take a ride aboard a climate-controlled semi-submersible boat. There is no more comfortable way to see the island's magnificent **Undersea Gardens** than from inside the *Starlight* or the *Emerald*, where the captain and crew describe the aquatic flora and fauna floating by outside the windows. Night tours are especially thrilling.

Back in Long Beach, a somewhat softer adventure awaits in the **Naples Island** district.

Extra Special Tip

Kid Cuisine The Blue Parrot at Metropole Market Place, Avalon; (310) 510-2465; www.blueparrotcatalina.com; is priced right. This second-floor restaurant has a terrific view of Avalon Bay, and the burgers are among the best in town. For dessert, walk over to the **Catalina Cookie Company** at 205 Crescent Avenue; (310) 510-2447 for an Eclipse, a fudge cookie dipped in white chocolate. It's just another delicious day in Catalina!

GONDOLA GETAWAY
5437 East Ocean Boulevard; (310) 433–9595; www.gondolagetawayinc.com.
$$$$

Locally famous, the Getaway features Venetian-style gondolas that cruise through narrow canals in the "backyards" of affluent home owners. Owner Michael O'Toole claims at least 300 marriage proposals have been proffered aboard his gondolas since they started plying the waters in 1982.

Long Beach offers countless ways to spend a pleasant morning or afternoon. The 15-block stretch of Second Street in the **Belmont Shore** area has swimming, lots of boutiques, and restaurants that range from Indian to Chinese to New York–style bagel shops. A mile and a half away, down **Ocean Boulevard**, downtown activity hustles and bustles along revitalized Pine Avenue.

LATIN AMERICAN ART MUSEUM
628 Alamitos Avenue; (310) 437–1689; fax (310) 437–7043;
www.molaa.com. Open Tuesday through Friday 11:30 A.M. to 7:00 P.M.; Saturday

11:00 A.M. to 7:00 P.M.; and Sunday 11:00 A.M. to 6:00 P.M. Call ahead for calendar of events.

This recently opened museum in downtown Long Beach is the only museum in the country that focuses on Latin American art. The 20,000-square-foot building was built in 1920 and houses the Robert Gumbiner Foundation collection of Latin American art, galleries for temporary showings, La Geleria (a gallery and shop), a research library, and a performance area. There's also a restaurant.

Where to Eat

Babouch, *810 Gaffey Street, San Pedro; (310) 831–0246; www.babouchrestaurant. com.* Familes share traditional Moroccan specialities such as couscous with vegetables and shrimp misharmel. The belly dancing performances are noisy and entertaining. Kids will find this a real cultural experience.

Claim Jumper, *Marketplace Shopping Center, 6501 East Pacific Coast Highway, Long Beach; (562) 431–1321.* For hearty family fare, it features wood-fired pizza, fresh fish, and large salads. $$

Home, *1760 Hillhurst Avenue, Los Feliz; (323) 669–0211.* Leave it to L.A. to open a real kid-haven restaurant. At Home, kids are encouraged to explore the patio, climb overstuffed sofas, check out the goldfish and doggies, and, in general, not follow the usual dining-out rules of "sitting still." Celebs' kids hang out here; Tim Roth's and rocker Anthony Kiedis's kids have been seen raiding the toy chests and like the cartoons in the playroom. The

four-page menu has everything but the kitchen sink, from My Sister the Tree Hugger (granola/fruit/yogurt) to a Mickey Mouse waffle. It's all happening right in Los Feliz, Madonna's neighborhood. Who knows, you just might see her daughter, Lourdes, there!

L'Opera, *101 Pine Avenue, at First Street, Long Beach; (562) 491–0066.* Exquisite early twentieth-century architecture sets the scene for sophisticated Italian cuisine. Best for age ten and older; this is not a pizza palace!

Parker's Lighthouse, *435 Shoreline Drive, Long Beach; (562) 432–6500, serves lunch and dinner daily.* Your best bet is the Sunday brunch. Just look for the lighthouse to find this family-friendly restaurant. The view is terrific from the patio: the Queen Mary and harbor. The down-to-earth menu includes fresh fish, mesquite-grilled with a choice of side sauces. And don't forget to save room for a slice of key lime pie. $$$

Where to Stay

Pavilion Lodge, *513 Crescent Avenue, Avalon; (800) 343–4491 or (310) 510–2500.* Beach lovers will like the Pavilion Lodge—it's just "14 steps from the beach." The 800 number is available between 8:00 A.M. and 5:00 P.M. for handling a variety of requests. You can use it to arrange to stay at the Pavilion Lodge or the Atwater Hotel or to check out Discovery Tours and Catalina Island camping.

Extra Special Tip

Leave the Driving to Someone Else

Riding the rails—it's the alternative to driving on your trip through Southern California. AMTRAK has excellent routes in the West, and it's the best way to circumvent the traffic! The train that does it best is called the San Diegans, with service between San Diego, Los Angeles, Santa Barbara, and San Luis Obispo.

Among the attractions along the route are Disneyland, Knott's Berry Farm, the missions at San Juan Capistrano, Sea World, Hollywood, and Beverly Hills.

Children's discounts offer savings for families. Kids ages two to fifteen are entitled to a 50 percent discount when traveling with an adult paying full fare.

Trains feature connections to **AMTRAK** motor coach service, commuter rail, and rapid transit.

Call **AMTRAK** at 800–USA–RAIL.

Redondo Beach

The South Bay is smaller than Long Beach and a mere twenty minutes' drive from downtown. You're within a forty-five-minute range of Disneyland, Knotts Berry Farm, Universal Studios, Six Flags Magic Mountain, the La Brea Tar Pits, Catalina Island terminals, and the Queen Mary Seaport. Redondo has the Galleria at South Bay (with 150 stores), superb sportfishing, and charters at the Redondo Beach Marina.

 PORTOFINO HOTEL AND YACHT CLUB
260 Portofino Way; (800) 468–4292 or (310) 379–8481; www.noblehouse hotels.com.

If you should base the family here, you'll have the best of both worlds—the atmosphere of a small, seaside village and the accessibility of most of Greater L.A.'s attractions. The oceanfront location places you but 6 miles from LAX and within walking distance of King Harbor, Seaside Lagoon, and a 27-mile-long coastal walking and biking path passing through Venice, Santa Monica, and Malibu. The Portofino's 163 rooms include 90 with views of the Pacific. Fifty-six rooms are smoke-free.

An assortment of complimentary family amenities is provided, from "baby joggers" and snugglies to high chairs and diapers. Phil Brown, president of Noble House Resorts and Hotels, declares, "The family amenities provide our guests with all the comforts and necessities of home, making family travel more convenient and relaxing." Way to go, Phil! We wish more hotel execs shared your enlightened attitude.

Where to Eat

Captain Kidd's, *209 Harbor Drive; (310) 372–7703. Open for breakfast, lunch, and dinner daily.* Fresh-from-the-market fish and crab are prepared grilled, Cajun-style, charbroiled, or deep fried and come with two generous side dishes. Check the Captain Kid's menu for seafood specialties. $$

The Fun Fish Market & Restaurant, *121 International Boardwalk; (310) 374–9982.* The Redondo Pier has an amusement center, which is good, but even more appealing around lunch- or dinnertime is Fun Fish, where fresh fish is served any way you like it. Kids will like selecting their fish from a tank. And don't forget the chowder! $$

Extra Special Tip

Fabulous Fixin's Before you start your food trek, it's wise to consult one of the guides available from Zagat (800–333–3421) or the L.A. guide to dining and nightlife free from the Los Angeles Convention and Visitor's Bureau (213-624-7300, fax 213-624-9746). Dining early will alleviate waiting; although it's always best to make a reservation whenever possible. Los Angeles restaurants are finally nonsmoking, thus making the environment family friendly.

And if you want to dine in, you will be pleasantly surprised at the marvelous array of takeout cuisines at many Los Angeles–area supermarkets such as Gelsons, Ralphs, and Bristol Farms. The colorful display of salads, hot and cold dishes, desserts, and deli specialties dazzles the eye and palate.

Coastal Los Angeles Where to Eat

As you move up and down the coast of Los Angeles County, you will find several good food establishments. Here are some that have been reviewed by "Junior Gourmet Zack." Zack is the son of restaurant critic Bob Gourley and gives the "thumbs up" to the following:

Aimee's, 800 Pacific Coast Highway, Redondo Beach; (310) 316–1081. The menu varies, everything from "spaghetti without green stuff" to osso buco and pork chops with whole-grain mustard sauce. Follow it up with a crème brûlèe. $–$$

King's Hawaiian Restaurant and Bakery, 2808 West Sepulveda Boulevard, Torrance; (310) 530–0050. Breakfast is available at King's. Zack gives the

French toast here the "thumbs up." Reasonable selections. Parents will enjoy dishes like Huli Huli chicken and standards like pot roast and fried chicken. $–$$

Papadakis Taverna, 301 West Sixth Street, San Pedro; (310) 548–1186. Greek food, dancing, and glass smashing. Sometimes there are belly dancers. Then you can sample the baklava for dessert. $$

Versailles, 1000 North Sepulveda Boulevard, Manhattan Beach; (310) 937–6829. Fine examples of Cuban cuisine. Share with the kids as the portions are huge. Nothing on the menu is over $10.95 except for the fresh lobster. $–$$

Annual Events

The following list of Greater Los Angeles-area events was made available courtesy of the California Trade and Commerce Agency Division of Tourism.

JANUARY

Tournament of Roses Parade—Pasadena. (626) 449–4100; fax (626) 449–9066. World-class parade of flowers features music and fantasy. The annual Rose Bowl game follows.

Dr. Martin Luther King Day Parade and Festival—Long Beach. (562) 570–6816. Parade, entertainment, and celebrations. Free.

Martin Luther King, Jr. Celebration—Santa Monica. (310) 434–4209; fax (310) 450–2387. Interfaith celebrations with music, dramatic readings, and inspirational messages. Free.

Golden Dragon Parade—Los Angeles. (213) 617–0396; fax (213) 617–2128. Chinese New Year parade. Colorful floats, multicultural performances, arts and crafts. Free.

FEBRUARY

Queen Mary Scottish Festival—Long Beach. *(562) 435–3511.* Pipe bands, Highland dancing, parades, competitions, performances, exhibits, and Scottish food and drink.

Camellia Festival and Parade—Temple City. *(626) 287–9150.* Children's festival and parade; floats decorated with camellias, carnival, and art show. **Free.**

Azalea Festival—South Gate. *(323) 563–5447; fax (323) 564–8632.* Festival features events, parade, talent shows, car show, arts and crafts, food.

APRIL

Toyota Grand Prix—Long Beach. (800) 4LB–STAY or *(562) 436–3645.* International field of world-class drivers and high-performance race cars negotiate the tight turns of the city in heated wheel-to-wheel competition.

Fine Arts and Crafts Fair—Santa Monica. *(310) 393–9825; fax (310) 394–1868.* Fair features one hundred of Southern California's finest artists and craftspeople. **Free.**

Pasadena Spring Art Show—Pasadena. *(626) 795–9311; fax (626) 795–9656.* Fine arts and crafts, children's amusement area, international food court. **Free.**

Glory of Easter—Garden Grove. *(714) 971–4000; fax (714) 750–3836; 12141 Lewis Street.* An annual Easter play with a cast of over 200 features special effects and live animals.

McDonald Fiesta-Broadway Fiesta—Los Angeles. *(310) 914–8308; fax (310) 914–8313.* Largest Cinco de Mayo celebration in the nation, covering 36 blocks with six stages of continuous entertainment. **Free.**

Carnaval Primavera Festival—Huntington Park. *(323) 585–1155; www.hp chamber1.com.* An international ambience blended together with color and excitement. Four city blocks with more than 120 food, arts and crafts, and commercial exhibitors, concerts, live entertainment, amusement rides, and more.

MAY

Cinco de Mayo—Los Angeles. *(213) 485–6855; fax (213) 485–5238.* Celebrate Mexico's 1862 victory over French forces in Pueblo, Mexico, with popular and traditional music, cultural presentations, dancing, and ethnic cuisine. **Free.**

Springfest—Alhambra. *(626) 282–5767; fax (626) 282–5596.* Street festival includes arts and crafts, entertainment, food, a car show, city displays, exhibits, and children's rides. **Free.**

Affaire in the Garden Show—Beverly Hills. *(310) 285–2537.* Quality hand-crafted arts and crafts. **Free.**

Museums of the Arroyo Day—Los Angeles. *(626) 796–2898; fax (626) 304–9652.* Open houses for the Southwest Heritage, Lummis, Pasadena Historical, and Gamble House Museums, with each one offering activities, exhibits, and entertainment. **Free.**

Old Pasadena Summer Fest—Pasadena. *(626) 797–6803; fax (626) 797–3241.* Festival includes Taste of Pasadena arts and crafts, children's activities, jazz festival, and entertainment. **Free.**

JUNE

Southern California Cajun and Zydeco Festival—Long Beach. *(502) 427–3717.* Cultural event features Cajun and Creole cuisine, dance and music workshops, and children's activities. **Free.**

San Fernando Valley Fair—Burbank. *(818) 557–1600; fax (818) 557–0600.* Live entertainment, rodeo, agricultural education, competitive exhibits, a carnival, arts and crafts, and an international food court.

Silent Film Benefit—Avalon, Catalina. *(310) 510–2414; fax (310) 510–2780.* Experience classic silent films with live music accompaniment held in the world-famous Casino building on Catalina Island.

Theater and Arts Festival—North Hollywood. *(818) 508–5155; (818) 508–5156.* More than fifteen theaters host two days of live theater and entertainment, arts and crafts, food booths, and a children's court. **Free.**

Old Pasadena Chili Championship—Pasadena. *(626) 795–9311; fax (626) 795–9656.* Cook-off features music and chili sampling.

JULY

Fireworks Extravaganza—Long Beach. *(562) 435–3511.* Features strolling entertainment and fireworks display. **Free.**

Celebration on the Colorado Street Bridge—Pasadena. *(626) 441–6333; fax (626) 441–2917.* Festival features bands, local restaurants, classic autos and motorcycles, art exhibits, and performance groups.

Art Festival—Malibu. *(310) 456–9025; fax (310) 456–0195.* Live music, food fair, orchid display and sale, pancake breakfast, and more than 200 artists on hand with exhibits. **Free**.

San Fernando Fiesta. *(818) 898–1200.* San Fernando's largest family event including food, games, carnival rides, top-name Latin entertainment, and a consumer trade show. **Free**.

Fourth of July Celebration—Avalon. *(310) 510–1520.* Golf car parade, dinner, and fireworks over Avalon Bay.

Lotus Festival—Los Angeles. *(213) 485–8745.* Experience a variety of Asian cultures, entertainment, art exhibits, ethnic cuisine, and children's activities.

Celebrate America—Santa Monica. *(310) 452–9209.* Celebrate July 4 Santa Monica style with music, booths, and spectacular fireworks. **Free**.

AUGUST

Catalina Ski Race—Long Beach. *(714) 994–4572.* World's largest water-ski race involving 110 boats pulling skiers from Long Beach's Belmont Pier to Catalina.

Taste of San Pedro—San Pedro. *(310) 832–7272; fax (310) 832–0685.* San Pedro restaurants present their signature entrees. Arts and crafts and a vintage car show are other highlights.

African Marketplace and Cultural Faire—Los Angeles. *(323) 734–1164; fax (323) 485–1610.* More than 2,000 performing artists, 300 vendors and exhibitors, fifteen cultural and ethnic festivals, seven stages of live performers, an international food court, and a children's village.

SEPTEMBER

Fine Arts and Crafts Fair—Santa Monica. *(310) 393–9825; fax (310) 393–1868.* Fair features a hundred of Southern California craftspeople. **Free**.

Salute to Route 66 Parade—Duarte. *(626) 357–3333.* Parade to honor the "mother road" of America includes classic car shows, stationary and marching bands, and floats. **Free**.

Catalina Festival of the Arts—Avalon. *(310) 510–2700.* Exhibits include mixed media, photography, crafts, and sculpture. **Free**.

Uptown Artwalk—Whittier. *(562) 696–2662; fax (562) 696–3763.* Artwork demonstrations, children's art activities, and live entertainment. **Free**.

Los Angeles County Fair—Pomona. *(909) 623–3111; fax (900) 865–3602.* California's sensational county fair you can't miss! It takes at least a full day to visit the flower and garden exposition, midway, and various entertainments. Kids can participate in educational activities.

Greek Festival—Arcadia. *(626) 499–6943; fax (626) 449–6974.* Authentic Greek festival with food, pastries, folk dances, music, dance lessons, and children's games.

OCTOBER

Affaire in the Garden Show—Beverly Hills. *(310) 285–2537.* Quality handcrafted arts and crafts. **Free.**

Catalina Jazz Festival–Avalon. *(818) 347–5299; www.jazztrax.com.* Contemporary jazz musicians and instrumentalists perform in the renowned Casino ballroom.

Lobster Festival—Redondo Beach. *(310) 374–2171.* Lobster feed, dancing, entertainment, kid's games, Pirate Camp, crafts, and seafood specialty booths.

Scandinavian Festival—Santa Monica. *(626) 795–9311; fax (626) 795–9656.* Daylong smorgasbord celebrates the riches of Denmark, Finland, Iceland, Norway, and Sweden with food, music, imports, costumes, arts, crafts, and a raffle.

Industry Hills Pro Rodeo—City of Industry. *(626) 961–6892; fax (626) 961–0691.* PRCA rodeo event, petting zoo, clowns, food and beverages, and western theme concessions.

Calabasas Pumpkin Festival—Agoura. *(818) 225–2227.* Wild West theme event includes games, music, handmade crafts, food, pumpkin contest, stage.

Village Venture Street Fair—Claremont. *(909) 624–1681; fax (909) 624–6629.* Arts and crafts, food, costumes, pumpkins, children's parade, and Halloween decorating contests. **Free.**

Arcadia Craft Faire and Carnival—Los Angeles. *(626) 447–2159; fax (626) 445–0273.* Rides, craft area, car show, food, games, entertainment, and attractions.

Oktoberfest—Huntington Beach. *(714) 895–8020; fax (714) 895–6011.* Old World village celebrates entire month with German food, drinks, and oompah bands. **Free.**

Octoberfest—Pasadena. *(626) 795–9311.* Music, dancing, German food, games, and a pumpkin patch. **Free**.

Sabor De Mexico Lindo Festival—Huntington Park. *(323) 585–1155; www.hpchamber1.com.* Cultural celebration that pays tribute to the heritage of Mexico, through music, dancing, food, displays, and arts and crafts. The festival brings together more than 125 foods, arts and crafts, and commercial exhibitors, plus concerts, live entertainment, two amusement and carnival areas, and a petting zoo. Three days and nights. **Free**.

NOVEMBER

Intertribal Marketplace—Los Angeles. (323) 585-1155; *fax (323) 224–8223.* Cultural event of music and dancing features more than ten artisans representing tribes throughout the nation.

Craftsman Weekend—Pasadena. *(626) 795–9311; fax (626) 795–9656.* Exhibition and sale of craftspeople's furnishings, accessories, and books, art exhibition, lectures, workshops, restoration and design demonstrations, and tours.

Fall Art Show—Pasadena. *(626) 795–9311; fax (626) 795–9656.* Fine arts and crafts, food court, entertainment, and children's amusement area. **Free**.

Doo Dah Parade—Pasadena. *(626) 795–9311; fax (626) 795–9656.* Eccentric parade features unique performing groups and artist teams; includes wacky costumes and cars. **Free**.

The Fabulous Christmas Lane—Huntington Park. *(323) 585–1155; www.hpchamber1.com.* This parade features professionally built floats designed with the parade's annual theme. Giant character balloons, equestrians, marching bands, colorful dance ensembles, plus other specialty units.

DECEMBER

Main Street Merchants Holiday Festival—Santa Monica. *(310) 395–3648.* Sand sledding, face painting, and loads of holiday festivities kids will enjoy. **Free**.

Christmas Parade—Whittier. *(562) 696–2662; fax (562) 696–3763.* Bands, floats, horses, and Santa. **Free**.

Holiday Open House. *(310) 510–2414.* Each year the Catalina Island Museum hosts open house at the Inn at Mount Ada, formerly the Wrigley Mansion. The Mansion is exquisitely decorated for Christmas. The event culminates with a raffle of an all-expense paid stay at the Inn to benefit the Catalina Island Museum. **Free**.

The Hollywood Christmas Parade. *(323) 469–2337.* This festive parade features celebrities, marching bands, classic cars, and, last but not least, Santa Claus!

The Glory of Christmas at the Crystal Cathedral—Garden Grove. *(714) 544–5697.* A blending of Christmas carols, live animals, flying angels, and special effects brings the nativity to life in this highly orchestrated stage show.

Orange County

The land on which the visionary Walt Disney built his Magic Kingdom in 1955 was discovered more than 150 years earlier by a Spanish explorer. Gaspar de Portolá gazed upon the magic river bringing life to the fertile valleys and fields leading to the Pacific Ocean and named it Santa Ana. In 1857, German immigrants bought portions of the area, at the time a Spanish land grant, for a mere $2.00 an acre. They called their new settlement Anaheim, which means "home of the Ana." With cuttings from their native Rhineland, the settlers began growing California's first grapes and making wine. In the late 1880s, the vineyards of California's wine capital in Anaheim were devastated by blight. So the settlers decided to plant oranges instead, and the current name Orange County was created.

Today's fastest-growing crops in the area are neither grapes nor oranges but amusement parks, sports attractions, and a galaxy of animated stars from Disney—all ready and waiting for the picking by you and your fun-starved entourage. If oranges thrive in this climate, so will you! Wintertime highs of 65 degrees rise to but 79 degrees in summer, and overnight lows—even in winter's darkest hours—rarely dip below 45 degrees. December through February is what passes for the area's "rainy season," although total annual rainfall is only 13 inches. Days are sunny and mild, nights clear and cool—that's the forecast for your Orange County visit.

Casual clothing is the way to go for 90 percent of your family fun here. Be sure to pack shorts, T-shirts, cotton pants, skirts, and really comfortable walking shoes or sandals. Bring a sweater or light jacket for evenings—along the waterfront it may get nippy. Don't forget your bathing suit and shades (but never fear, you can always buy the latest beachwear and gear at one of the numerous malls or gift shops).

Your family can still visit the city of Orange itself, with its historic district featuring a nineteenth-century soda fountain; relax on the beaches of Newport

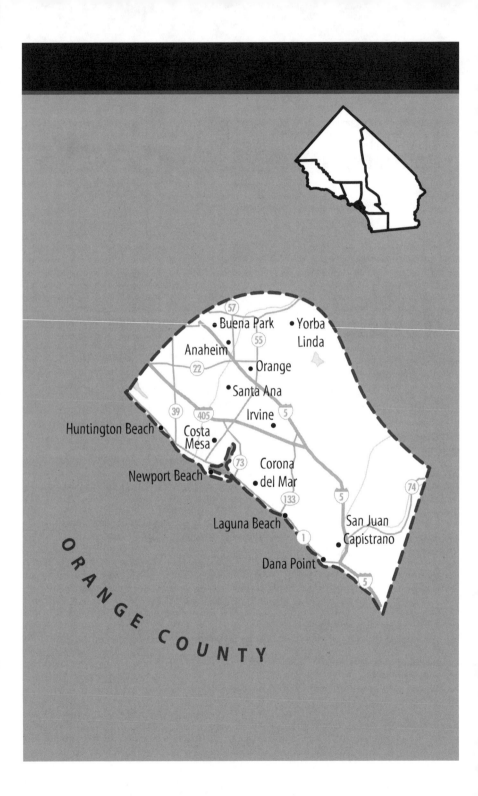

Buena Park
Yorba Linda
Anaheim
Orange
Santa Ana
Huntington Beach
Irvine
Costa Mesa
Newport Beach
Corona del Mar
Laguna Beach
San Juan Capistrano
Dana Point

ORANGE COUNTY

and Laguna; check out the world-class surfing at Huntington Beach; shop 'til you drop in Costa Mesa; see the swallows in Capistrano and the marine life in Dana Point. By popular kid demand, however, you will doubtless make your first Orange County stop in Anaheim at "Uncle Walt's place"—the unparalleled Disneyland Resort, which includes the original Disneyland and the new Disney's California Adventure parks, plus the Downtown Disney District.

Anaheim Resort Area

From Los Angeles, drive south on Interstate 5 to the city of Anaheim and vicinity, the family fun center of Orange County. Using Disneyland Resort as your Orange County starting point makes much sense geographically and economically. Family-style lodging and restaurants are plentiful and very affordable in Anaheim and neighboring Buena Park. Make room reservations as far in advance as you can, especially for summertime and holiday periods, since Anaheim attracts 17 million-plus visitors every year, including many who visit at the West Coast's largest exhibition center, the Anaheim Convention Center. Many hotels and motels provide package plans that include Disneyland Resort tickets (passports) as well as free breakfasts and transportation services.

DISNEYLAND PARK

1313 South Harbor Boulevard, at the intersection of Interstate 5; (714) 781–4565; www.disneyland.com. $$$$

Hours: During the fall, winter, and spring, hours are generally Monday through Friday 10:00 A.M. to 8:00 P.M., Saturday 9:00 A.M. to midnight, and Sunday 9:00 A.M. to 10:00 P.M. Summertime hours are usually 8:00 A.M. to midnight every day. Extended hours are in effect during holiday periods. Very Important Note: Hours are subject to change, so call ahead for exact opening and closing times on your preferred days to avoid disappointment.

Directions: Follow the signs to designated parking areas. Trams are provided to the main entrance. (Parking is $7.00 per car per day).

The magic of Disneyland exists in eight "themed lands." Begin with your entrance on Main Street USA, a composite of America in the 1900s. Move along to Adventureland, housing Tarzan's Treehouse, one of our favorites, the Indiana Jones Adventure, and the Jungle Cruise. New Orleans Square features the classic Pirates of the Caribbean and Haunted Mansion. Critter Country has the wettest ride—Splash Mountain—and Many Adventures of Winnie-the-Pooh. Fantasyland is highlighted by Sleeping Beauty's Castle, King Arthur's Carousel, Mr. Toad's

Wild Ride, Peter Pan's Flight, and the breathtaking Matterhorn Bob-sleds. Next comes Frontierland with the cool Big Thunder Mountain mine ride. Mickey's Toontown is basecamp for all your young ones' favorite Disney characters. See Mickey's and Minnie's residences and Goofy's Bounce House, and ride Roger Rabbit's Car Toon Spin. Tomor-rowland is the launching pad for space-age attractions. Here you will thrill to classics such as Star Tours and Space Mountain, plus the Astro Orbitor, Rocket Rods, Innoventions, interactive water fountain, and 3-D "Honey I Shrunk the Audience."

Extra Special Tip

Doing Disneyland With three attractions—the original Disneyland, the new Disney's California Adventure, and the Downtown Disney District—this trip can be a visual and physical overload for you and your family. We advise a minimum two-night stay and three days to really enjoy all the fun available. (It's practically impossible to do both parks in one day; even one overnight and two full days can be tricky, depending on your stamina.) For first-timers, begin with the original Disneyland early in the day. Take a short break midday for lunch and naps, then return for the afternoon and evening shows (such as the fireworks over the Magic Castle). You'll need a second full day to really explore DCA (Disney's California Adventures) because many of the activities are live stage shows and movies presented at specific times. On the third day, revisit favorite attractions at either park and get in some shopping at Downtown Disney. Always check park operating hours and plan your visit around your kids' eat-sleep schedule. The best new timesaving option is the FASTPASS, a computerized ticketing system that allows you to reserve a time slot for the most popular rides. When you arrive at your designated time period with your computer-gener-ated pass, you'll go to a special line and get on within minutes. Highly recommended!

DISNEY'S CALIFORNIA ADVENTURE PARK

1313 Harbor Boulevard, at the intersection of Interstate 5 (you can also exit at Disneyland Drive); (714) 781–4565; www.disneyland.com. Open year-round, generally Monday through Friday from 10:00 A.M. to 8:00 P.M.; Saturday from 9:00 A.M. to 10:00 P.M. and Sunday from 9:00 A.M. to 10:00 P.M. Extended *hours during the summer and holiday periods. Note: Hours are very subject to change; call ahead for exact opening and closing times on your preferred days to visit. Admission fees are also subject to change. Many special packages and promotions are offered throughout the year. $ $ $ $*

Opened in Feburary 2001 with much fanfare; this new fifty-five-acre theme park celebrates the great state of California—from Disney's imaginative perspective. You'll enter the park, affectionately known as DCA for short, from the promenade area under a replica of San Francisco's Golden Gate Bridge to explore four distinct lands. Paradise Pier re-creates a beachfront amusement zone reminiscent of Santa Monica Pier or the Santa Cruz boardwalk. Check out California Screamin'—a super-fast steel roller coaster that loops you upside down around a Mickey Mouse head icon. The 150-foot Sun Wheel Ferris wheel, Orange Stinger, Jumpin' Jellyfish, and Golden Zephyr rides get family fun points here, along with plenty of concessions and food vendors along the midway.

The second land, dubbed the Hollywood Pictures Backlot, has huge soundstages that hold attractions such as Jim Henson's *Muppet Vision* 3-D movie; Hyperion Theater's live hip musical/dance performances; the Superstar Limo ride; and the Animation Center with its five separate options to discover the magic behind cartoons and films.

The Golden State land features the must-do Soarin' Over California experience, where you will hang with feet dangling as you fly like an eagle—visually—around an 80-foot dome-shaped motion picture screen

Extra Special Tip
Disneyland Resort Fun Facts

- 21,000 men and women are employed as cast members at the peak of summer season.

- 7,000 gallons of paint are used each year to spiffy up the park.

- 150,000 lightbulbs are used to brighten up the park.

- More than 7,500 trees, 50,000 shrubs, and 900 species of plants can be found here. It takes a 110-person landscaping staff to maintain it all.

- Park guests buy in one year: 4 million hamburgers, 1.6 million hot dogs, 3.4 million orders of fries, 1.5 million servings of popcorn, and 1.2 million gallons of soft drinks to wash it all down.

- Annual trash totals approximately 17 million pounds. However, Disneyland does recycle 5 million pounds of cardboard, 1 million pounds of office paper, and 14 million pounds of aluminum cans every year.

filled with an amazing view of the best California scenery. Don't miss Grizzly River Run, a white-water-rafting ride that swirls you down two waterfalls; Bountiful Valley Farm with its demonstration veggie and fruit gardens; Robert Mondavi's Golden Vine Winery (with wine tasting for us adults); Pacific Wharf, where you can watch Boudin's Bakery make sourdough bread and mission tortillas pop out; and a movie starring Whoopi Goldberg in the Golden Dreams Theatre.

October 2002 saw the opening of "A Bug's Land," a fourth area including five attractions inside Flik's Fun Fair. Plenty of food and beverage options inhabit DCA, and be prepared to spend some gold nuggets to enjoy the diverse range of fare, ranging from traditional burgers, dogs, and fries to sushi, chowder, pizza, and Chinese and Mexican cuisine. Disney's California Adventure certainly embraces Walt's original promise: "Disneyland will never be complete as long as there is imagination left in the world."

EDISON INTERNATIONAL FIELD

2000 Gene Autry Way, Anaheim. Baseball season runs April through September; call (714) 634–2000 for a schedule and ticket prices; www.angelsbaseball.com.

The 70,000-seat stadium is home to baseball's Anaheim Angels (2002 World Series champions) and a variety of other sporting events, concerts, and festivals.

ARROWHEAD POND OF ANAHEIM

2695 East Katella Avenue, Anaheim. (714) 704–2400; www.arrowheadpond. com.

This 19,200-seat enclosed arena hosts many events and concerts and is home to the National Hockey League's Mighty Ducks, who skate from October to April (714-704-2701). Call for ticket prices and event schedules.

STADIUM PROMENADE

Adjacent to the Arrowhead Pond Stadium on East Katella Avenue, Anaheim. (714) 288–9845. Open daily, hours vary by season.

This impressive dining and entertainment complex includes twenty-five movie theaters; a Penske Racing Center where you can ride full-size interactive car simulators; dining at the Gordon Biersch Brewery, King's Fish House, Chili's Grill, and Acapulco Cantina; free live entertainment on weekends, and more. Free shuttle service to all Mighty Ducks hockey home games, too.

Extra Special Tip

Downtown Disney District Opened in January 2001, this 20-acre dining, shopping, and entertainment area is located between the original Disneyland and the new Disney's California Adventure and encircles three Disneyland Resort hotels. The district is free and open to the public year-round. It features nicely landscaped gardens and promenades interspersed with 300,000 square feet of retail shops, restaurants, and twelve movie theatres. Some highlights: excellent pastries and espresso at La Brea Bakery; wood-fired pizza at Naples Ristorante; tapas at Catal Restaurant; Ralph Brennen's Jazz Kitchen for Cajun food; the House of Blues for live entertainment (the Sunday gospel brunch is inspiring!); Y Arriba! Y Arriba! for Latin cuisine and dance shows; Rainforest Cafe for tropical treats; and the ESPN Zone for a fantastic sports fix (live sports broadcasts, interactive games, and food at the Studio Grill). Shopping includes the ubiquitous World of Disney store, plus plenty of other gift, souvenir, music, jewelry, and fashion emporiums. For more information, contact (714) 300–7800 or www.disneyland.com.

GLACIAL GARDEN ICE ARENA

1000 East Cerritos Avenue, Anaheim; (714) 502–9185. Open daily, with varying times and fees for open-figure skating, instruction, and hockey matches.

This is the place to go if your family would rather participate than watch ice sports. Head over to this dual-rink facility, complete with a pro shop, snack bar, locker rooms, and skate rentals.

THE ANAHEIM FAMILY FUN CENTER

1041 North Shepherd off the 91 Riverside Freeway; (714) 630–7212 for times and current fees. Open daily. Note: Height restrictions apply to all rides and activities.

This huge complex has batting cages, bumper boats, go-carts, rollerskating, and an arcade and snack bar.

ADVENTURE CITY (ages 2 to 12)

1238 Beach Boulevard between Cerritos Avenue and Ball Road, on the outskirts of Anaheim; (714) 236–9300 for current operating hours or check the Web at www.adventurecity.com. Generally open daily in summer from 10:00 A.M. to 10:00 P.M. and in winter from Friday through Sunday, but hours are subject to change without notice. $ $ $

Opened in August 1994 by the Ansdell family, Adventure City, "the Little Theme Park Just for Kids," resembles a storybook village designed and proportioned for children two to twelve. For a wonderfully relaxing experience, consider visiting this two-acre park with its sixteen kid-sized rides that are quiet yet still zoom and thrill, as well as hourly puppet shows, a new 25-foot climbing wall, live theater, storytelling, and face painting. Parent-child interaction is made easy here because the atmosphere is very casual and low-hype. There are plenty of park benches for us parental units to sit and relax on while the kids go brave the Kid Coaster or the carousel.

Extra Special Tip

Getting in the Swing The ever-popular **Golf N'Stuff** is conveniently located across the street from Disneyland at 1656 South Harbor Boulevard (714-778-4100) and has two beautifully landscaped eighteen-hole miniature golf courses and an arcade center open seven days a week. Real golf enthusiasts can swing out under the instruction of PGA pros at the **Islands Golf Center**, 14893 Ball Road (714-630-7888), on eighteen acres of practice tees, greens, and a fairway. There are more than twenty other Orange County golf options, including **Pelican Hill Golf Club**, in Newport Beach (949-759-5103 or www.pelicanhill.com) and the **Tustin Ranch Golf Club** in suburban Tustin (714-730-1611). Call for tee times and directions.

If your family wants to swing out with a racket, you can choose from twelve championship hard-surface tennis courts at the **Anaheim Tennis Center Inc.**, located at 975 South State College Boulevard (714-991-9090). The center is open year-round and offers computerized, self-loading ball machines as well as professional instruction. More than fifty tennis courts can be found at hotels and in Orange County's public parks. Call (714) 771-6731, ext. 220, www.ocparks.com for information.

HOBBY CITY

1238 Beach Boulevard between Cerritos Avenue and Ball Road, on the outskirts of Anaheim, adjacent to Adventure City; (714) 821–3311; www.hobbycity.com. $

This mini-town was founded in 1955 by Bea DeArmond and her husband (the grandparents of the creators of Adventure City). The nine-acre parcel contains twenty-three different hobby and collectible shops—most remarkably, a half-scale reproduction of the White House that shelters the Doll and Toy Museum. Browse the Cabbage Patch Kids

Official Adoption Center, complete with doctors and nurses. Visit the American Indian Trading Post, located in a log cabin, and find your new favorite stuffed animal at the Bear Tree.

CHILDREN'S MUSEUM AT LA HABRA (ages 2 to 10)

301 South Euclid Avenue, La Habra, approximately 30 minutes from Disneyland; (562) 905–9793; www.lhcm.org. Hours: 10:00 A.M. to 5:00 P.M. Monday through Saturday and 1:00 to 5:00 P.M. on Sunday; closed major holidays. $

Opened in 1977 as California's first children's museum, this facility is located in a renovated 1923 Union Pacific train depot. It contains fifteen permanent exhibits including a nature walk, science station, dino dig, kids on stage, and preschool play park. Temporary exhibits change at least three times a year.

CRYSTAL CATHEDRAL OF THE REFORMED CHURCH IN AMERICA

13280 Chapman Avenue, Garden Grove. Call the Visitor Center at (714) 971–4000 to check tour times or (714) 544–5679 to reserve tickets for the extremely cherished holiday pageants; www.crystalcathedral.org. **Free** *tours are generally available daily, but times are subject to change due to church services and events. Donations appreciated.*

For some religious and architectural history, visit the dramatic, all-glass sanctuary designed by Philip Johnson, considered a dean of American architects. This incredible place features 10,000 glass panes covering a weblike steel frame resembling a four-point star. The 2,890-seat cathedral hosts the annual Glory of Christmas and Glory of Easter pageants, with live animals, flying angels, and incredible special lighting reflected from the twelve-story glass walls and ceilings.

RICHARD NIXON PRESIDENTIAL LIBRARY, MUSEUM, AND BIRTHPLACE

18001 Yorba Linda Boulevard, Yorba Linda. From Anaheim, take the Riverside Freeway Route 57 northbound and exit Yorba Linda Boulevard, then travel about 5 miles east to the library, on the left-hand side (watch carefully for signs); (714) 993–5075 or (800) 872–8865; www.nixonfoundation.org. Open Monday to Saturday from 10:00 A.M. to 5:00 P.M. and Sunday from 11:00 A.M. to 5:00 P.M. $$

Be sure to schedule at least half a day to let your family experience a view of political and world history depicted at the nine-acre site. This was the first presidential library and museum built using no tax dollars.

The user-friendly, well-thought-out facility was first opened and dedicated on July 19, 1990. It features a self-guided tour, beginning with the twenty-eight-minute film *Never Give Up: Richard Nixon in the Arena.* Propaganda? Let your taste decide! Continue through galleries focusing on "The Road to the Presidency" and "The Wilderness Years," life-size statues of world leaders, a portion of the Berlin Wall, a re-creation of the White House's Lincoln sitting room, gifts from supporters, the Watergate years, and personal memorabilia. The exhibits portray America's thirty-seventh commander in chief right up until his death on April 22, 1994. Both President and Mrs. Nixon are buried here in the tranquil First Lady's Garden. You may visit the grave site, the reflecting pool, and the white clapboard farmhouse where Nixon was born on January 9, 1913. It remains precisely as it was when Nixon and his family lived there, right down to the bed where he was born. The intimate museum store on the premises contains commemorative souvenirs, postcards, and a selection of Nixon's books.

Extra Special Tip

All-Suite Hotels Near Disneyland Like California wildflowers, an amazing variety of all-suite hotels have sprung up near the park in recent years. This trend really is a boon for traveling families like us, who like to have a private bedroom for the adults and a multifunction living room/dining area with hide-a-bed arrangements for the kids. Each suite hotel has varying amenities such as Free breakfasts, kitchenettes, pools, and spas. However, all feature Free shuttle buses to Disneyland and Free parking. You might want to investigate the **Castle Inn & Suites,** (714) 774–8111, the **Peacock Suites Hotel** at (714) 535–8255, or **Portofino Inn and Suites** (714) 782–7600.

Where to Eat

Disney's PCH Grill at Disney's Paradise Pier Hotel, *1717 Disneyland Drive; (714) 999–0990. Open daily for breakfast, lunch, and dinner. Hours vary seasonally.* PCH stands for Pacific Coast Highway, California's prime and celebrated coastal route. Dining in the PCH Grill for lunch and dinner celebrates all the foods and beverages that make up California cuisine. Menu maps plot your meal course by course and feature fresh seafood, pastas, oak-fired pizzas, and some exotic Asian specialties. If you're looking for traditional American fare, this is probably not the best spot for you, but you know what they say: "When in California, eat like the Californians do," or something like that. Your best bet for the family at the PCH Grill is breakfast, because Minnie Mouse is the star here. She is the "hostess with the mostest" for this fun-filled Disney dining experience that also features a magic act onstage with Mr. Wizard. (Kids get to help perform tricks between bites.) You can order off the menu or cruise the buffet for your favorite breakfast items.

Goofy's Kitchen at the Disneyland Hotel, *1150 Magic Way, Anaheim; (714) 778–6600.* Your kids will not want to miss Goofy's, one of the eight restaurants on-site. Open every day—breakfast and dinner. Call for specific hours as they vary seasonally. You can dine with Disney characters (and get your picture taken!), eat Disney Character Meals, try out the all-you-can-eat buffet, and receive a **Free** souvenir button. Our kids insist on this "dining experience" every time! $$$

Where to Stay and Eat

Anaheim Hilton Hotel and Towers, *777 Convention Way, Anaheim; (714) 750–4321.* Only two blocks from Disneyland, this AAA three-diamond property features 1,576 guest rooms and suites in a colorful, bright motif. The hotel has a heated outdoor pool, four whirlpools, three rooftop garden sundecks, and the Sports and Fitness Center with its indoor pool, health spa, basketball gym, sauna, tanning beds, and massage services. Retail shops, a duty-free shop, a beauty salon, eight restaurants and lounges, and foreign currency exchange complete your experience. **The Hilton Vacation Station** program is specially created for kids zero to twelve. From Memorial Day through Labor Day, there is a separate check-in desk in the lobby, with trained personnel and a character mascot. Here you will find an impressive lending library of 300 handheld video games and toys from Kenner, Hasbro, and Playskool. At 4:00 P.M. daily, kids (and parents if accompanied by a kid) can take a behind-the-scenes hotel tour, including the massive kitchens and

laundry. All Vacation Station activities are gratis for hotel guests. **Cafe Oasis,** open for breakfast, lunch, and dinner off the main lobby, has an outstanding children's menu that is very affordable. The hotel offers a **Free** shuttle bus to Disneyland Resort every thirty minutes and running daily according to park opening/closing times. $$$$

Disney's Grand Californian Hotel, *1600 South Disneyland Drive, Anaheim, 92802. (714) 635–2300.* Opened in February 2001, this luxurious 751-room hotel with its striking California Craftsman architectural design is located on the northwest corner of the new Disney's California Adventure. This hotel is the only one to offer direct access straight into the park, a wonderful timesaving feature for your family. More than 160 of the guest rooms feature solid wooden bunk beds—great fun for kids of all ages! From the moment you arrive (and are offered valet parking), you are treated with outstanding hospitality and service. Hotel dining options include 24-hour room service and the excellent **Story-teller's Cafe** with its tasty breakfast buffet and American cuisine for lunch and dinner daily (and visits from Disney characters such as Chip'n Dale), plus the stunning **Napa Rose Restaurant** (with an open exhibition kitchen), **Hearthstone Lounge,** and **White Water Snacks Poolside.** You'll appreciate Pinocchio's Workshop, a supervised kids activity center, and the Mickey Mouse–shaped kiddy pool plus two other swimming pools (one with an awesome redwood slide), whirlpools, exercise suite, and Eureka Springs Health Spa. We really like this property and feel the higher room rates are justified given the ease of park accessibility combined with the outstanding amenities and service. $$$$

Disneyland Hotel, *1150 Magic Way, Anaheim; (714) 778–6600 or direct to reservations at (714) 956–6400.* Just west of Disneyland and connected by the futuristic monorail, this hotel opened at the same time as the park in 1955 and has continued to evolve. It features 990 guest rooms and suites in three high-rise towers surrounding the magical Peter Pan–themed Neverland pool complex (with water slides, bridges, and shallow play areas); a kids' playground; and a sandy beach with rental pedal boats, remote-control tugboats, and dune buggies. There are several restaurants and lounges to choose from, plus four swimming pools, a hot tub, the

Team Mickey Fitness Center, gift shops, and an eighty-game video arcade.

This hotel is a destination within itself, and you should plan some time to enjoy all the amenities. Family-friendly features include no charge for children under seventeen staying in same room as parents; **Free** roll-aways and porta-cribs, and baby-sitting referrals to licensed "grandmother types." Value-priced hotel and park package plans are prevalent and include early admission into both parks one and a half hours before the regular opening. Be sure to ask what's available when making reservations. Another great service is the Package Express, which delivers all your park purchases to your hotel room for **Free**. $$$$

Disney's Paradise Pier Hotel (formerly Disneyland Pacific Hotel), *1717 Disneyland Drive; (714) 999–0990 or direct to reservations at (714) 956–6400.* This fifteen-story, full-service hotel was acquired by Disney in December 1995 and underwent a complete renovation and name change in 2001. It now overlooks the festive Paradise Pier area at Disney's California Adventure. Choose from 502 nicely furnished guest rooms and suites. There are four restaurants and lounges, an outdoor pool and spa deck, a game arcade, convenient indoor/outdoor parking, and gifts shops. There is no charge for children under eighteen staying in the same room as parents.

For More Information

Anaheim/Orange County Visitor and Convention Bureau. *800 West Katella Avenue, 92802. (714) 765–8888 or (888) 598–3200; mail@anaheimoc.org; www. anaheimoc.org.*

Buena Park

Now it's time to gear up for another round of great family adventure in nearby Buena Park—only fifteen minutes from Anaheim and Disneyland. This area's development began in 1920, when Walter and Cordelia Knott and their three young children arrived and started farming on twenty acres of leased land. The Knotts set up a roadside produce stand on Beach Boulevard to sell their crops, and in 1932 Walter Knott started propagating a cross blend of raspberry, blackberry, and loganberry plants that he named boysenberry. In 1934, to help make ends meet during the Great Depression, Cordelia Knott began serving chicken dinners for 65 cents on her wedding china to passing motorists. Soon Knott's Berry Farm boysenberry fruits, jams, jellies, and pies, along with the Chicken Dinner Restaurant, became so popular that the family decided to build an attraction to keep waiting patrons amused. In 1940 Walter Knott began moving old buildings to the site from various ghost towns. The Calico Mine Ride followed in 1960, and a recreation of Philadelphia's Independence Hall was constructed in 1966. In 1968 the amusement park area was enclosed, and for the first time a general admission fee was charged. Knott's Berry Farm forms the nucleus for many attractions in this commercial section of Orange County. Plan on spending at least two days here in order to do it all "berry good."

KNOTT'S BERRY FARM

8039 Beach Boulevard at the corner of La Palma Avenue; (714) 220–5200 or www.knotts.com. Open daily except Christmas. Summer hours 9:00 A.M. to midnight. In winter the park operates weekdays, 10:00 A.M. to 6:00 P.M., Saturday 10:00 A.M. to 10:00 P.M., and Sunday, 10:00 A.M. to 7:00 P.M. Extended hours are offered during holiday periods. All admissions after 4:00 P.M. are reduced year-round. Parking across the street and accessed by a special walkway or tram is $7.00 per car. Be absolutely sure to call in advance for current ticket prices and schedules since all are subject to change without notice. $$$$

Knott's Berry Farm was family-owned and -operated until its 1997 purchase by Cedar Fair, L.P. It attracts more than five million guests each year to its entertainment park and marketplace, featuring 165 attractions, rides, live shows, restaurants, and shops. The lushly landscaped 150 acres have plenty of flowers, trees, waterfalls, and shady spots.

Six theme areas include the original Ghost Town, where you can pan for gold and go for a great log ride and take the Ghost Rider, the longest wooden coaster in the West; Camp Snoopy, the official home of the Peanuts gang including Woodstock's air mail ride; and Fiesta

Village, prowling ground for the Jaguar!—a 2,700-foot-long steel roller coaster that winds its way above the park and loops through Monte-zooma's Revenge (another thrilling coaster with its own 76-foot-high loop). The Boardwalk has a dolphin and sea lion show, Xcelerator, Perilous Plunge, the Hammerhead ride, the Boomerang (ever been on a roller coaster that rolls backward? Definite queasy alert!), and the Windjammer dual surf-racer roller coaster and Supreme Scream—312 feet of vertical excitement. The Mystery Lodge is a magical multisensory show focusing on native North American culture located in the Wild Water Wilderness. Come here at the end of your day if you plan on riding Bigfoot Rapids. Speaking from personal experience, heed the warning signs—you *will* get wet on this ride —most likely drenched! It may feel great on a hot summer day, but squishy shoes and clothing can get mighty uncomfortable mighty fast. "Indian Trails" gives you a chance to dry off and watch Native American arts, crafts, and music.

KNOTT'S SOAK CITY U.S.A.

Across the street from Knott's Berry Farm, 8039 Beach Boulevard at La Palma Avenue, (714) 220–5200, adjacent to Knott's Independence Hall, Buena Park. Open daily Memorial Day to Labor Day; open Saturday and Sunday in May, September, and October. $$$$

Open in summer 2000, this California-beach-theme water park features twenty-one separate water rides and attractions, including tube and body water slides, a wave pool, a lazy river, a family funhouse, restaurants, snack bars, a sand beach, a pier, and gift shops.

RIPLEY'S BELIEVE IT OR NOT! MUSEUM

7850 Beach Boulevard, one block north of Knott's Berry Farm along the Buena Park entertainment corridor; (714) 522–7045; www.ripleysbuenapark.com. Open Monday to Friday from 11:00 A.M. to 5:00 P.M.; Saturday and Sunday from 10:00 A.M. to 6:00 P.M. year-round. $$

Use your parental discretion on the age appropriateness of this attraction. In our opinion, mouse fetus wine, edible maggot jewelry, and a four-eyed man might be a little disconcerting to the very young.

One of the many Ripley's around the country, this 10,000-square-foot structure opened in 1990 with an "Odditorium" featuring a unique collection of the bizarre, the strange, and the beautiful found during the worldwide travels of adventurer Robert Ripley, born on Christmas Day 1893. Some of the exhibits are educational, like the 200 B.C. Venus de Milo statue, Chinese art, and primitive currency.

THE MOVIELAND WAX MUSEUM

7711 Beach Boulevard, just down the street from Ripley's; (714) 522–1155;
www.movielandwaxmuseum.com. Open daily from 9:00 A.M. to 7:00 P.M. Go for
the combination ticket with Ripley's for considerable savings. $$$

This is America's first wax museum and one of the world's largest
collections (more than 400) of life-size wax images of celebrities from
the 1920s until today. If you have seen these stars only on the silver
screen or television, you will be able to see them "up close and per-
sonal" here. The figures are so realistic you will want to reach out and
touch. Don't do it, but take plenty of pictures during your self-guided
tour through incredibly detailed sets and originally costumed stars,
ranging from Gary Cooper and Bette Davis to Michael Jackson, Whoopi
Goldberg, Kevin Costner, and Tom Hanks (as Forrest Gump). The *Star
Trek* set is certainly a winner, but young children may want to avoid the
Chamber of Horrors, featuring Dracula and Frankenstein as well as
Jason and Norman Bates. Since its inauguration in 1962, the museum
has been a must-visit on every Southern California tourist's agenda. Put
it on yours.

MEDIEVAL TIMES DINNER AND TOURNAMENT

7662 Beach Boulevard, across the street from Movieland Wax Museum; (714)
521–4740 or (800) 899–6600; www.medievaltimes.com. Open nightly year-
round with special Sunday matinees. $$$$

Included is a four-course meal of twentieth-century food (appetizer,
vegetable soup, chicken, ribs, baked potato slice, and apple turnover) in
medieval style (no modern knife, fork, or spoon to assist you). Make
sure you bring plenty of extra cash to buy banners ($1.00 each) to wave,
souvenir programs ($7.50), and photos taken during dinner ($10.00).
Beer, wine, sodas, and coffee are included in the admission price; how-
ever, these prices are subject to change and do not include gratuity for
your hardworking serving wenches and serfs. Call the colorful castle for
daily show times—advance reservations are **required.** Make sure you
arrive at least one hour before your scheduled show time to navigate the
parking lot with your chariot and negotiate the check-in line.

This is outstanding family fun that is not to be missed—you and the
kids can release all kinds of pent-up vocal energy as you yell for "your"
knight in armor during a pageant of excellent horsemanship and tour-
nament games of skill and accuracy. You'll eat in an arena filled with
more than 1,100 people, divided into six sections, wearing colored hats,
waving streamers, and cheering their favorite knight on to victory over

the course of a two-hour eleventh-century show. A pricey outing, but we think you definitely will agree that "your day's not over until you've seen those knights!"

WILD BILL'S WILD WEST DINNER EXTRAVAGANZA

7600 Beach Boulevard, at the intersection of the Riverside Route 91 Freeway; (714) 522–6414 or (800) 883–1546. Show times vary depending on season and run seven nights a week, year-round. Reservations are required. $$$$

This Hollywood-style, family-oriented, two-hour dinner and show experience will have you and the young ones whooping it up. The non-stop action begins the moment you sit down in the 800-seat "barn" at long tables facing an elevated stage. Wild Bill and his sidekick, Miss Annie, serve as master and mistress of ceremonies for the entertainment on stage, which is complete with high-tech lighting and effects and includes singers, cancan girls, roping artists, and Native American dancers. Your servers will provide tableside entertainment as they distribute the hearty family-style menu of soup, salad, fried chicken, ribs, baked potatoes, biscuits, baked beans, corn on the cob, and apple pie topped with vanilla ice cream. The meal includes your choice of soft drinks, beer, or wine. Plenty of audience participation is encouraged during the fun production, including sing-alongs and whooping contests. Wild Bill's is definitely a Southern California version of "how the West was fun."

Where to Eat

Knott's California Marketplace, *Just outside the main entrance of Knott's Berry Farm, 8039 Beach Boulevard at the corner of La Palma Avenue; (714) 220–5200.* This area is filled with shops and restaurants for your family's pleasure, but the best is Mrs. Knott's original **Chicken Dinner Restaurant.** Hearty American fare is served for breakfast, lunch, and dinner at very reasonable prices. The kids' menu comes complete with crayons and a coloring book. We recommend eating here for lunch (go early or late to avoid crowds). Don't plan on taking any rides anytime near your consumption of that delicious chicken, mashed potatoes, and boysenberry pie. (We speak from experience here. Trust us!) $$

Where to Stay

Radisson Resort Knott's Berry Farm, *7675 Crescent Avenue, adjacent to Knott's Berry Farm. Buena Park. (714) 995–1111; www.radisson.com/buena parkca.* 320 units recently renovated and upgraded with a limited number of "Peanuts" theme-rooms with nightly Snoopy character turndown service. Free Snoopy gift for kids at check-in. Outdoor kiddy pool, adult pool, whirlpool, fitness center, sauna, and steam room. Festive Italian family food at **Cucina! Cucina! Cafe.** Gift shops. 𝐅𝐫𝐞𝐞 parking. $$$

For More Information

Buena Park Convention and Visitors Office. *6601 Beach Boulevard, Suite 200, 90261-2904. (714) 562–3560 or (800) 541–3953; fax (714) 562–3569; tourbp@ buenapark.com; www.buenapark.com.*

Orange

How would you like to find a slice of the midwestern United States buried in the heart of Orange County? Look no further than the historic city of Orange, sandwiched between Santa Ana and Anaheim, the two largest cities in all of Orange County. Approach the city of Orange by way of eastbound Chapman Avenue, off Interstate 5 or from State Route 57. As you enter downtown, cobblestone, tree-lined thoroughfares take you into the intersection of Chapman and Glassell Streets, where you will discover a circular central plaza. The "Plaza City" boasts a 1-square-mile historic district, where nineteenth-century architecture is preserved and cherished, and the appeal is decidedly homespun and friendly. Check out the living history lessons presented in the myriad antiques shops scattered around the plaza.

WATSON'S DRUG AND SODA FOUNTAIN

116 East Chapman; (714) 633–1050. $

The best place to soak up the flavor of Orange is on a stool at a joint that has been continuously serving heaping scoops of ice cream, traditional American meals, and remedies at its Plaza Square location since 1899. Prices for hand-dipped cones start at around $1.00, and the root beer floats are so frothy you will wonder how you lived this long without one. Breakfast, lunch, and dinner daily, featuring a kids' menu

for those twelve and under, with all items less than $4.00. Go in any
time to see an authentic soda fountain in action and watch the servers
in their period outfits and hairdos play soda jerks.

For More Information

City of Orange Chamber of Commerce. *531 East Chapman Avenue, Suite A,
Orange, 92866; (714) 538–3581 or (800) 938–0073; www.orangechamber.org.*

Santa Ana

Orange County's largest city is also the county seat of government and home
to the **John Wayne/Orange County Airport** (949) 252–5200. Downtown
Santa Ana combines Fiesta Marketplace, a bustling Latino-style pedestrian
mall, with a contemporary $50 million civic center and about a hundred his-
toric buildings that would make the Spanish explorer Portola proud of the city
he christened in 1796.

BOWERS MUSEUM OF CULTURAL ART AND KIDSEUM
*2002 North Main Street; (714) 567–3600. Open Tuesday through Friday from
10:00 A.M. to 4:00 P.M., Saturday and Sunday 10:00 P.M. to 6:00 P.M. Open hol-
idays except Christmas, Thanksgiving, and New Year's Day. Closed Monday. $$*

A significant part of Santa Ana's past is found in its first museum,
created in 1936 through a bequest from Charles and Ada Bowers to
preserve the local history of Orange County. Through gifts and acquisi-
tions, the Bowerses' collections have grown over the years, and the
museum has enlarged its space three times. It is now considered one of
the finest cultural arts repositories in the West. The museum specializes
in the arts of the Americas, the Pacific Rim, and Africa, along with its
ongoing commitment to chronicle the story of Orange County. The
museum store has unique art treasures, cards, and gifts not readily
available in traditional museum gift shops. Increasing community inter-
action and family demand have caused the recent expansion into an old
bank building two blocks away.

In December 1994, the 11,000-square-foot **Bowers Kidseum**
opened two blocks away at 1802 North Main Street. This amazing cen-
ter has been competently designed for ages six to twelve as a place
where children can learn about other cultures, music, art, and history
through interactive, hands-on exhibits. Hours of operation for the gen-

eral public run Tuesday through Friday from 1:00 to 4:00 P.M., Saturday and Sunday from 10:00 A.M. to 4:00 P.M. Admission fees are identical and reciprocal with the Bowers Museum. Thematic "explorers' backpacks" covering various cultural differences are just one example of this outstanding opportunity for your kids to actually learn something valuable while vacationing. The Kidseum perfectly bridges the gap between amusement and education.

DISCOVERY MUSEUM OF ORANGE COUNTY

3101 West Harvard Street. (714) 540–0404. Open Wednesday through Friday from 1:00 to 5:00 P.M. and Saturday and Sunday from 11:00 A.M. to 3:00 P.M. Closed major holidays. $

This historic museum, located in the fully restored, 1898 Victorian Kellogg House, is your family's chance to step back in time to the 1800s. Kids can try on Victorian costumes, wash clothes on a scrub board, play a pump organ, or talk on a hand-cranked telephone. This is a very fun yet informative way to learn early California history.

THE SANTA ANA ZOO AT PRENTICE PARK

1801 East Chestnut Avenue; (714) 835–7484; www.santaanazoo.org. Open daily 10:00 A.M. to 4:00 P.M., extended hours in summer. Closed holidays. $

This charming zoo will calm your kids' animal urges with its 250 species of primates, other mammals, and birds. Refreshments are available in the food court, and vendors around the grounds sell snacks and ice cream. A playground and miniature train rides are available. Call for current programs and times.

DISCOVERY SCIENCE CENTER

2500 North Main Street (at the corner of Interstate 5 and the Santa Ana Freeway), Santa Ana. (714) 542–CUBE; www.discoverycube.org. Open daily from 10:00 A.M. to 5:00 P.M.; except major holidays. $$$

"The Amusement Park for Your Mind" opened in 1998 in a 59,000-square-foot multistory facility devoted to sparking children's natural curiosity and increasing everyone's understanding of science, math, and technology. Over 100 highly interactive exhibits make you think, search for answers, and participate in the learning process. Eight themed areas include Perception, Dynamic Earth, Quake Zone, Exploration Station, Principles of Flight, Performance, Space, and KidStation (a special area for those under five). Our personal favorites include the Shake Shack to experience an earthquake, lying down on a bed of nails, and dancing on the musical floor. This is a marvelous family activity that you should not miss! Highly recommended.

Irvine and Costa Mesa

The city of Irvine is the largest master-planned community in the United States. It was first developed in 1959 as a site for the University of California-Irvine on an old Spanish land grant. Billboards, overhead power lines, and TV antennas are banned here in an area divided into 38 urban villages featuring a plethora of parks, all connected by greenbelts and bike paths. Shopping centers and services are all conveniently located nearby. The central corridor of high-rise buildings like the Irvine Spectrum and Koll Center provide headquarters for plenty of Fortune 500 firms as well as some family fun.

The adjacent city of Costa Mesa, also home to many corporations as well as a popular residential community, became a player on the Orange County shopping and entertainment scene in 1967 with the opening of the South Coast Plaza Mall, a great place for your family to satisfy those shopping urges.

IRVINE SPECTRUM CENTER

At the intersection of Interstate 405 (exit Irvine Center Drive) and Interstate 5 (exit Alton), Irvine. Open daily from 11:00 A.M. to 11:00 P.M., hours can vary during holiday periods and special events. Call (949) 789–9180 for more information.

This premier outdoor entertainment plaza offers 21 IMAX movie cinemas, the Nascar Silicon Motor Speedway, Sega City, laser light shows, world-class restaurants, nightlife, and specialty shops from around the globe.

WILD RIVERS WATERPARK (over age 3)

8770 Irvine Center Drive, Irvine; (949) 768–WILD. Open daily throughout the summer season from 10:00 A.M. to 8:00 P.M.; call for weekend and winter hours. $$$$

 Your high-tech children will definitely want to take advantage of the twenty-acre park with more than forty water rides, including the Edge, the Ledge, and the Abyss; two wave pools, kiddie wading pools, sunbathing areas, a water slide, log flumes, picnic areas, and a video arcade to complete the family-fun mix.

PALACE PARK

3405 Michelson Drive, Irvine; (949) 559–8336; www.so-cal.com/palace. Open daily, hours vary according to season and holidays. $$

This indoor/outdoor facility has more than six acres of family entertainment, including miniature golf, batting cages, laser tag, bumper boats, and a state-of-the-art, 25,000-square-foot video arcade with the new Galaxian virtual-reality challenge machines, where up to six people compete against the computer. The Palace Playland is specifically created for the younger set, with a large squishy maze.

SOUTH COAST PLAZA AND THE CRYSTAL COURT

3333 Bristol Street, at the intersection of Interstate 405 and Bristol Street, Costa Mesa. (800) 782–8888 or call the concierge at (949) 435–2034 for a current special event and promotion schedule.

More than 100 world-renowned stores call this internationally recognized address home, as do restaurants, art galleries, and even a day spa. The kids will clamor to check out the fabulous toys of FAO Schwartz, the Disney Store, and the Sesame Street Store.

TRINITY BROADCASTING NETWORK INTERNATIONAL HEADQUARTERS

3150 Bear Street (across Interstate 405 from the South Coast Plaza Mall); (714) 708–5405; www.tbn.org.

This striking, classically inspirational building houses broadcast studios and the popular gift and bookshop of this Christian television network. The Virtual Reality Theater presents free motion pictures daily. Call for current titles and show times. All ages are welcome.

ORANGE COUNTY PERFORMING ARTS CENTER

600 Town Center Drive, South Coast Plaza, Costa Mesa; (714) 556–2121 or www.ocpac.org for current events and admission charges.

Opened in 1986, the 3,000-seat Segerstrom Hall is where major symphony concerts, operas, ballets, and Broadway musicals are presented year-round. Children's programs dominate around the Christmas holidays. Call for a schedule of **Free** backstage tours.

ORANGE COUNTY FAIR AND EXPOSITION CENTER

88 Fair Drive, Costa Mesa; (714) 708–1567 or www.ocfair.com for current activities.

Discover a variety of fun family events, including swap meets, automobile and motorcycle speedway races, and concerts. In July, the Orange County Fair takes over, featuring top name entertainment, livestock, carnival rides, rodeo, foodstuffs, arts, crafts, contests, and demonstrations.

For More Information

Costa Mesa Tourism and Promotion Council. *Box 5071, Costa Mesa, 92628. (800) 399–5499; www.costamesa-ca.com.*

Irvine Chamber of Commerce. *17755 Sky Park East, #101, Irvine, 92614. (949) 660–9112; www.irvinechambercom.*

Huntington Beach

Waterfront action or just plain relaxation will provide a respite from all your inland encounters. Orange County's beaches are part of the defining Southern California experience. Traveling along the Pacific Coast Highway, commonly known as PCH or just the Coast Highway, begin your waterside explorations at Huntington Beach, Orange County's third largest city (after Santa Ana and Anaheim). It is growing into a thriving resort area with more than 8 miles of uninterrupted shoreline. Between Goldenwest Street and Brookhurst Street along PCH, the Bolsa Chica and Huntington Beaches provide plenty of area for safe swimming, picnicking, and surfing. Beach parking fees are charged and vary according to time and season.

Huntington is one of the surf capitals of Southern California. Your kids will probably know this because of the mega-television coverage afforded the surfing championships and international competitions held here every summer. You can easily spend a day on the beaches of Huntington, just enjoying the beautiful surf, sand, and sea. (Do remember to use your sunscreen liberally. Ask any Huntington Beach surfer dude—sunburn is not cool!) The town's ambitious redevelopment efforts along Main Street, just off PCH, contain postmodern shopping plazas and condos alongside the original turn-of-the-last-century waterfront clapboards, which now house trendy clothing stores, beach shops, and bistros. Strolling the 1,583-foot municipal pier is a favorite pastime. Pier Plaza, on PCH at Main, hosts a farmer's market on Friday and live entertainment.

INTERNATIONAL SURFING MUSEUM

411 Olive Street; (714) 960–3483; www.surfingmuseum.org. Displays, admission fees, and opening and closing hours change like the tides (well, not really that frequently!), so call for the current schedule and low admission donations, dudes.

An art deco-ish building downtown, home of radical exhibits, artifacts, and memorabilia ranging from vintage surfboards to surf wear and surf films.

BOLSA CHICA ECOLOGICAL RESERVE AND INTERPRETIVE CENTER

Between Warner Avenue and Goldenwest Street on the Pacific Coast Highway, just opposite the entrance to Bolsa Chica State Beach; (714) 846–1114. Open daily, dawn to dusk. **Free**.

It is both relaxing and educational to walk through the 300-acre reserve, one of the largest salt marsh preserves in Southern California. The reserve supports such rare migratory waterfowl as avocets, egrets, plovers, and terns. A 1.5-mile walkway with explanatory signs leads the way throughout the ecosystem. **Free** guided public tours are given the first Saturday of each month.

SHIPLEY NATURE CENTER AT HUNTINGTON CENTRAL PARK

Goldenwest Street between Slater and Ellis Avenues; (714) 960–8847. Center generally open daily 9:00 A.M. to 5:00 P.M.; park open 5:00 A.M. to 10:00 P.M. **Free** *admission.*

For another view of plants and animals, the park is home to hundreds of bird species. For human guests there are picnic areas and playgrounds, plus walking and bicycling trails that wind past ponds, waterways, and woodlands.

Where to Stay and Eat

Hilton Waterfront Beach Resort and Palm Court Restaurant, *21100 Pacific Coast Highway, across from beach; (714) 960–7873 or (800) 822–7873.* Almost every one of the 290 rooms at this modern, beachfront high-rise has an ocean view. Right in the center of all the action, yet surrounded by luxury, this AAA-rated four-diamond property is a beautiful place to call home for your Orange County beach explorations. Heated pools, a sauna, a spa, tennis courts, and an exercise room all beckon when you are tired of the Pacific Ocean sand and surf across the street. **Palm Court** has a fine kids' menu, with breakfast and lunch (casual) and dinner (more formal, not great for young children) daily. There's also a deli here that packs a yummy picnic lunch. Room service on your balcony overlooking the ocean isn't such a bad deal either! $$$

For More Information

Huntington Beach Conference and Visitors Bureau. *417 Main Street, 92648. (800) 729–6232 or (714) 969–3492; www.hbvisit.com.*

Newport Beach Area

Just south of Huntington Beach along the glittering Pacific lies a city of villages, islands, and private enclaves first incorporated in 1906. The Newport Beach area comprises Balboa, Balboa Island, Lido Isle, Newport Heights, Harbor Island, Bay Shore, Linda Isle, and Corona del Mar. It includes one of the West Coast's most famous yacht harbors, containing approximately 9,000 pleasure craft. In addition, a 6-mile "inland" beach lies along the peninsula between Newport Bay and the ocean. You and your family will discover what many believe to be the trendiest Southern California beach life here.

BALBOA PAVILION

400 Main Street, located at the Newport Bay end of Main Street, on the Balboa Peninsula. Open daily. **Free**.

Begin your exploration of the waterfront action at this classic building constructed in 1905 and now listed in the National Register of Historic Places. Here you will discover a marine recreation center offering ferries to quaint Balboa Island and Catalina Island and charter boats for sailing, whale-watching, sightseeing, and sportfishing. The Fun Zone has a carousel, Ferris wheel, and arcade.

DAVEY'S LOCKER SPORTFISHING

400 Main Street, Balboa Pavilion, Balboa; (949) 673–1434; www.daveyslocker. com. Open daily; hours vary according to season.

Your headquarters in Newport Beach for harbor excursions, whale-watching, and half-, three-quarters-, and full-day fishing excursions for catching yellowfin tuna, bonito, sand bass, and rockfish. Twilight fishing trips are offered in the summer, too. These folks are the pros and will make you feel very comfortable and safe on the water.

Cruising to Catalina from Orange County
The Catalina Passenger Service operates the *Catalina Flyer*, its 500-passenger catamaran vessel, from Balboa Pavilion in Newport Beach. It offers in-season (March through October) seventy-five-minute cruises daily to neighboring Santa Catalina Island, a pristine, unspoiled isle only 26 miles out to sea yet a world away. (See Chapter Two for Long Beach/San Pedro embarkation choices.) Fares and departure times are subject to change seasonally. Reservations are required. Phone for current schedules (949) 673–5245 or (800) 830–7744 (in California) or www.catalinainfo.com. $$$$

CATALINA PASSENGER SERVICE/PAVILION PADDY CRUISES
400 Main Street in the Balboa Pavilion, Balboa; (949) 673–5245; www. catalinainfo.com. Call for sailing times. $$

At the end of the Balboa Peninsula and Pier, do not miss taking a sightseeing cruise aboard the old-fashioned riverboat *Pavilion Paddy*. You will wind your way through the meandering channels of Newport Harbor and see some imposing homes and dazzling yachts of the rich and famous (like the late John Wayne and Shirley Temple). Tours run mostly year-round. Sunday brunch cruises are also available in season. This is also the dock for *Catalina Flyer* service to Catalina Island offshore. (See Extra Special Tip.)

THE NEWPORT HARBOR NAUTICAL MUSEUM
151 East Coast Highway, Newport Beach; (949) 673–7863. Call for seasonal hours and entrance fees.

This interesting museum gives a photographic history of the harbor, a fascinating ships-in-a-bottle exhibit, and a display of navigational instruments and model ships housed in the 190-foot *Pride of Newport*, docked near the Back Bay Bridge. The **Riverboat Cafe** serves lunch and brunch.

HORNBLOWER CRUISES AND EVENTS
2431 West Pacific Coast Highway, Suite 101, Newport Beach; (949) 646–0155; www.hornblower.com. Cruises on climate-controlled large yachts offered year-round. Evening and Sunday brunch cruise schedules vary according to season and demand for private charters. Brunch cruises sail for two hours and include an all-you-can-eat buffet with champagne for adults; ages four to twelve half-price. Gratuity and cocktails additional. $$$$

Excellent service from nautically attired crew and California cuisine prepared fresh onboard make this an upscale cruising, dining, and sightseeing experience to remember. Recommended for older children; for our families, we like the Sunday brunch cruises best.

SHERMAN LIBRARY AND GARDENS

2647 East Pacific Coast Highway, south of Newport Beach in Corona del Mar; (949) 673–2261. Gardens are open daily from 10:30 A.M. to 4:00 P.M. $

This two-acre cultural center has botanical gardens displaying tropical and subtropical flora in addition to its research library of southwestern history. The touch-and-smell garden is a major wow for your kids; you will enjoy the respite in the tea garden.

Extra Special Tip

Shopping and More with an Ocean View Luring you away from the Newport Beach and harbor area, but with the ocean firmly in sight, the 600-acre **Newport Center,** just above the Pacific Coast Highway between MacArthur Boulevard and Jamboree Road, is an office, luxury hotel, and entertainment complex built in 1967. It hosts a must-stop shopping center—the trendy **Fashion Island.** Contact (949) 721–2000, the concierge contact number, or www.irvineco. com (click on shop), for schedules of children's activities, fashion shows, and great promotions. Containing more than 200 major chain stores and regional specialty shops, Newport Center is also home to the luxurious AAA five-diamond rated **Four Seasons Hotel** (949–759–0808; www.fourseasons.com/newportbeach), as well as forty restaurants in the Atrium Court. This is where you and the kids can chill out after a hard day at the beach!

Where to Eat

Hard Rock Cafe Newport Beach, *451 Newport Center Drive (Fashion Island), Newport Beach; (949) 640–8844. Open daily 11:30 A.M. to 11:00 P.M.* This is the Orange County version of one of the most famous rock-and-roll restaurants in the world, featuring memorabilia of major rock stars as well as their platinum and gold records. Be sure to make your pilgrimage to at least one of these emporiums for the fun of it! $$$

Tale of the Whale, *400 Main Street, in the Balboa Pavilion, Balboa; (949) 673–4633; www.taleofthewhale.com.* Open daily 11:00 A.M. to 11:00 P.M., serving lunch, dinner, and cocktails overlooking the magnificent harbor area. Dressy casual, but a fine children's menu makes this a super spot to dine on the best fresh seafood. Our favorite is cioppino, a fish stew that is a feast. $$

Where to Stay

Hyatt Newporter Resort Hotel,
1107 Jamboree Road, one-half mile from Pacific Coast Highway, Newport Beach; (949) 729–1234 or (800) 233–1234. This 410-room California casual property has spacious, beautifully landscaped grounds. Some of the rooms need some refinishing, but the value is here for your family, with package plans and special rates. There are three heated pools, a wading pool for the kids, a nine-hole, par-three golf course, plus an exercise room if you're feeling flabby from laying on the beach. Two restaurants serve daily meals. You'll appreciate the shuttle service to nearby shopping and attractions. $$$

The Newport Dunes Resort Park,
1131 Back Bay Drive, just off PCH and Jamboree Boulevard; (949) 729–3863 or (800) 288–0770. Beach hours are 8:00 A.M. to 10:00 P.M. daily. Overnight camping site and a seven-lane boat launch ramp are open twenty-four hours. This hundred-acre waterfront RV resort provides more than 400 hookups for recreational vehicles and campers, each separated by tropical vine-covered fences. Day-trippers will enjoy a private day-use beach on a waveless inland lagoon. You can rent kayaks, windsurfers, paddleboats, and sailboats here for hours of fun. Call for current prices. $$

For More Information

Newport Beach Conference and Visitors Bureau. *3300 West Coast Highway, 92663. (949) 722–1611 or (800) 94–COAST; www.newportbeach-cvb.com.*

Laguna Beach

Unspoiled by time or tide, the dazzling white sands of Laguna Beach, combined with its artist-colony heritage and year-round mild climate, add up to a unique Orange County destination resort worth exploring. All the major beach action along the Pacific Coast Highway can be found here—your kids will "dig" the sand and the playground at Main Beach downtown, while you stroll the art galleries, boutiques, and bistros that line the Pacific Coast Highway.

 FESTIVAL OF ARTS AND PAGEANT OF THE MASTERS
In Irvine Bowl Park, 650 Laguna Canyon Road, near the ocean. The annual festival is staged July and August. For a complete program and brochures call (800) 487–3378 or (949) 494–1145; www.foapom.com. $$$$

The **Festival of Arts** features 150 of the area's most accomplished artists in a rigorously juried show requiring that all pieces on display or for sale be original, including paintings, sculpture, pastels, drawings, serigraphs, photographs, ceramics, jewelry, etched and stained glass, weaving, handcrafted furniture, musical instruments, model ships, and scrimshaw.

Each summer evening the park's natural amphitheater is the site of the **Pageant of the Masters,** a world-famous event, where amazingly faithful re-creations of famous artwork are presented on stage by live models. Narrators and a full orchestra make these **tableaux vivants** (living pictures) an extraordinary dramatic experience, particularly the finale—a stunning live portrayal of Leonardo da Vinci's *Last Supper.* There is so much for your kids to see and do, including participating in hands-on workshops, watching performing artists, listening to music, even viewing the junior art displays of local schoolchildren.

THE SAWDUST ART FESTIVAL WINTER FANTASY
935 Laguna Canyon Road; (949) 494–3030 for this year's Winter Fantasy dates and nominal admission fees. $

This favorite Laguna Beach event is held on four consecutive weekends in November and December in a fragrant eucalyptus grove. Wander three acres of paths containing 150 booths filled with holiday arts and crafts while your kids play in the snow (trucked in daily!). A children's art workshop, food, and entertainment make this a wonderful addition to your wintertime vacation experience in Southern California.

THE LAGUNA ART MUSEUM
307 Cliff Drive; (949) 494–6531. Open Tuesday through Sunday, 11:00 A.M. to 5:00 P.M. $

This small but interesting museum has rotating exhibits within several spacious galleries that focus on both contemporary and traditional paintings and sculpture by California artists.

Where to Stay and Eat

Hotel Laguna and Claes Restaurant, *425 South Pacific Coast Highway, Laguna Beach; (949) 494–1151 or (800) 524–2927.* This historic, sixty-five-room property right on the sand in the absolute center of town was built in 1930. The three-story old girl has undergone several facelifts over the years but remains a favorite. Don't expect ultra-modern furnishings but revel in the California-beach quirky atmosphere. Be sure to request a room on the ocean side, because the street side is way too noisy. Private beach access, complete with your own beach chairs and food/drinks/towel attendant, make this the ultimate place to people-watch while the kids create sand castles. We really enjoy **Claes Restaurant** on the patio for breakfast, lunch, or early dinner (the bar gets a little hectic later on). You can dine overlooking the beach and all the action. $$$

For More Information

Laguna Beach Visitor Center. *252 Broadway (State Route 133), 92651. (800) 877–1115 or (949) 497–9229; www.lagunabeachinfo.org.*

Dana Point

At the turn of the nineteenth century, Dana Point (named after Richard Henry Dana, author and mariner) was the only major port between Santa Barbara and San Diego. Now this natural cove has picturesque and modern marinas hosting 2,500 craft. It is famous for its whale-watching cruises from late December through March. The town celebrates its annual Harbor Whale Festival in March with street fairs and plenty of outdoor activities.

ORANGE COUNTY OCEAN INSTITUTE

24200 Dana Point Harbor Drive; (949) 496–2274. Open daily from 10:00 A.M. to 4:30 P.M., closed major holidays. Ship tours are Sunday from 10:00 A.M. to 2:30 P.M. Admission fee is voluntary; donations are gladly accepted.

Be sure to investigate this fun place that has outstanding sea life exhibits, tide pool tours, and a hands-on aquarium touch tank. While you're there, take a tour of the tall ship *Pilgrim*, a replica of the vessel on which Richard Henry Dana, author of the book *Two Years Before the Mast*, sailed to Southern California in the 1830s. In July and August, musical and dramatic productions with a nautical theme are presented on the *Pilgrim*'s deck. Your kids will love the chance to really see sea life in action!

DANA POINT HARBOR INFORMATION SERVICE

Post Office Box 701, Dana Point, 92629; (949) 496–1094; www. danapointharbor.com.

Your best point of contact for waterfront activities and special events, including whale-watching; rentals of Jet Skis, kayaks, canoes, and sailboats; parasailing; and windsurfing.

Where to Stay

Doubletree Guest Suites Dana Point, *34402 Pacific Coast Highway, across from Doheny State Beach, next to the Yacht Harbor; (949) 661–1100.* This full-service, 196-suite hotel is located along a 10-mile stretch of beautiful white sand beach. All suites have a bedroom and a sitting room (our fave floor plan) with a wet bar, microwave, fridge, two remote control TVs, a VCR, and panoramic views to boot.

If you get bored with the beach (heresy), you can always take a dip in the pool or work out in the fitness center. The restaurant **Tresca** has a Mediterranean menu, open daily for all three meals and Sunday brunch. $$$

For More Information

Dana Point Chamber of Commerce. *24681 La Plaza #115, Box 12, 92629. (949) 496–1555; www.danapoint-chamber.com.*

San Juan Capistrano

The village of San Juan Capistrano is just inland along Interstate 5 north from Dana Point, set in rolling hills between the Santa Ana Mountains and the sea. It has many old adobe buildings, and the 1895 Santa Fe Railroad depot has been lovingly restored and is now an AMTRAK station and restaurant. Since San Juan Capistrano is good enough for thousands of swallows to return to every year, you know you cannot go wrong here, or for that matter anywhere in Orange County—the ultimate family vacation destination.

MISSION SAN JUAN CAPISTRANO AND CULTURAL CENTER
Two blocks west of the junction of State Route 74 and Interstate 5 at 31882 Camino Capistrano; (949) 248–2048. Open every day except Good Friday, Christmas, and Easter, 8:30 A.M. to 5:00 P.M. $$

This "jewel of the missions" was founded on November 1, 1776, by Father Junipero Serra and is seventh in his famous chain of twenty-one missions along the California coast. On your self-guided walk through history, you will first enter the Serra Chapel, the oldest building still in use in California; then tour the ruins of the Great Stone Church, which was destroyed by an earthquake in 1812; view the padres' quarters, soldiers' barracks, an Indian cemetery, and the mission kitchen. You can also view the site of an ongoing archaeological dig as well as revel in the majestic gardens. Even the crankiest toddlers seem to unwind here.

Today the mission is famous for the swallows that arrive every March 19 (St. Joseph's Day) and leave on October 23. These remarkably constant birds fly approximately 6,000 miles from Goya, Argentina, to nest and rear their young in San Juan Capistrano. As early as 1777, a record of their return was first noted in the mission archives, spawning ceremonies and celebrations each year since (not to mention the celebrated song "When the Swallows Come Back to Capistrano").

For More Information

San Juan Capistrano Chamber of Commerce. *31871 Camino Capistrano, Suite 306, 92675. (949) 493–4700.*

Annual Events

The following list of Orange County events was made available courtesy of the California Trade & Commerce Agency.

FEBRUARY

Festival of Whales—Dana Point. *(800) 290–DANA.* Coastal whale-watching cruises and arts/crafts exhibition. **Free**.

MARCH

Swallows Day—San Juan Capistrano. *(949) 248–2048.* This fiesta celebrates the annual return of the swallows to Capistrano, featuring pageantry, entertainment, and food.

APRIL

Glory of Easter—Garden Grove. *(714) 971–4069.* This annual Easter play features special events, live animals, and a cast of more than 200 in the dramatic presentation of the last seven days of Christ on earth.

MAY

Strawberry Festival—Garden Grove. *(714) 638–0981.* Festival features strawberry dishes including strawberry shortcake, pie, and tarts; entertainment, beauty contests, arts, crafts, and rides. **Free**.

JUNE

Art-a Fair—Laguna Beach. *(949) 494–4514.* National juried competition and show of outstanding arts and crafts.

JULY

Sawdust Festival—Laguna Beach. *(949) 494–3030, fax (949) 494–7390.* Laguna Beach becomes a magical village created by artists. The two-month (July and August) festival includes handcrafted treasures, entertainment, jugglers, storytellers; jazz, country, rock, and contemporary musicians. Become an artist yourself by attending one of the many hands-on workshops.

Fourth of July Celebration—Huntington Beach. *(714) 536–5496, fax (714) 374–1551.* Red, white, and blue bash with a 5k run, parade, and fireworks. **Free**.

Festival of Arts and Pageant of the Masters—Laguna Beach. *(800) 487–3378 or (949) 494–2685, fax (949) 494–9387.* Colorful exhibit of fine, strictly original creations by 160 South Coast artists; includes the world-famous Pageant of the Masters "living pictures" performances.

Orange County Fair—Costa Mesa. *(949) 708–1543, fax (949) 641–1360.* This rural fair in an urban setting offers livestock, a carnival, a rodeo, commercial wares, themed attractions, and fiber arts.

AUGUST

Pow Wow—Costa Mesa. *(714) 663–1102.* Annual event weekend features Native American dancers, singers, and food.

U.S. Open of Surfing—Huntington Beach. *(714) 366–4584, fax (714) 366–9224.* Watch the best surfers in the world compete for a large sum. **Free**.

SEPTEMBER

Newport Beach Sandcastle Contest—Newport Beach. *(949) 729–4400, fax (949) 729–4417.* Event features sandcastles and sculptures built by amateurs and professionals. **Free**.

Taste of Newport Beach—Newport Beach. *(949) 729–4400, fax (949) 729–4417.* Savor the cuisine of more than thirty Newport Beach restaurants; entertainment.

OCTOBER

Oktober Fest—Huntington Beach. *(714) 895–8020.* **Free**. Old Worlde Village features German food, drink, and oompah bands.

Silverado Days—Buena Park. *(800) 541–3953 or (714) 562–3560, fax (714) 562–3569.* Fair includes arts and crafts, carnival rides and games, contests, live entertainment, a cook-off, and food booths. **Free**.

NOVEMBER

Glory of Christmas—Garden Grove. *(949) 544–5679.* Living Nativity scene includes animals, flying angels, holiday music, and pageantry.

Sawdust Festival Winter Fantasy—Laguna Beach. *(949) 494–3030, fax (949) 494–7390.* Unique holiday arts and crafts festival features 150 artists and craftspeople from around the country; artist demonstrations, hands-on workshops, children's art activities, continuous entertainment, Santa Claus, and a snow playground. Continues through December.

DECEMBER

Glory of Christmas—Garden Grove. *(714) 544–5679.* Living Nativity scene includes animals, flying angels, holiday music, and pageantry.

Christmas Boat Parade—Newport Beach. *(800) 94–COAST or (949) 729–4400 or (949) 729–4417.* More than 200 illuminated and decorated boats cruise the harbor. **Free**.

Christmas at the Mission—San Juan Capistrano. *(949) 248–2048.* Holiday celebration includes music, entertainment, and refreshments. **Free**.

The Inland Empire and Beyond

Residents of Greater Los Angeles often think of everything else in California—with the exceptions of San Francisco, San Diego, and a handful of other cities—as "the great outdoors." Indeed, the presence of gold (somewhere) in "them thar hills" aside, what makes California such a gold mine for the nature enthusiast is the wealth of opportunities for outdoor excitement afforded by its vast expanses of wooded mountains, pristine lakes, and other natural areas. As with so many other lifestyle considerations, when it comes to out-of-doors fun, Southern California truly has the edge.

Even those areas with the most striking natural beauty, however, have rich cultural heritages stretching back to the days of the Spanish explorers and Native Americans before them. A wide variety of museums—many geared toward children—sprinkle the scenic splendor of the Southern California wilds. The combination of history, festive special events, and towering above it all those glorious mountain peaks makes for an unforgettable family adventure.

When considering which areas to travel to or through, it helps to think like a native Southern Californian: In other words, think big! We tend to take wide open spaces for granted, but in a state where many counties are bigger than entire states, can you blame us? We like to drive, and we consider many areas easily within the orbit of Greater L.A. These include, among others, the sizable chunks of San Bernardino and Riverside Counties east of L.A. (a 28,000-square-mile region known as the Inland Empire); vast Kern County north of the city, with its celebrated Kern River; Tulare, farther north, gateway to Sequoia and Kings Canyon National Parks; and the ski resort of Mammoth, at the southern end of the Sierra Nevada range. The latter areas may be more Central than Southern California, but a true Californian just hops in the car, puts the top down, and goes. Getting there is easy, and with landscapes like these, easily half the fun.

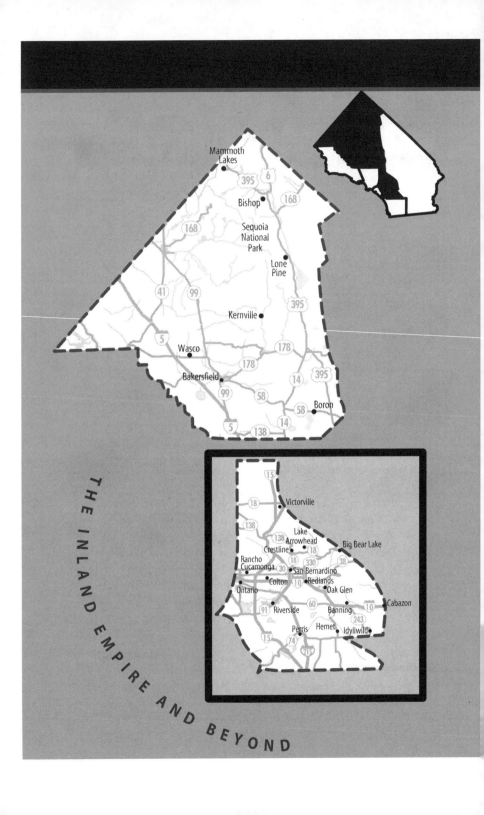

Mammoth
Lakes

395 6

Bishop

168

168

Sequoia
National
Park

Lone
Pine

41 99

395

Kernville

5

Wasco

178

178

395

Bakersfield

14

99

58

58 Boron

5 138 14

THE INLAND EMPIRE AND BEYOND

15

18 Victorville

138

138
Lake
Arrowhead 18
Crestline 18 Big Bear Lake

Rancho 18 330 38
Cucamonga 30 San Bernardino
Colton 10 Redlands
Ontario Oak Glen

60 Cabazon
91 Riverside Banning 10

243
Perris Hemet Idyllwild
15 74

215

It is California's Inland Empire that furnishes the archetypal images of the Golden State: acre upon acre of lush orange groves guarded by snowcapped mountains in the not-so-far-off distance. To the East Coast eye—that is, one accustomed to cities arranged on neat grids and self-contained countryside speckled with small towns—the Inland Empire can be a bit overwhelming. The valley floor is an immense patchwork of farmlands and small cities. It's sometimes hard to tell where one town ends and another begins. Malls, museums, and roadside fruit stands all vie for the motorist's attention. There are over 660,000 acres of national forest. All this makes for a slightly rough-and-tumble atmosphere, but a relaxed one, too. Though still growing, the palm-studded Inland Empire is a less pressured kind of place than adjacent L.A. County. It's about as far away from stuffy as you can get—and that's *very* Southern California.

If the sight of citrus crops right and left is quintessential Southland, those snowcapped mountaintops house a part of the state perhaps less well known to the visitor. Mountain vacation spots such as Lake Arrowhead and Big Bear, with its 7,000-foot-high lake, are like old-fashioned New Hampshire lakeside resorts à la California. They offer calm, cool respite from the L.A. basin and surrounding valleys and loads of outdoor activities from the simple to the simply adventurous. But to really appreciate the roominess of the Inland Empire, we recommend that you make stops along the way. Those who value the journey as well as the destination won't be disappointed, and during road trips kids need as much stretch-run-and-have-fun time as itineraries allow.

Ontario

If, like most people, you enter the Inland Empire via Interstate 10, heading east out of Los Angeles, you'll want to make a couple of stops in the Ontario area. With its bustling international airport, Ontario is the hub of this region within a region.

Welcome to the new **Ontario International Airport,** a terrific gateway for families on the grand Southern California tour route! The airport is serviced by Continental, Delta, Northwest, Southwest, American, United, United Express, Alaska, America West, Jet Blue, and Aeromexico. You can start your itinerary from here without the hassle that is LAX. This new state-of-the-art $270 million terminal is a major link in Southern California's air transportation network. You can easily rent a van or car from here and head for the hills, mountains, desert, and beyond. Hertz (800–654–2210; www.hertz.com) now has the Magellan Neverlost system for an extra $8.00 a day, which means you can enjoy the gorgeous Southern California views instead of studying a road map. Beware of the airport parking; an hour will set you back $5.00. If you are being picked up, have your friend wait for you curbside at the baggage claim area and use the $5.00 you saved to buy a number three at the In-N-Out Burger, which is on Interstate 10 and Vineyard near the airport.

Extra Special Tip

Mall Break! If you have visions of a megamall, with everything the kids could ever imagine, you'll be glad to know that the **Ontario Mills,** (1 Mills Circle), Southern California's largest entertainment and outlet mall, is open seven days a week (www.ontariomills. com). At the intersection of Interstate 15 and Interstate 10, Ontario Mills has it all. It's mere minutes from the airport, thirty minutes from Disneyland, and forty minutes from downtown L.A. Start with a noisy lunch at the **Rainforest Cafe** (909–941–7979), where you'll find animated wildlife, environmental education, and a spunky menu with hamburgers, salads, and more. You'll hear the sounds of the rain forest as you dine. **Dave & Busters** is another hit here with state-of-the-art interactive games and simulators, (909) 987–1557. Snackers will like the food court, which is near the Virgin Megastore. Parents will love the smooth-as-silk cheesecake in more flavors than you thought possible at the **Cheesecake Factory.** Dig in!

GRABER OLIVE HOUSE
315 East Fourth Street, Ontario; (909) 983–1761 or (800) 996–5483. Open Monday through Saturday 9:00 A.M. to 5:30 P.M.; Sunday 9:30 A.M. to 6:00 P.M. Free admission.

This is a fitting place to visit just in case the area's warm Mediterranean-like breezes have put thoughts of—what else?—olive oil in your mind. They've been doing wonderfully delicious things with homegrown olives at Graber House since 1894. An on-site olive processing and packing plant and a museum will enlighten kids and adults alike.

PLANES OF FAME AIR MUSEUM/FIGHTER JET MUSEUM
7000 Merrill Avenue, Chino (just south of Ontario on Highway 60); (909) 597–3514. Open daily 9:00 A.M. to 5:00 P.M. except Thanksgiving and Christmas. $$

This two-in-one museum houses a very impressive collection of both vintage World War II airplanes and military aviation memorabilia. It's a vivid reminder of the pivotal role the aviation industry has played in California's history.

Where to Eat

Cucina! Cucina! Italian Cafe, *960 North Ontario Mills Drive, Ontario; (909) 476–2350.* Known for its festive atmosphere, Cucina! Cucina! is a popular place in Ontario. Moderate prices and great tasting food. $–$$

New York Grill, *950 North Ontario Mills Drive, Ontario; (909) 987–1928.* Upscale dining and a great Sunday brunch. Special children's menu features hamburgers, hot dogs, and grilled cheese sandwiches. $–$$

Where to Stay

Doubletree Hotel Ontario, *222 North Vineyard, Ontario, (909) 937–0900 or (800) 222–8733; www.doubletree.com.* The Doubletree boasts 340 guest rooms, a restaurant, a pool, and a spa. $$$

Ontario Airport Marriott, *2200 East Holt, Ontario, (909) 975–5000 or (800) 228–9290; www.marriott.com.* This 293-room property is within walking distance of the Ontario Convention Center and restaurants and is close to the Ontario International Airport. $$

Historic Route 66

It's now called Historic Route 66, but in the 1920s it was the Mother Road, which in Southern California started in Santa Monica and made it possible for generations to travel through Los Angeles, Pasadena, Monrovia, Rialto, and beyond. Route 66 buffs celebrate the era with parades and rallies. (More information, **Historic Route 66 Association,** *P.O. Box 66, Kingman, AZ 86402; 520–753–5001.*)

If you start your Historic Route 66 excursion at the Vineyard exit in Ontario and exit on Citrus (or the reverse), you can get a good idea of how this legendary stretch of highway once looked. Today it's punctuated by shopping centers blending into one another, erasing the once colorful structures that gave definition and a sense of place to this inimitable stretch of road. If your family wants to delve into Historic Route 66's golden past, visit the **California Route 66 Museum** at 16849 D Street, Victorville; (760) 261-8766. See Victorville for more information.

Rancho Cucamonga

Rancho Cucamonga, northeast of Ontario, has a name kids love to make fun of. But there's also fun to be had in the town. There's a monument here to Jack Benny (you'll have to explain to the kids who Jack Benny was), as he often mentioned Rancho Cucamonga on radio and television shows.

Where to Eat

Bono's, *15395 Foothill Boulevard, Fontana; (909) 822–4036.* Coming from the east, take the Citrus exit off Interstate 10. In about 8 miles, you'll see this landmark family-owned-and-operated institution that has been around since 1936. Today it provides the perfect breakfast or lunch for families. Breakfast features farm fresh local eggs and omelets (try the Italian sausage) for $4.95 and under. Other favorites are oversized grinders (2-, 4-, and 6-foot sizes) and huge portions of spaghetti with soup or salad and garlic bread. There's an exhibit of Historic Route 66 memorabilia and a lot of Italian-imported specialties for sale—from *torrone* to pepperoni!

Magic Lamp Inn, *8189 Foothill Boulevard, Rancho Cucamonga; (909) 981–* 8659. If you want to get more kicks on Route 66 around the dinner hour, visit this legendary, classic 1950s restaurant with its comfortable red banquettes and the look and feel of yesteryear. The menu includes old favorites such as chicken marsala and roast prime rib of steer *au jus.*

Sycamore Inn, *8318 Foothill Boulevard, Bear Gulch, Rancho Cucamonga; (909) 982–1104.* This historic inn, just across the street from the Magic Lamp, opened in 1848. The children's menu includes the Hot Dogger, Burger Master, Mr. Chicken, and the Big Cheese. Tell your kids this restaurant was in business a long time before McDonald's and Burger King—even before the California burger was invented.

Colton

 FIESTA VILLAGE
1405 East Washington Street, Colton; (909) 824–1111. Sunday through Thursday 10:00 A.M. to 10:00 P.M.; Friday and Saturday 10:00 A.M. to 11:00 P.M. Nominal admission fee varies by activity.

This is an eminently doable amusement park, well endowed with miniature golf, race cars, batting cages, and water slides. Kids can't seem to get enough of the new Blast Off! slide.

All right. You've taken in a bit of culture, a bit of sunshine, and hopefully a bite of something to eat from one of the myriad fast-food establishments along the interstate (**In-N-Out**, 800-786-1000 for locations, makes the best burgers.Try the number three, it's a $3.89 bargain and includes a burger, fries, and drink.) Now, why not get away from it all, or above it all, as the case may be? There are three main resorts in the mountains framing the northern tier of the Inland Empire: Crestline, Lake Arrowhead, and Big Bear. Choose according to taste: a day for a detour, two or three for a mini-vacation.

Crestline

On your way to or from Lake Arrowhead, you'll pass through Crestline, a smallish, rather funky, no-nonsense mountain village that lures passersby in for a meal or a lakeside stroll.

LAKE GREGORY COUNTY REGIONAL PARK
24171 Lake Drive, located off Route 18; (909) 338–2233.
     The 86-acre Lake Gregory is Crestline's centerpiece, a popular though rarely crowded spot for swimming, shore fishing, and paddle-boarding. Some scenes from Disney's new *Parent Trap* were filmed here as well. From May through September, Friday night in Crestline means **Lakeside Family Market Night**, a festival of fun that features not only plenty of food and fresh produce but also kids' rides, crafts vendors, and entertainment.

HIGHLAND SPRINGS RESORT AND GUEST RANCH
10600 Highland Avenue, Beaumont, 92223; (909) 845–1151; fax (909) 845–8090.
     This 900-acre ranch offers horseback riding, cookouts, hayrides, and BBQs. Once a stagecoach stop for gold panners headed for the Colorado River, this rustic resort is a good choice for a family vacation. Palm Springs is 30 miles east, and Idyllwild is 20 miles south.

EDWARD–DEAN MUSEUM AND GARDENS
9401 Oak Glen Road; (909) 845–2626. Take I–10 east to Beaumont Avenue, head east to Oak Glen Road. Open 10:00 A.M. to 5:00 P.M. Friday, Saturday, and Sunday.
     J. Edward Eberle and Dean W. Stout began this beautiful museum in 1950. It is a treasure trove of sixteenth- through nineteenth-century

decorative arts. This could easily be considered a "mini Huntington Library."

Extra Special Tip

No Earplugs Required If you're near Claremont, home of Claremont Colleges, and have an evening free, consider tickets for **Ben Bollinger's Candlelight Pavilion Dinner Theatre** (455 West Foothill Boulevard), exiting from Interstate 10.

This is a far cry from a rock concert, so let the kids know in advance. This is where musicals of yesteryear such as *Singin' in the Rain* (based on the MGM film), *The Sound of Music,* and *Ain't Misbehavin'* come alive. Dinner is served a la carte with appetizers, entrees, desserts, and a selection of kid-friendly, nonalcoholic beverages, such as the Melinda May (with coconut cream) and the Show Stopper (a frozen raspberry piña colada and cream concoction).

The box office is open Tuesday and Wednesday, 11:00 A.M. to 5:00 P.M., Thursday and Friday 11:00 A.M. to 7:00 P.M., and Sunday, 10:00 A.M. to 6:00 P.M. Call (909) 482–0871 for performances, times, and cost of tickets.

This is a large theater, which was once a gymnasium. The seating is spacious and comfortable, and the sight lines are excellent, even if you sit in the back at a banquette. It's a perfect way for the family to enjoy live theater and to learn about the marvelous vintage musicals, where you could really hear the words and they meant something, too.

Where to Eat

Mulberry Tree, 23794 Lake Drive; (909) 338–2793. Open Thursday through Saturday, lunch 11:00 A.M. to 4:00 P.M.; dinner 4:00 to 9:00 P.M.; Sunday brunch is served holidays only. Closed Monday, Tuesday, and Wednesday. Serves lunch and dinner. Gift shop next door.

Twin Peaks

Where to Eat

Antlers Inn Restaurant, (909) 337–4020. Dinner Tuesday through Sunday, lunch on Saturday, and brunch on Sunday. If you want to prolong your mountain meanderings, try Highway 189 between Blue Jay and Agua Fria and visit this restored inn.

Lake Arrowhead

Summer days find many folks at nearby **Lake Arrowhead Village**, a hundred-year-old resort area named for the arrowhead landmark at the base of the San Bernardino Mountains. No one knows exactly how the 1,115-foot-tall, 396-foot-wide geological imprint got there, but it certainly helps those with a less-than-stellar sense of direction. Virtually every imaginable aquatic activity—swimming, waterskiing, fishing, sailing—is available on the lake, which is ringed by accommodations ranging from camping facilities (daily use fees $7.00 to $12.00) to a deluxe room in the waterfront Hilton.

MCKENZIE'S WATERSKI SCHOOL

At the marina; (909) 337–7862.

The longest-running school of its kind in the United States, McKenzie's offers lessons for children of all ages (summertime only).

THE LAKE ARROWHEAD CHILDREN'S MUSEUM

Lake Arrowhead Village, lower level; (909) 336–3093, fax (909) 336–5815. Open daily. $

Features fun hands-on exhibits, including an ever-popular climbing maze.

RIM OF THE WORLD HISTORICAL SOCIETY

(909) 336–3093. 10:00 A.M. to 5:00 P.M. winter hours; 10:00 A.M. to 6:00 P.M. summer hours.

Newly opened after a recent fire, the society has exhibits teaching kids about old-growth forests, from Cedar Pines Park to Green Valley Lake.

THE ARROWHEAD PINE ROSE CABINS

Highway 189 at Grandview; (800) 429–PINE or (909) 337–2341. $$

Individuality reigns supreme at this great base camp for sightseeing. It's centrally located between Lake Arrowhead and Lake Gregory. Seventeen cabins (one, two, and three bedrooms) and a five- to seven-bedroom lodge are scattered around five forested acres. No charge for cribs. Children welcome and stay 𝐅𝐫𝐞𝐞 in same cabin as parents.

ARROWHEAD QUEEN

Lake Arrowhead Village waterfront; (909) 336–6992. $$$

A great summertime way to experience the lake. The Louisiana-style paddle-wheel vessel departs hourly.

Where to Eat

Belgian Waffle Works, *A few steps from Woody's; (909) 337–5222, fax (909) 337–7862.* Open for breakfast, lunch, and dinner. This cozy spot, winner of the Table for Two award in 1997, is filled with the irresistible aroma of—no surprise—Belgian waffles! $

Casa Coyote's Grill & Cantina, *Lake Arrowhead Village, Lower Level, Lake Arrowhead, (909) 337–1171.* This is a full-service family restaurant with southwestern/Mexican favorites. $

Cliffhanger Restaurant, *Highway 18, Arrowhead Highlands, (909) 336–4488.*

This restaurant features fine dining with a view of the mountains and valley. $–$$

Woody's Boat House, *Lake Arrowhead Village, lower level; (909) 337–2628, fax (909) 337–9562.* Dockside merchants offer another view of the lake, so spend some time exploring this corner of the village. If you are a fan of the Chris Craft boats of the '50s, stop by for breakfast, lunch, or dinner. Woody's has a salad bar, a separate kids' menu, and fair prices. Beautifully restored Chris Craft boats serve as booths and your platform for viewing the lake. $$

Where to Stay

Lake Arrowhead Resort, *Lake Arrowhead Village, (909) 336–1511.* Located on Lake Arrowhead, this resort has all of the amenities, including its own beach. $$$

Big Bear Lake

If you follow Highway 18 east from Lake Arrowhead to Big Bear Lake, you'll be cruising along the **Rim of the World Scenic Byway**, with its spectacular vistas of thick forests and the sprawling valley below. It's a fitting entry to the 5-mile-long lake, the perennial favorite of choosy citizens of the Inland Empire.

Big Bear is many things to many people: Some come for the great water sports, others for the chance to see the stars and meteor showers during the refreshingly cool nights, and others for the hiking opportunities. Hiking trails abound in the area, including a section of the 2,600-mile Pacific Crest Trail that extends from Canada to Mexico. In winter—and often well into spring—Big Bear means top-notch skiing, plus sledding, tubing, and snowball fights.

BIG BEAR DISCOVERY CENTER
San Bernardino National Forest, P.O. Box 66, Fawnskin, 92333; (909) 866–3437; fax (909) 866–1781; ctennisr5/_sanbernardino@fs.fed.us.

Get your family to the marvelous Big Bear Discovery Center before you make any decisions on where to go and what to do. Try one of the tours, such as the Grout Bay Canoe Tour, Mountain Mining Tour, or Woodland Trail Tour; children are welcome! The U.S. Forest Service has made great strides in opening this area to tourists. There is an orientation video, a gift shop, exhibits, an amphitheater, and information on over fifty activities, from horseback riding, hiking, and backpacking to fishing and bird-watching. Ask about the Children's Forest, a 3,400-acre site on Highway 18 between Running Springs and Big Bea Lake, where kids learn about the preservation of our magnificent wildlands.

BIG BEAR QUEEN

(909) 866–3218; www.bigbearmarina.com.

Enjoy the water up close during a ninety-minute cruise aboard a paddle-wheeler.

Cruise the Lake with Captain John *(909) 866–2455, Pleasure Point Boat Landing is at 603 Landlock Landing Road (Cienega Road off Big Bear Boulevard at Metcalf Bay). It is open from 6:00 A.M. daily from May 1 to November 1. Captain John, a real mountain man, casts off daily from the Pleasure Point Marina at noon, 2:00, and 4:00 P.M. for a two-hour cruise around the scenic shoreline of Big Bear Lake. There are also canoes, pedal boats, pontoons, and eight-, ten-, and fifteen-horsepower motorboats at the landing.*

SNOW SUMMIT

*880 Summit Boulevard, P.O. Box 77, Big Bear Lake, 92315; (909) 866–5766; info@snowsummit.com; www.snowsummit.com. For **Snow Summit Snow Reports**, call (888) SUMMIT–1 or (909) 866–4621. $$$$*

Here is a paradise for snow seekers. Take it all in from View Haus, where rustic dining will enchant you and the kids with a marvelous mountain view. If there is no natural snow, don't worry, they will make it happen for you! There is a children's school and a mountaintop family park. Ample free parking.

BEAR MOUNTAIN

43101 Goldmine Drive, Big Bear; (909) 585–2519; www.bearmtn.com.

They offer nearly fifty runs, 28 miles of trails, and snowmaking systems that cover all the cleared ski trails. Bear Mountain boasts a vertical drop of 1,700 feet; Snow Summit has a drop of 1,175 feet. Excellent and inexpensive ski instruction centers abound, and plenty of rental companies make downhill and cross-country skiing or snowmobiling easy for those without equipment of their own.

ALPINE SLIDE AT MAGIC MOUNTAIN

800 Wild Rose Lane, Big Bear; (909) 866-4626. Slide open daily 10:00 A.M. to 4:00 P.M. $$

A Big Bear must. Few can resist the lure of "bobsledding" down the concrete runs. The maximum attainable speed is fast enough to thrill, but not fast enough to frighten. Actually, you control your own pace as you glide down the hillside. In winter, kids can inner tube down a mountain of snow, then be rope-towed back to the top again.

MOONRIDGE ANIMAL PARK

Goldmine Drive, Big Bear Lake; (909) 584–1171; www.moonridgezoo.org. Open year-round 10:00 A.M. to 5:00 P.M. $

Kids will love this zoo, which is a home to many orphaned and injured wild creatures, from ringtail cats, wolves, and foxes to raccoons and cougars. There's even a grizzly bear family in residence.

Big Bear Adventure Passport Here's how to get the kids their own Big Bear (the plush, stuffed kind that is). Get yourself a thirty-two-page Adventure Passport (call 800–4 BIG BEAR). Earn ten Adventure Stamps, including one for lodging, then stop by the **Visitor's Center** at 630 Barlett Road in Big Bear and pick up your bear! There are discounts galore with the passport, such as 10 percent off the entire check every day between 7:00 A.M. and 2:00 P.M. at the **Grizzly Manor Cafe** in Big Bear Lake and a free scenic sky-chair round-trip ride without a bike (or one-way with a bike) at Snow Summit.

Where to Eat

Mozart's Bistro, *40701 Village Drive, Big Bear, (909) 866–9497.* Serving lunch and dinner daily, this great stop has American and German cuisine. Try the salmon! $

Stillwell's (in Northwood's Resort), *(909) 866–3121, www.northwoodsresort. com/stillwells.htm.* Serving breakfast, lunch, and dinner in a unique, rustic mountain atmosphere. $

Where to Stay

Holiday Inn-Big Bear Chateau, *42200 Moonridge Road, Big Bear, (909) 866–6666; fax (909) 866–8988.* All of the eighty units contain gas fireplaces for coziness. $$$

The Northwoods Inn, *40650 Village Drive, Big Bear Lake, 92315; Reservations: (800) 866–3121.* The long-awaited opening of this 1930s-style, 141-room mountain lodge is good news for fami-lies! There are even Golden Getaway Grandparents packages that include a full American breakfast plus a box lunch for four to go, mountain bike rental, and a half-day pass at Snow Summit or a two-hour pontoon boat rental. You are right at the village, where there are inviting shops and restaurants, all amid those enchanting whispering pines. $$$

Victorville

If you take Interstate 15 a bit north of the San Bernardino Mountains (another section of the Route 66 Heritage Corridor), before you get too far into the Mojave Desert you'll come across the little town of Victorville. In addition to its role as a gateway to the Mojave, it has a few worthwhile stops.

CALIFORNIA ROUTE 66 MUSEUM

16825 D Street, take Exit D off Interstate 15; (760) 951–0436; fax (760) 951–0509; www.califrt66museum.org. Open Thursday through Monday, 10:00 A.M. to 4:00 P.M. **Free.**

Kids may not appreciate the incredible array of memorabilia gathered by Route 66 fans, but this museum will make them wonder and ask questions about what travel was like before freeways. That alone is worth making the stop. From the high desert landmark called Hulaville (once an open-air museum along Route 66 on Victorville's southern fringes built by an eccentric ex-carney) to cute Route 66 fanny packs (for sale), the curiosities displayed here reveal an era of American travel left to the pages of history.

The museum recently moved into a 5,000-square-foot building, which was formerly the old Les Pyrenees bar and restaurant.

While in the area, don't pass up the opportunity to visit **Bob's Big Boy,** a successful revival of the 1950s family-type restaurant many Californians thought vanished from the dining scene. You'll note the funky, bigger-than-life

Bob holding the Big Boy hamburger at the entrance. The Big Boy version of a hamburger now costs $2.99. In bygone days it was less than a buck!

There's a small gift shop to the left of the cashier with the Big Boy logo emblazoned on coffee mugs and pins and a bakery selling chocolate chip cookies, perfect for backseat munching. If you're in a hurry, check the other side of the freeway, and you'll find an In-N-Out (for hamburgers, fries, and lemonade), a Dairy Queen, and Popeye's Chicken. Make sure you have a portable Dust Buster ready to clean up the crumbs in the backseat!

You are now about 5 miles from the Roy Rogers–Dale Evans Museum, so you might want to visit both museums on the same day.

ROY ROGERS–DALE EVANS MUSEUM

15650 Seneca Road; (760) 243–4547; www.royrogers.com/museum.html. Open daily except for Christmas, Thanksgiving, and Easter 9:00 A.M. to 5:00 P.M. $$

Interstate 15 between Las Vegas and Hesperia may seem uneventful unless you make one important detour, and that's to visit this wonderful museum. Take the Roy Rogers Drive exit off Interstate 15. You can easily make this into a three-hour tour if you factor in lunch.

As you approach the "fort" (this is no ordinary museum!), you will see that famous horse Trigger immortalized, maybe 12 feet high, at the museum entrance. There's no way of getting lost trying to find this California landmark, a perfect stop for your family.

Plan to spend at least one hour perusing this vast collection of cowboy-era memorabilia, from lapel pins with portraits of Trigger and Buttermilk (the kids will be more impressed with the stuffed Trigger, a feat of taxidermy) to the original car that took the Rogers family from Ohio to California way back when. It's as if Dale and Roy cleaned out their attic and archived everything from boots to buttons for future generations to see. The Rogers had nine children and a deep commitment to family values, which is evident as you meander through this museum.

This fascinating museum, filled to the gills with cowboy boots, dime store Triggers (rides costing a dime), movie posters, and even a stuffed elephant head trophy, gives kids an idea of what America was like so many years ago. Save about fifteen minutes to visit the gift shop, which is well stocked with Rogers-era merchandise, which kids will find curious and parents will find nostalgic.

MOJAVE NARROWS REGIONAL PARK

18000 Yates Road, off Bear Valley Road; (760) 245–2226; fax (760) 245–7887; www.co.san-bernardino.ca.us/parks/mojave.htm.

This picturesque, not-quite-yet-the-desert site spans 840 acres and overlooks the Mojave River. With an 87-unit campground (with 38 full utility pads), year-round fishing, and rowboat rentals, the park is well equipped for families interested in a little communing with nature. Mojave Narrows Regional Park is home to the Huck Finn Jubilee during Father's Day weekend. This festival is loaded with toe-tappin' bluegrass music, a watermelon seed spittin' contest, arts and crafts booths, and a catfish derby.

ADVENTURE FLIGHTS INC.

(909) 678–4334; www.advflights.com.

One of several ballooning firms servicing the area with very reasonably priced flights. Sometimes you can get a ride on the spot, but it's always best to call ahead. One of the longest-running companies in "these parts."

San Bernardino

On the other side of the mountains, via Interstate 15 to Interstate 215 south, lies sprawling San Bernardino. "San Berdoo," as it's called locally, offers pleasures of a more municipal, but certainly no less stimulating, nature.

A SPECIAL PLACE

1003 East Highland Avenue; (909) 881–1201. Open Tuesday through Friday 9:00 A.M. to 1:00 P.M. and Saturday 11:00 A.M. to 3:00 P.M. $

A family-oriented museum worth a detour if your kids enjoy hands-on type exhibits.

HISTORIC SITE OF THE WORLD'S FIRST MCDONALD'S HAMBURGERS

1398 North E Street. Open Monday through Sunday 9:00 A.M. to 5:00 P.M.

In 1948 Dick and Mac McDonald opened their original restaurant on this site on the business district loop of Route 66. There is a display of early McDonald's memorabilia. No food here, though.

RENAISSANCE PLEASURE FAIRE

Glen Helen Regional Park, at the foot of the San Bernardino Mountains where Interstates 15 and 215 meet; (909) 880–0122 or (800) 52–FAIRE. Open 9:00 A.M. to 6:00 P.M. on eight weekends plus Memorial Day from beginning of May to early June. $$$

This is indeed a pleasure—a lively re-creation of a sixteenth-century English country fair. Sponsored by the **Living History Centre**, this is the largest outdoor theatrical event of its kind. But for the conspicuous absence of fog, you'd swear you were in merry olde England. How often do you get the chance to toast the arrival of Queen Elizabeth I on her royal barge, see knights in shining armor battle one another in a royal joust, and ride an elephant all in the same day?

Then there's the **Elizabethan theater,** music, and country dance on six stages, old English-style crafts, and historically accurate foodstuffs to partake of (mega-sized turkey legs are a perennial favorite). You can also opt to get your palm read by a gypsy, have a fortune teller teach you all about tarot cards, or just pause to chat with a strolling, fully costumed jester. The festive atmosphere at the fair is simply contagious, an unforgettable treat for both youngsters and older youngsters.

GLEN HELEN REGIONAL PARK

2555 Glen Helen Parkway; (909) 887–7540; fax (909) 887–1359 for park information and (909) 880–6500 for concert information.

The "jewel in the crown" of the area's regional parks, 1,425-acre Glen Helen comes complete with a half-acre swimming lagoon, a 350-foot water slide, and a beach. And proof positive that Southern Californians think big, the park also boasts the **Blockbuster Pavilion** outdoor concert venue, the largest amphitheater in the United States (total capacity is 65,000).

ROUTE 66 RENDEZVOUS

(800) 867–8366.

If you're up for a healthy dose of nostalgic honky-tonk (150,000 people were so inclined last year), check out this four-day affair that kicks off every year in mid-September. Southern Californians have always had a special relationship with their automobiles; what wine is to the French, cars are to us—sacred objects, worthy of adulation. This is clearly in evidence as squeaky-clean vintage Corvettes, Cobras, and Chevys cruise the sunny streets of downtown San Bernardino (some of those streets have replaced the fabled old Route 66). Drag races, an auto sound challenge, and an antique performance parts swap are also on the annual activity roster. Dozens of vendors hawk their wares, which range from antique milk caps and Elvis clocks to new stereo equipment. And to put a little honk into the tonk, celebrities come to life via ongoing **Legends in Concert** performances. The rendezvous, which is 𝕱𝓻𝓮𝓮 to spectators, is held in conjunction with the **Taste of San Bernardino Food Fair.**

NATIONAL ORANGE SHOW

689 South E Street; (909) 888–6788. Held from Thursday to Monday (Memorial Day Weekend). Admission is 𝕱𝓻𝓮𝓮.

Here's an event you'll never find in Kansas. Started way back in 1911, the show has been getting juicier ever since. Today it features fireworks, top entertainment, a rodeo, livestock shows, art exhibits, kid-friendly rides, and, of course, a broad range of oranges and orange food products.

Where to Eat

Guadalaharry's, *280 East Hospitality Lane, San Bernardino. (909) 889–8555.* Specializing in fajitas, Guadalaharry's is also known for its fried ice cream dessert. $-$$

Isabella's, *201 North E Street, #101, San Bernardino. (909) 884–2534.* Tasty Italian cuisine in a relaxing atmosphere.

Pinnacle Peak, *2533 South La Cadena, Colton. (909) 783–2543.* Mesquite-grilled Cowboy and Cowgirl Steaks.

Don't wear a tie!—it will be cut off at the door! Many ties decorate the inside of this ranch-style restaurant. $

Yamazato of Japan, *289 East Hospitality Lane, San Bernardino. (909) 889–3683.* Teppenyaki chefs are very entertaining as they prepare your meal on a grill at your table. It's fun to watch them flip an egg into their hat or a shrimp into their pocket! Delicious teriyaki, tempura, and sushi dishes. $

Where to Stay

Hilton-San Bernardino, *285 East Hospitality Lane, San Bernardino, (909) 889–0133 or (800) 445–8667; www.hilton. com.* Located off the I-10 at the North Waterman exit. As the street name suggests, this area of San Bernardino is visitor friendly. You'll find an extensive variety of restaurants on Hospitality

Lane within walking distance of the hotel, including Guadalaharry's, Yamazato, and others. $$$$

La Quinta Inn, *205 East Hospitality Lane, San Bernardino, (909) 888–7571.* La Quinta is adjacent to the Hilton and close to restaurants. $$$

Radisson Hotel and Convention Center, *295 North E Street, San Bernardino.* A complete meeting and entertainment center located in down-town San Bernardino. Close to shopping at Carousel Mall, which really does have a carousel. $$$$

Redlands

Quiet little Redlands, home of the eponymous and highly regarded university, awaits exploration just a few minutes east of San Bernardino on Interstate 10. If you're on the way to, say, Palm Springs and only have time for one detour, make it Redlands. You'll be in excellent company, for in the latter part of the nineteenth century, Midwesterners and East Coasters of certain means began a time-honored tradition of wintering in Southern California, and one of their favorite spots was Redlands. Among the city's attractions are several mansions that bear witness to the Golden State's brief Victorian renaissance.

SAN BERNARDINO COUNTY MUSEUM

2024 Orange Tree Lane, near the California Street exit from Interstate 10; (909) 307–2669 or (888) BIRD-EGG. Open Tuesday through Sunday 9:00 A.M. to 5:00 P.M. $. Children under five, **Free***.*

This local landmark is easily recognized by its large geodesic dome (actually a seminar room). Here you'll find exhibits on early Californian ranch life and the Native Americans who once lived in these parts. But the real strong suits of the museum are the earth and biological science exhibits, which also happen to be among the most popular with younger children. For starters, there are more than 40,000 birds' eggs, the state's only dinosaur tracks, and a dazzling collection of minerals and gemstones. Kids are captivated by the live insect, reptile, and amphibian displays. Both kids and adults can contemplate the forces that formed the Inland Empire's beautiful mountains by keeping an eye on the always-on seismometer.

KIMBERLY CREST HOUSE AND GARDENS

1325 Prospect Drive; (909) 792–2111; www.kimberlycrest.org. Open Thursday through Sunday 1:00 to 4:00 P.M. September through July. $

With its commanding views of the San Bernardino Valley, this six-acre estate, purchased in 1905 by J. Alfred Kimberly and his wife, Helen (of Kimberly-Clark fame), features Louis XVI decor on the inside and formal Italian gardens and lush orange groves on the outside. See if you can spot the great southern magnolia, for years the Kimberlys' outdoor

Christmas tree. The most impressive of the city's mansions, this French château-style home is off Interstate 10 at the Ford exit. Closed August. Average visit: one hour.

THE FRUGAL FRIGATE

9 North Sixth Street, (909) 793–0740; www.frugalfrigate.com. Monday through Friday 10:00 A.M. to 6:00 P.M.; Thursday 10:00 A.M. to 8:00 P.M.; Saturday 10:00 A.M. to 5:00 P.M., and Sunday 12:00 to 5:00 P.M.

A delightful source for "carefully chosen children's classics," this unique bookstore is located in historic downtown Redlands.

Extra Special Tip

Pizza, Pizza, and More Pizza The Gourmet Pizza Shoppe (120 East State Street; 909-792-3313) boasts ninety different combinations of pizza, including peanut butter and jelly. Their beverage list features sodas from all over the world including cream sodas, root beers, black cherry sodas, and six varieties of orange soda! You won't find noisy arcade games or a TV in the dining room. This family-style pizza parlor has seating areas with children's books available for kids to read while they await their favorite pizza.

A. K. SMILEY PUBLIC LIBRARY

125 West Vine Street; (909) 798–7565; www.akspl.org. Monday and Tuesday, 9:00 A.M. to 9:00 P.M.; Wednesday and Thursday, 9:00 A.M. to 7:00 P.M.; Friday and Saturday, 9:00 A.M. to 5:00 P.M.

A grandiose library over one hundred years old and built in the Moorish style. The children's section offers storytelling and a wealth of books for the two to twelve set. It's better, but a lot smaller than those behemoth bookstores!

PHARAOH'S LOST KINGDOM THEME PARK

1101 California Street (I–10 and California), 92374; (909) 335–PARK. Prices vary. The Sky Coaster costs extra. Open Sunday through Thursday 10:00 A.M. to 11:00 P.M.; Friday and Saturday 10:00 A.M. to midnight.

An eye-catching eighteen-acre Egyptian-style amusement park with rides, a water park, pyramids, and sphinxes. Some might regard Pharaoh's as yet another Disney imitation (or to others, a monstrosity). Regardless, it's a gauche, comic, replication of history plastique. For a moment, when you catch a glimpse of the stately ersatz gold pharaoh, you'll think you've escaped the freeways for Egypt. And just wait until you've journeyed further along Interstate 10 toward Cabazon. You'll encounter a couple of life-sized dinosaurs. Holy Victor Mature!

At any rate, Pharaoh's is open daily. If your tastes run toward video arcades (which we believe are a preparatory course for later-life gamblers), the one here is colossal, with the incentive of **Free** admission for kids. Once inside, you'll find the tariff rises sharply. We recommend steering the young ones to the rides, the water park, and other activities like the King's Pond (bumper boats) and Chariots of Thunder (race cars).

Extra Special Tip

Hot Rod Fans will love the new **National Hot Rod Association Motorsports Museum** that opened at Fairplex in Pomona in 1998. This 28,500-square-foot museum, which shares grounds with the Los Angeles County Fair, is highlighted by fifty vintage and historical cars and memorabilia ranging from fire suits and helmets to photos chronicling the history of drag racing. In case your kids don't know what this is, here's a good place to give them their basic education in this national pastime. For information call (909) 623–3111 or contact them at fairplex.com.

Where to Eat

Martha Green's Doughlectibles,
105 East Citrus Avenue (909) 798–7321.
The bakery has all varieties of fresh pastries and breads. The restaurant serves breakfast, lunch, and dinner. The French toast is worth the calories. Lunch choices include a great patty melt. This Martha has her own line of cookbooks as well. $

Oscar's Mexican Restaurant, *19 North Fifth Street, (909) 792–8211.* Oscar's is an institution in downtown Redlands, serving great Mexican food that is sure to satisfy your appetite. They have great "lite combos" for $6.25. $

Riverside

If one views the Inland Empire as a vast stage, its outdoor attractions tend to steal the show. Maybe that's why so few people seem to know much about Riverside, the city built on oranges. Riverside is accessible via Highway 60 or

Highway 91, both south of Interstate 10. By 1895 more than 20,000 acres of navel orange trees had made then-sleepy Riverside into the nation's wealthiest city per capita. This distinctly Californian heritage is still evident, thanks to the presence of a handful of old California-style structures: the old **City Hall** (3612 Mission Inn Avenue), restored **1892 Heritage House,** the finest example of Victorian lifestyle in the West, and the city's landmark, the restored **Mission Inn** (3649 Mission Inn Avenue). Originally a twelve-room adobe built in 1875 (a very long time ago by Californian standards), this grand hostelry expanded along with the town.

RIVERSIDE MUNICIPAL MUSEUM

3580 Mission Inn Avenue; (909) 826–5273. Open Monday 9:00 A.M. to 1:00 P.M., Tuesday through Friday 9:00 A.M. to 5:00 P.M., Saturday and Sunday 1:00 to 5:00 P.M.; admission **Free.**

The area's roots are on display at this museum, with its large collection of Native American artifacts and early citrus industry exhibits.

JURUPA EARTH-SCIENCE MUSEUM AND CULTURAL CENTER

7621 Granite Hill Drive; (909) 685–5818. Open Saturday 8:00 A.M. to 4:30 P.M. $

If you missed the San Bernardino County Museum (above) and it's Saturday, bring the kids here for an educational guided nature walk. Along with excellent fossil and crystal exhibits, the museum has a cache of moon rocks.

CALIFORNIA CITRUS STATE HISTORIC PARK

Take Riverside Freeway (Route 91) to Van Buren Boulevard at Dufferin Avenue, look for the big orange; (909) 780–6222.

This California state park was built to celebrate 100 years of citrus production in Riverside with support from Sunkist growers. Located on the 377 acres are the Varietal Grove, which has a hundred different species of citrus, an outdoor amphitheater where concerts are held on Friday evenings during summer (the last concert is the first Friday in August), and new in the spring of 2002, a larger visitor center. Many weddings and events are held in the California Craftsman–style building. As you walk around the park, you will encounter interpretive displays and picnic areas.

BOTANIC GARDENS AT UCR

University of California at Riverside, (909) 787–4650; www.gardens.ucr.edu. Open daily from 8:00 A.M. to 5:00 P.M.

These gardens are nestled in the foothills of the Box Springs Mountains in East Riverside and cover forty hilly acres. The gardens boast more than 3,500 plant species from around the world. More than 200 species of birds have been observed in the gardens. From the 60/I–215, exit at Martin Luther King Boulevard and turn right. Turn right again at Canyon Crest Avenue and enter the UCR campus. Follow signs to the gardens and park in Lot 13. Admission is 𝐅𝐫𝐞𝐞, although donations are appreciated.

RANCHO JURUPA PARK

4600 Crestmore Drive; (909) 684–7032.

There are thirty-five parks in Riverside County's Regional Park and Open Spaces system. Rancho Jurupa Park is located just outside the city limits of Riverside and provides fishing, biking, hiking, and equestrian trails as well as camping. Don't forget to stop into the Luis Robidoux Nature Center on the park grounds. Only a mile (as the crow flies) from Rancho Jurupa is the Jensen-Alvarado Ranch. This was the first non-adobe building in the Riverside area. Many school groups come to learn how to make homemade ice cream and tortillas (on a potbellied stove!). The Jensen-Alvarado Ranch is located at 4307 Briggs Street in Rubidoux. Take Freeway 60 west from Riverside, exit at Rubidoux Boulevard, drive south to Tilton Avenue, and head west on Briggs.

CASTLE AMUSEMENT PARK

3500 Polk Street; (909) 785–3000; www.castlepark.com. No admission fee; ride tickets and game tokens can be purchased inside the park.

Hold on to your collective hats! This twenty-five-acre park has it all. It was built in 1976 to be the "Ultimate Family Entertainment Park." The three-level castle houses more than 400 state-of-the-art games. The rare Dentzel carousel (built in 1898) is one of the oldest in America and has fifty-two hand-carved, brightly painted animals and two sleighs on highly polished brass poles (one of our family advisers had the family photographed here for a Christmas card). Add to these four world-class, eighteen-hole, championship miniature par-four golf courses surrounded by gorgeous palm trees. The Big Top Restaurant has everything from a salad bar to super sundaes. This place could be as good as Disneyland!

Where to Eat

Anchos Southwest Grill and Bar,
*10773 Hole Street, Riverside; (909)
352–0240. Take Freeway 91 to La Sierra,
head north to Hole, and turn right.* Delicious Mexican and southwestern cuisine. Watch the flour tortillas being
made and rotating in the warmer. Try
the Ribs and Diego Shrimp, which isn't
listed on the menu. Wonderful! $

Ciao Bella, *1630 Spruce Street, Riverside;
(909) 781–8840.* This restaurant is
famous for its California cuisine. Tasty
pasta dishes. $$

Gram's Mission Barbeque Palace,
*3527 Main Street, Riverside; (909) 782–
8219.* Gram's reigns supreme in barbe-
cue and Cajun cuisine. $

Mario's Place, *3646 Mission Inn
Avenue, Riverside; (909) 684–7755.* Some
of the most savory Italian dishes avail-
able. The Palagi family has made
Mario's Place a landmark in Riverside.
$$–$$$

Sevilla Restaurant & Club, *3252
Mission Inn Avenue, Riverside; (909) 778–
0611. Take Freeway 91 to the Mission Inn
Avenue exit.* This restaurant specializes
in Spanish (not Mexican) food. Enter-
tainment includes flamenco dancers
and offers nightlife when the children
go to sleep. $$

Where to Stay

The Historic Mission Inn, *3649 Mission Inn Avenue, Riverside; (909) 784–
0300.* This European-style hotel encom-
passes an entire city block in downtown Riverside. Come stroll the halls of
this great inn, which has hosted several
of our nation's presidents.

Holiday Inn Select, *3400 Market
Street, Riverside; (909) 784–8000.* Adjacent to Riverside's Convention Center,
the Holiday Inn is within walking distance of the historic downtown area.

Perris

For a taste of the real Riverside County, you have to delve into deep Riverside—in other words, let the country roads be your guide. If you take Interstate
215 south from State Highway 60 (which runs right through Riverside), in
about twenty traffic-free minutes you'll come across the little town of Perris.
The locals always say there's nothing like Perris in the springtime—a reference
to the California golden poppies and other wildflowers that carpet these parts
round about April. Even if your visit doesn't happen to coincide with the
annual flora show, Mother Nature won't disappoint. Rambling about the

Temecula Valley, in which Perris lies at the northern head, is like entering a time warp to old California. Bring your camera.

The Perris area is well known for the outdoor activities afforded by its laid-back country setting. The early morning and late evening stillness, coupled with mild temperatures, spells paradise for aviation buffs. Hot-air balloon, sailplane, hang glider, and even skydiving outfitters abound in the area. It can be quite a spectacle simply to watch these folks in action at the Perris Valley Airport. At ground level, campers, swimmers, boaters, fishers, hikers, and bikers will enjoy a detour to the **Lake Perris State Recreation Area**, 1781 Lake Perris Drive; (909) 657-0676. Visit the YA-I Heki Museum for information on Native American history of the area. It's located at Lake Perris Recreation Area.

ORANGE EMPIRE RAILWAY MUSEUM

2201 South A Street; (909) 657-2605; oerm@Juno.com. Nominal fees for trolley and train rides. $$

This is the West's biggest railway museum, with electric cars, buildings, and other artifacts. The museum covers sixty acres, so there is plenty of room for a family picnic among streetcars, trains, and municipal buses from yesteryear.

More than 150 historic train cars, locomotives, and streetcars are on display indoors and outside. Are you ready to ride the rails, kids? Each Saturday and Sunday from 11:00 A.M. to 5:00 P.M., vintage streetcars circle the museum property (it takes about seven minutes), and antique Southern Pacific train cars make a ten-minute trip to the Perris Depot and back.

Hemet

If you're heading from the Perris area to Hemet or Idyllwild (more on that next), you could take either Highway 74 east or drive along the **Juan Bautista de Anza National Historic Trail**. This scenic corridor, which skirts Lake Perris, dairy farms, and other quiet farmlands, follows the tracks de Anza made when he explored the region for Spain in 1775.

RAMONA PAGEANT

2400 Ramona Bowl Road; (909) 658-3111 or (800) 645-4465. Late April/early May.

Performed by more than 350 of the town's residents, the play is adapted from an 1884 novel that depicts the romantic spectacle of early California. It has been an annual event for more than seventy years, earning it the designation as the official outdoor play of California. The play runs on weekends from 3:30 to about 6:30 P.M.

DIAMOND VALLEY LAKE

300 Newport Road, Hemet; (909) 765–2612. Exit 215 south at 74 east toward Hemet. Head south at State Street to Newport Road. Turn right.

These 4,000 square acres of water storage and recreation land are the great attraction of the Hemet Valley. Inside the visitor center you can see the mastodon exhibit as well as other artifacts retrieved from excavations made as this lake began to fill in 1999. The lake will be completely filled by 2004.

Idyllwild

Take Highway 74 east out of Hemet to Highway 243, which leads to the hamlet of Idyllwild. You will be traveling on the **Palms to Pines Scenic Highway**, and as the name indicates, you'll observe desert palm and oak trees giving way to pine and fir forests as the elevation increases. Idyllwild, which looks like a village from the Swiss Alps dropped into the heart of the **San Bernardino National Forest**, makes for one of the most enchanting detours in the Inland Empire, especially in winter. Since the town is nestled 5,400 feet up, Idyllwild nights are cool and crisp, even in the summer. Get ready to tackle the great outdoors by ordering up a savory Belgian waffle first—any time of day—at the **Idyllwild Cafe**, 26600 Highway 243, next to Idyllwild School; (909) 659-2210. Or try the home-baked pies at **Granny's Pies** at the Fort; (909) 659-6344.

JAZZ IN THE PINES

(909) 659–4885 for ticket information and (909) 659–3774 for general information; info@idyllwildjazz.com.

This musical event takes place in late August, amid lofty pines and clear skies.

LIVING FREE ANIMAL SANCTUARY

54250 Keen Camp Road, at Mountain Center on Highway 74; (909) 659–4684; www.living-free.org. Saturday only 10:00 A.M. to 4:00 P.M. Other days by appointment. Plan to arrive before 3:30 P.M. if you would like time to walk one of the resident dogs. Admission **Free***; donations welcome.*

This is a most unusual retreat for dogs and cats, a nonprofit animal sanctuary founded by Emily Jo Beard on 180 bucolic acres. The retreat is home to a variety of dogs, such as Sparkes, Kingdom, and Pike, plus cats such as Oprah, Bandit, and Kira. They have found a new life and home in this caring environment. The emphasis is on education, and children will find the dogs "living in harmony" and the cats "contented," enjoying spacious yards, play structures, and shady trees.

🍴 SUGARLOAF CAFE AND MARKET

70–111 Highway 74 at Mountain Center; (760) 349–9020. Open Tuesday through Sunday 8:00 A.M. to 8:00 P.M. $

It's a 15-mile drive from Palm Springs and fifteen degrees cooler, too. At these two rustic roadhouses, you can order anything from barbecue chicken hot off the rotisserie to sandwiches in a basket. Try one of their homemade soups, the perfect way to start your dining adventures in this majestic region of Southern California. Outside dining on the patio is a nice way to take in the scenery. And the market has a deli and takeout, too.

Extra Special Tip

Idyllwild This town, at an altitude of 5,400 feet with zero days of smog, is a mile-high oasis nestled in the San Jacinto Mountains and this author's favorite choice for a well-balanced family vacation in Southern California. It is devoid of fast-food joints (and their comforts), but the exceptional opportunities for family recreation more than compensate! Check it out by contacting the **Idyllwild Chamber of Commerce** at 54295 Village Center Drive, 92549; (909) 659-3259; fax (909) 659-6216; www.idyllwild.org; chamber@idyllwild. org. For lodging call (909) 659-2201, (909) 659-2869, or (909) 659-5520.

HIDDEN VILLAGE

25840 Cedar Street; (909) 659–2712.

What a discovery in this mountain village—a quaint Chinese restaurant owned by internationally-known chef Freeman Ye.

IDYLLWILD ARTS

P.O. Box 38, 92549; (located at the end of Tollgate Road); (909) 659–2171; www.idyllwildart.org.

Idyllwild Arts offers a family camp in late June and early July. There are separate activities for children, teenagers, and adults, including hiking, wilderness activities, swimming, and just relaxing. Evening activities include concerts, folk dancing, and family talent night.

Oak Glen

Washington State doesn't have a monopoly on apples. Oak Glen, just north of Yucaipa, is the core of the Inland Empire's tranquil apple country, which both tourists and natives are often surprised to find. September through December means apple-picking time at the 900-acre **Los Rios Rancho**, 39610 Oak Glen Road; (909) 795-1005 and **Parrish Pioneer Ranch**, 38561 Oak Glen Road; (909) 797-1753.

In the summer, you can pick raspberries instead—not a bad alternative. The New England atmosphere of Oak Glen is particularly strong in wintertime, when snow often coats the apple orchards. But any time of year, the place is simply charming.

RILEY'S FARM AND ORCHARD

12253 South Oak Glen Road; (909) 790-2364; www.rileysfarm.com.
"Villagers and country folk" are cordially invited to "come and be one hundred years behind the times." During apple season you can take the kids on a hayride that includes a farm tour, cider pressing, and hot-caramel-dipped apples.

Are you there yet? The town of Oak Glen is like a West Coast version of Sleepy Hollow, with its antiques stores and scent of fresh apple pie wafting out of the windows of little restaurants. The pace is slower up here, and residents seem to like it that way. Not everything's coming up apples, though. At the **Mously Museum of Natural History**, 35308 Panorama Drive; (909) 790-3163, seashells, minerals, and fossils take center stage.

Where to Eat

Parrish Pioneer Apple Ranch, *38561 Oak Glen Road, Yucaipa; (909) 797–4020.* Parrish Pioneer Apple Ranch is home to Apple Annie's Restaurant. Stop in for lunch (they have a great selection of sandwiches) and hot apple pie àla mode! $

Banning/Cabazon

GILMAN RANCH HISTORIC PARK AND WAGON MUSEUM

Wilson and Sixteenth Streets in Banning, off Interstate 10 heading toward Palm Springs; (909) 922–9200. Open Sunday 10:00 A.M. to 4:00 P.M.

Stop here for a peek into California's ranching past.

Farther along Interstate 10, the kids will make you pull over in **Cabazon** (population 1,400) the instant they see two hulking dinosaurs stalking drivers on the left (exit at Main Street). One's a brontosaurus with a mini-museum and gift shop tucked into his belly. His friend is a not-too-friendly-looking *Tyrannosaurus rex*. Like Pee Wee Herman in *Pee Wee's Big Adventure* (if you haven't seen it, your kids probably have), you can climb up to the dinosaur's jaw to take in the view. These Jurassic monstrosities are California camp at its best. They seem to be made expressly for family vacation fun.

There are two more attractions in Cabazon, both easily visible from Interstate 10. The first is **Hadley's Fruit Orchards**, an all-natural dried fruit and produce emporium famous for its deliciously frosty date shakes. The other is **Desert Hills Premium Outlets and New Cabazon Outlets** (48400 Seminole Road, 909-849-6641), three rambling outlet complexes. If your kids have been pining for a new pair of Nikes, or you have designs on some off-price Ralph Lauren apparel or home furnishings, you've hit the jackpot. And this isn't even Las Vegas!

Kern County

Unlike many other states, California never quite seems to end. If you thought the sweeping vistas stopped after the San Bernardino Mountains, think again. Just north of them lies Kern County, nestled between the Sierra Nevada and the coastal range. With its 8,073 square miles, Kern is the largest county in California and is as large as Massachusetts. It forms the southern tier of the agriculture- and oil-rich Central Valley, the one of *Grapes of Wrath* fame, acre for acre the richest in the world. No matter what time of year you happen to be driving through, you'll see boundless fields of grapes, almonds, carrots, apples, watermelons, tomatoes, and more. The fruits and vegetables grown here are shipped all over the world, but you can sample them first at any of the numerous roadside farmer's markets.

Even if you've never been to Kern County before, you or your kids may feel as though you have, because of the numerous movies that have been filmed here over the years, from *Star Packer* (with John Wayne, 1934) to *Jurassic Park*. This portion of the vast, semiarid valley is perhaps best known, though, for white-water river rafting on the Kern River. It was the river, in fact, that put the region on the map: Gold was discovered in the riverbed in 1851. There is even more to explore, but basically the area is less tourist intensive than the California that lies farther south. It is, above all, a place to appreciate the great outdoors, slow down a bit, and smell the roses.

Boron

TWENTY MULE TEAM MUSEUM
26962 Twenty Mule Team Road; (760) 762–5810; www.rnrs.com/20muleteam. Open daily 10:00 A.M. to 4:00 P.M. Kids welcome. **Free**.

If you find yourselves on Highway 58 at the junction of Highway 395 ("Four Corners") and think you're in the middle of nowhere, think again. Another 6 miles and you're here. Should you have that Thomas Guide we recommended, you won't get lost. Your kids may not remember the TV series *Death Valley Days* or the product Borax (it used to make our wash sparkle), but here's a good way to refresh your memory. The museum, located in a renovated house from the old Baker Mine campsite, depicts borax mining and early life in Boron. There are plans to add an air and space museum here, so look for an F4D airplane that was retired here. There's also a train station that was brought in from Kramer. Keep your road map handy and your eyes open—there's no telling what you'll find in these parts.

THE BORAX VISITOR CENTER
4486 Borax Road, off Highway 58 at the Borax Road exit; www.borax.com. Open seven days a week from 9:00 A.M. to 5:00 P.M., excluding major holidays and weather permitting. Parking, $2.00.

Everyone who finds his or her way to this center gets a sample of "TV rock." After watching the seventeen-minute video on the worldwide uses of borax, the kids will understand why there really is a treasure in "them thar hills." And it's borax!

Wasco

There's no better place to start smelling the roses than Wasco, which has the most extensive miniature-rose-growing facilities in the world. As you drive along the roads that inspired Jack Kerouac, roll down the window and let the aroma of 20 million blossoming buds waft on in.

If you'd like to learn about the agricultural history of the area and you're traveling on a Saturday, pay a visit to the **Wasco Museum**, 918 Sixth Street (805) 758-8949, for a good, small-town introduction. Open Saturday 1:00 to 3:00 P.M.

Kernville

Have you been contemplating a **white-water river-rafting adventure** for your family? If so, you're in the right place. From its headwaters at Lake South America in the Sierra Nevada (elevation 11,800 feet), the Kern River falls more than 12,000 feet in 150 miles. That makes it one of the fastest-falling rivers in North America. But the pace of the rapids ranges from wild to mild. According to the International River Classification System, rapids ratings range from Class I—very easy, like a swimming pool with a current—all the way up to Class VI, which is virtually unrunnable. Class I and II rapids are perfectly suitable for most children; older ones who enjoy a good soaking can take on Class III. The important thing to remember is that you don't just drive up to the river and hop in with an inner tube. There are several professional rafting outfitters whose sole purpose is to orchestrate a fun, safe time for everyone who signs up.

Most of these outfitters are based in Kernville, the traditional jumping-off point for rafting trips. If you've never done this kind of thing before, ask them about one-day instruction sessions, usually available for $50 to $100.

SIERRA SOUTH MOUNTAIN SPORTS OUTFITTERS
11300 Kernville Road; (760) 376–3745 or (800) 376–2082; paddle@Sierra-south.com; www.sierrasouth.com. Prices vary.

This company offers a wide range of rafting and kayaking excursions, including a two-and-a-half-hour Lickety-Blaster run. On this eminently manageable aquatic jaunt, rafters experience Class II and III rapids. Lake kayaking is an alternative to river rafting, for those traveling with kids under twelve say the folks at Sierra South, because it is more relaxed and there is swimming at Lake Isabella. It's a family paddle adventure at a mellow pace.

WHITEWATER VOYAGES

(800) 400–RAFT; www.whitewatervoyages.com. $$$$

Offers Class I and II family trips that accommodate kids as young as four. Whitewater's guides were stunt doubles for Meryl Streep and Kevin Bacon in *The River Wild*.

MOUNTAIN AND RIVER ADVENTURES

(760) 376–6553 or (800) 861–6553; fax (760) 376–1267; www.mtnriver. com. $$$$

Offers mountain-biking and rock-climbing rambles in addition to white-water rafting trips—all under expert supervision by guides who know the lay of the land (and water) inside out.

If you happen to be in Kernville in late February (before the rafting season kicks in), enjoy the carnival atmosphere of **Whiskey Flat Days**, when the town travels back in time to the gold rush days. With a parade, rodeo, whisker and costume contests, and frog races, the event is designed for families in search of a little quality fun time. Call (760) 376-2629 for dates and other information.

Extra Special Tip

Cheryl's Diner Let's talk turkey now, and not turkey vulture! For a down-home meal try Cheryl's Diner, 11030 Kernville Road. Open from 6:00 A.M. to 9:00 P.M. Breakfast, lunch, and dinner served at family-friendly prices.

Kernville straddles the northern end of Lake Isabella, built in 1953 for flood control and as a hydroelectric source and reservoir. It is Southern California's largest freshwater lake. With up to 11,000 surface-acre feet, it also happens to be a prime body of water for Jet Skiing, waterskiing, windsurfing, sailing, and fishing.

KERN VALLEY TURKEY VULTURE FESTIVAL

Contact Kernville Chamber of Commerce, (760) 376–2629 or (800) 350–7390; fax (760) 376–4371.

Just when you think you've heard about the most unusual festival imaginable (for instance, the tobacco spitting competition in Calico), along comes this one. Held between September 1 and October 31, depending on when the big birds decide to fly through Kern Valley (some 33,000 passed through in 1996), the festival offers such activities as a turkey vulture slide show, workshops on raptor rehabilitation, a bird-banding demonstration, and an official Turkey Vultures Lift-Off. There are turkey vulture T-shirts to buy, designed by John Schmitt, and enough information to satisfy the most rabid bird-watcher (or turkey vulture buff). The festival takes place in Weldon at Audubon's Kern River Preserve.

The region around the lake is surrounded by the **Sequoia National Forest**; for camping information and details about other outdoor activities, stop by the **U.S. Forest Service's** new visitor center off Highway 155, just south of the lake's main dam, 4875 Ponderosa Road; (760) 379–5646.

Where to Eat

The River View Lodge, *P.O. Box 745, Kernville, 93238; (760) 376–6019.* This historic eleven-room inn welcomes families and pets. You'll find refrigerators in every room and a picnic area, too. The country-style rooms with two queen beds are ideal for families.

Bakersfield

There are several points of departure in and around the pleasant city of Bakersfield, Kern's county seat. Honored by President Clinton as an "all-American city," Bakersfield has an unexpected culinary surprise: numerous Basque restaurants. One of the largest Basque communities outside the Pyrenees is in Kern County, and no chance to sample their singular cuisine should be missed.

BUCK OWEN'S CRYSTAL PALACE

2800 Buck Owens Boulevard, Bakersfield; (661) 869–BUCK; (661) 328–7500 for dinner reservations. Call (808) 855–5005 or (661) 328–7560 for show reservations; www.buckowens.com. Daily tours are available. **Free**.

Opened in 1996, this all-in-one restaurant, museum, and theater is a must-see! Even if the kids are unaware that Buck Owens starred in *Hee Haw*, they'll love the smashingly sensational decor. You'll be amazed by what's over the 50-foot-long bar: the car Elvis never drove, a vintage 1970s Pontiac and yacht, studded with silver dollars! It's mounted at a tilt so you can check out its luxurious interior.

Buck Owens and others perform country favorites evenings, matinees, and weekends. State-of-the-art sound, and lighting and giant screens throughout make this a visual marvel. And we haven't even mentioned the 35-foot mural showing Buck's rise from the cotton fields to

THE INLAND EMPIRE AND BEYOND

Carnegie Hall to entertaining presidents at the White House. Country music has found a home in Bakersfield.

KERN COUNTY MUSEUM AND LORI BROCK CHILDREN'S DISCOVERY CENTER

3801 Chester Avenue; (661) 852–5000. Open Monday through Friday 8:00 A.M. to 5:00 P.M. and Saturday 10:00 A.M. to 5:00 P.M. $

The museum provides more than a glimpse into the history of Bakersfield and its environs. Kids have room to roam here, for it's a fourteen-acre walk-through site with over sixty historic and refurbished structures, ranging from the Havilah Courthouse and Jail (1866) and the Calloway Ranch Blacksmith Shop (circa 1880) to an 1898 Southern Pacific locomotive. The Spanish Mission–style main museum building houses permanent and changing exhibitions that chronicle Kern County's history, natural history, and culture. The Lori Brock Children's Museum, with hands-on displays and activities for kids, is also located on the premises.

CALIFORNIA LIVING MUSEUM (CALM)

Just north of Bakersfield, 14000 Alfred Harrell Highway; (661) 872–2256. Open Tuesday to Sunday 9:00 A.M. to 5:00 P.M. $

Whereas the Kern County Museum focuses on the human history of the area, the natural environment occupies center stage here. This is an ideally situated spot for a family-oriented wildlife experience. The thirteen acres house a botanical garden, petting zoo, and natural history museum. The animal exhibits assemble fauna native to California: coyotes, desert tortoises, shore birds, and birds of prey, including hawks, raptors, owls, and eagles. The *Mammal Round* exhibit features mountain lions, raccoons, foxes, and bobcats—yes, all native to the Golden State! The Living Museum merits at least a ninety-minute visit.

TULE ELK STATE RESERVE

Twenty-seven miles west of Bakersfield, 4 miles west of Interstate 5, and off the Stockdale Highway, south of Buttonwillow; (661) 764–6881 or (661) 248–6692.

For a slightly wilder look at the wild kingdom, head to this 953-acre site. Tule elks were once as common in California as the antelope of South Africa are today, but they are now a rare species. The State Division of Beaches and Parks keeps a herd of about thirty adult elk at the park, which is equipped with a shaded picnic and viewing area. With the sweeping grassland forming a backdrop, gawking at the elks' regal antlers (which only the males have) is rather like taking a mini-safari. The best times to view the elk are in summer and fall.

FORT TEJON STATE HISTORIC PARK

Interstate 5, 36 miles south of Bakersfield. Living history programs held the first Sunday of each month; Civil War reenactments, third Sunday, April through October. (661) 248–6692. Exit off Interstate 5, 70 miles northwest of Los Angeles at the top of Grapevine Canyon.

The fort is well worth a few hours' stop.

Extra Special Tip

California State Parks The time has come to let you in on a California secret, the **state parks annual pass,** which allows an unlimited number of entries for one full year from the date of purchase, "provided the park is open and the space is available." Request a free copy of the California State Parks Magazine, which includes activities, maps, and facilities. Contact **California State Parks Store,** P.O. Box 942896, Sacramento, 94296-0001 or call (800) 777–0369. Also try **California State Parks Information** at ceres.ca.gov/parks/.

Interested in camping along the way? Family campsites accommodate up to eight people and may include anything from fire rings and showers to picnic tables and a water supply. Southern California campsites include **South Carlsbad** (premium beachfront), open year-round, where sites are available at a higher fee ($19–$22). The **National Park Reservation Service** handles camping and tour reservations at twenty-six national park sites, including **Channel Islands** ($2.50), **Death Valley** ($16.00), **Joshua Tree** ($10.00), **Sequoia,** and **Kings Canyon** ($16.00). These are camping fees only and the rates listed are per night. Check information at (800) 365–2267 or reservations.nps.gov or www.nps.gov. Reservations can be made up to five months in advance and can be done by mail or phone. And don't forget California's 430 lakes! They span the state from the desert to a high alpine setting.

CalTour has everything you need to put your family odyssey together, write to: **California Tourism,** P.O. Box 1499, Dept. 200, Sacramento, 95812-1499 or try www.visitcalifornia.com or call (800) 862–2543, ext. 200. Call (800) 444–PARK (7252) 8:00 A.M. to 5:00 P.M. Pacific time for further information.

Where to Eat

A highlight of any meal is the scrumptious Basque salsa, made of chopped tomatoes, yellow and jalapeño chiles, garlic, onions, and salt. Try it at:

Benji's French Basque Restaurant, *4001 Rosedale Highway; (661) 328–0400.*

Chalet Basque, *101 Union Avenue, (661) 325–1316;* $$

Chalet Basque, *200 Oak Street, (661) 327–2915.*

Pyrenees Cafe, *601 Sumner Street, (661) 323–0053.* $$

Noriega Hotel, *525 Sumner Street, (661) 322–8419. One seating at noon and one seating at 7:00 P.M.* Our favorite family-style dining spot. Make sure you know how to get there, as first-timers have some trouble. Hungry diners sit at long tables (you may not know who'll be next to you), sharing up to seven courses of hearty Basque food. No set menu. We've tried soup, salad, chicken, ribs, fresh-cut french fries—all excellent. The ambience is, well, plain, but the service is efficient and the fare is robust. Only the most ravenous will have room for dessert. $–$$

Walker's Basin

QUARTER CIRCLE U RANKIN RANCH

Minutes north of Bakersfield in Walker's Basin; (661) 867–2511. Take Interstate 5 north to the Lamont-Lake Isabelle exit. The ranch is 38 miles from the exit, past the town of Caliente.

If your kids spot some elk, they may be disappointed to learn that no, they can't ride or even pet them. However, they can pet and ride horses to their hearts' content here. Members of the Rankin family have been ranching at their Quarter Circle U for 132 years, and they've got the western way of life down pat. This is a working 31,000-acre, cattle and guest ranch where kids and adults can help out with farm chores and horseback ride at their leisure. From Bakersfield, take Highway 58 east 22 miles to Caliente. Drive 2 miles through town, take a left at the fork in the road, then drive 10 miles to the ranch. Call for current rates (which include riding, lodging, and three meals a day) and other information.

Tulare County

SEQUOIA NATIONAL PARK AND KINGS CANYON NATIONAL PARK

The parks are open twenty-four hours a day, year-round. Call (559) 565–3341 for general information on wilderness hiking, camping, lodging, or road and weather conditions; or contact Sequoia Guest Services, authorized concessionaire of the National Park Service, (559) 561–3314; www.nps.gov.

Tulare County is best known as the home of these parks. Even though it's part of Fresno County, Kings Canyon shares its east-west boundary with Sequoia, and the two parks are generally referred to together. If the wooded retreats of Big Bear and Lake Arrowhead in the Inland Empire are imbued with an "escape from the city" atmosphere, up here you'll really feel a zillion miles away from it all. This is nature at its most unbridled, God's country with a very capital G. With more than 800 miles of marked hiking trails and 1,200-plus campsites and other lodging options, it's no wonder Sequoia and Kings Canyon are a California family favorite for camping and nature trips. However, the biggest attractions can be seen in a day.

The attractions are trees. Autumn in New England may be prime leaf-peeping time, but the trees of the central Sierra Nevada are marvels to behold any time of year. This is mainly due to their gargantuan size. Giant sequoias, which can reach 311 feet and an age of up to 3,200 years, grow naturally only on the west slope of the Sierra Nevada. Of the thirty-seven largest sequoia trees in the world, twenty giants roost here in Sequoia and Kings Canyon. You'll find the most stupendous grove of sequoias in the Giant Forest, longtime home of the **General Sherman Tree**. Weighing in at 2.7 million pounds, the 275-foot-tall tree is the largest living thing in the world. At more than 2,300 years, it's also one of the oldest. Each year the venerable Sherman grows enough wood for another 60-foot-tall tree. Imagine the tree house possibilities! For an easy, rewarding hike the whole family

Extra Special Tip

Wuksachi Lodge Check out the new 103-room Wuksachi Lodge, (888) 252–5757. Imagine a high-tech hotel room in the midst of the Sequoia wilderness. It's real, and it's all here—complete with computer data ports!

will enjoy, try the 2-mile, two-hour Congress Trail, which begins at the Sherman and circles around the grove.

Kings Canyon is where the **General Grant Tree**, the earth's third-largest, has its roots. It's also known as the "Nation's Christmas Tree." Annual Noel celebrations are held beneath its considerable and magnificent canopy.

Conservationist John Muir called Kings Canyon a rival to Yosemite, and it's not hard to see why. The depths of the canyon at Cedar Grove, where the Kings River gushes between sheer granite walls, bottom out at 8,000 feet. Both Sequoia and Kings Canyon offer incomparable vistas, hiking trails, and other natural wonders, including more than a hundred caves.

Mammoth Lakes Area

The Mammoth Lakes area is California's answer to the Alps. Southern Californians have been known to schlep their ski equipment to locales as far off as Chile and Chamonix, but most will agree that some of the best skiing anywhere is found 300 miles north of Los Angeles at **Mammoth Mountain Ski Area** in the heart of the Sierra Nevada. The statistics bespeak world-class thrills: an 11,053-foot summit, a 7,953-foot base, 30 lifts, 150 trails, and 3,500 acres of skiable terrain. The ski season often extends as late as July. Don't let the fact that the U.S. Ski Team trains at Mammoth each spring deter you from coming: Fully 30 percent of the ski runs are rated for beginners. Plus, Mammoth boasts one of the finest ski schools in the country, with family lessons and a children's ski school offered regularly.

Mammoth is one of the best choices for a family vacation—summer or winter. Children can be dropped off as early as 8:30 A.M. for activities before lessons begin.

Summer means even more activities to keep the family fit. Everyone can ride the gondola to Mammoth Mountain's 11,053-foot summit for the best view in town. Call 888–GO–MAMMOTH.

MAMMOTH MOUNTAIN SKI AREA

Open Monday through Friday 8:00 A.M. to 4:00 P.M., and weekends and holidays 8:00 A.M. to 4:00 P.M. Call (760) 934–2712 for more information; www.visit mammoth.com; mammothmtn@aol.com. Information hotline: (888) GO–MAMMOTH or (888) 466–2666; ask for a free travel planner.

Extra Special Tip

ENTERTAINMENT Editions *2125 Butterfield Road in Troy, MI 48084; (800) 445–4137 or (800) 374–4464; wwwentertainment.com.* Offers substantial savings throughout Southern California. The firm has books covering San Diego, Santa Barbara, and Orange Counties; the San Fernando and San Gabriel Valleys; plus Long Beach, Bakersfield, Riverside/Palm Springs, and the Inland Empire. Their typical hotel discounts for advance bookings can save you 50 percent off published room rates for a variety of hotels and resorts. Among these: Hotel Atwater, Catalina Island, Hilton Hotels, Holiday Inns, Best Westerns, Comfort Inns, Vagabond Inns, Doubletree Hotels, and Days Inns—all suited for families. You must identify yourself as an Entertainment member when making reservations. Along with accommodations they offer a long list of "two-for-one" deals at hundreds of restaurants, from Bananaz Grill and Bar in Palm Desert and Scancella's Italian Grill in Temecula to old standbys like Shakey's, McDonalds, El Pollo Loco, Dairy Queen, and our personal favorite, Krispy Kreme doughnuts.

Historic Hotels of America

If you want to delve into the history of California's hostelries, the best starting place is *Historic Hotels of America*, a membership directory. There are fourteen "historic" hotels in California; eight in Southern California (800-678-8946). One is the **Mission Inn** in Riverside, the heart of the Inland Empire. The inn is more of a resort, filling an entire city block. There's a scrumptious Sunday buffet, marvelous museums just across the street, and something for every member of the family. Besides the Mission Inn, others include the legendary **Hotel del Coronado** (San Diego), the **El Encanto** (Santa Barbara), the **Georgian** (Santa Monica), the **Regal Biltmore** (downtown L.A.), the **Ojai Valley** (Ojai), and the **La Valencia** (La Jolla). Among these, the Hotel del Coronado stands out. Perfect for a memorable family vacation experience, it has a stunning beach (where *Some Like It Hot* was filmed), a terrific romping ground for the kids. Contact www.historichotels.nationaltrust.org.

California Historic Country Inns

If your preferences run toward country inns, **California Historic Country Inns** (P.O. Box 568, Carmel Valley, CA 93924; www. california inns.com) lists a number of bucolic hideaways where children are welcome. Of their seventeen options, we recommend two in particular: the **Upham Hotel** in Santa Barbara (800–727–0876) and **La Casa Del Zorro** in Borrego Springs (800–824–1884). You might consider their new "Passport to Free Nights" deal offering a 𝔉𝔯𝔢𝔢 night's accommodation at any country inn if you stay at five different listed inns.

When getting ready for your trip, think about subscribing to the **Family Travel Times**, the ultimate newsletter for traveling families. We followed their tips to a delightful family day touring East Anacapa Island from Santa Barbara. Available through Dorothy Jordan & Associates, Inc., 40 Fifth Avenue, New York, NY 10011; (212) 477–5524 (twych@tiac.net), it's published quarterly. Subscriptions $40 per year.

WOOLLYWOOD CHILDREN'S SKI SCHOOL
In the Main Lodge, (760) 934–0685, or in the Canyon Lodge, (760) 934–0787.

The school is divided into Mammoth Explorers (ages four to six and seven to twelve), the Big Kahuna Snowboard Club (seven to twelve), children's private lessons (four to twelve), the Custom Kid's Camp (seven to twelve), and a three-day ski/snowboard camp.

DJ'S SNOWMOBILE ADVENTURES
(760) 935–4480.

Families will enjoy one- and two-hour backcountry self-guided tours or half-hour introductions to snowmobiling rides in the flats.

SLEDZ
(760) 934–7533.

Perfect for kids who love grappling with gigantic inner tubes. Well-matched for kids three and up. Older kids (4 feet tall and up) can ride the authentic bobsleds with adult supervision.

INYO NATIONAL FOREST
(760) 873–2400 or (760) 873–2500 for permits and updated information.

Open to "snow play" in designated areas. Families must park off road and while at play, the U.S. Forest Service warns, "watch out for the trees!"

CHILDREN'S FISHING FESTIVAL (ages 1 to 15)

At Snowcreek Pond every June.

Kids learn how to fish for alpers trout. Best of all, the event is **Free** and tackle is provided.

MAMMOTH MOUNTAIN BIKE PARK (ages 4 and up)

(760) 934–0706 or contact Mammoth Lakes Park and Recreation, (760) 934–8989, ext. 237, for details.

This is a great haven for kids four and up wanting to learn to ride mountain bikes. Many trails are ideal for younger riders.

RED'S MEADOW PACK STATIONS

P.O. Box 395, Mammoth Lakes, CA 93546; (760) 934–2345 or (800) 292–7758; www.mammothweb.com/redsmeadow/

If you're in the market for a modern A-frame cabin, these new but rustic cabins are furnished with butane heating, running water, large bathrooms with showers, gas ranges, and refrigerators. Rates are $450 per week for two; $25 per week for each additional guest. Motel-style rooms with bedrooms and modern bathrooms are $49 per night for two; $10 per night for each additional person. From Red's Meadow there are various group riding and hiking trail trips to such places as the **John Muir Wilderness, Bishop to Bodie** (camping along the old stage-coach route via saddle horse, mule, and wagon), and the other off-the-beaten-path tours your family will long remember. These tours begin in late May and end about the first of October. If you're into more comfort, reserve a condominium for the family. Rates are surprisingly reasonable.

CHATEAU DE MONTAGNE

(800) 242–8330 or (760) 934–6374. $$$

One- to four-bedroom condos starting at $95 per night during the spring/fall season. There are lodging/lift packages as well. This condo rental is within walking distance of shopping, movies, and the Snow-creek Golf Course. There's a **Free** shuttle bus to the Mammoth Mountain Ski Area. Some nonsmoking units are available, and cribs are provided for a nominal charge.

PAUL SCHAT'S BAKERY & CAFE

3305 Main Street; (760) 934–6055. $

If the name sounds familiar, you're right. Father Erick has a "bakkery" in Bishop. From delectable caramel-encrusted pecan rolls to scintillating sweet rolls with sweet sliced apples, this place, near the outlets in Mammoth, is an absolute must. Drop by for breakfast or lunch in Cafe Vermeer, where you can order sandwiches on the freshest bread on the planet. The kids will appreciate a bag of M&M cookies to share (however reluctantly) in the backseat.

TAMARACK CROSS-COUNTRY SKI CENTER

Located 2 miles from the town of Mammoth in the Mammoth Lakes Basin on Twin Lakes Road. $$$$

A great bet for families, with its groomed trails that weave through pine forests. It's also home to the **Tamarack Lodge Resort,** (800) 237-6879; www.tamaracklodge.com. Ask about mid-week winter ski packages.

DOG SLED ADVENTURES

(760) 934–6270 or (800) MAMMOTH.

Tours (on an honest-to-goodness dogsled) mush off from the Main Lodge at Mammoth Mountain Inn.

SIERRA MEADOWS RANCH

1 Sherwin Creek Road; (760) 934–6161.

You can spend some quality time on one of several theme horse-drawn sleigh rides through Mammoth Meadow (moonlight rides, breakfast rides, etc.) or take a hay or trail ride in summer. The warm months, by the way, are when Mammoth's majesty welcomes back the hiking, fishing, and mountain-biking crowd. Closes Labor Day weekend and opens again Memorial Day weekend.

Lone Pine

How can you not stop in Lone Pine, in southern Inyo County, once you realize you can explore one of the earth's oldest geological formations by car? Among others, these fantasmagoric formations resemble a bullfrog, a polar bear, Hannibal the Cannibal, and an owl. Hundreds of rock sculptures can be imagined in these bizarre hills, and you can drive the route in about half an hour.

You're on historical turf here; this is where Republic Pictures filmed dozens of spaghetti Westerns during the '40s and '50s. Chase scenes from these cowboy flicks, with such stars as Hopalong Cassidy, were immortalized in this stunning landscape. Recently, scenes for *Maverick* (starring Mel Gibson) were shot here. If you see *The Shadow* with Alec Baldwin, you'll recognize the Alabama hills backdrop. Many stars return for the mid-October **Annual Lone Pine Film Festival**. You might just see Virginia Mayo, Rand Brooks, Penny Edwards, Ann Rutherford, or Loren James (Steve McQueen's double for twenty-two years). Of course, the kids may never have heard of these stars. Spending a few hours or a few days here, within view of the majestic Mount Whitney, is to enter a time warp with California charisma.

You might stop for lunch at the **Totem Café**, 131 South Main Street, or for a burger at the **Mount Whitney Restaurant,** 227 South Main Street.

Overnight accommodations aren't a problem, as so many people stop here to mountaineer for a few days.

Where to Stay

Best Western's Frontier Motel, *1008 Main Street at Highway 395, one-half mile south of Lone Pine; (760) 876–5571, (899) 528–1234, or (800) 428–2627;* www.bestwestern.com. Rates include continental breakfast at this 73-room hotel. $$

For More Information

Lone Pine Chamber of Commerce. *126 South Main Street, 93545. (760) 876–4444; toll free (877) 253–8981, fax (760) 876–9205; www.lone-pine.com.*

Bishop

Chances are quite good you'll pass through the town of Bishop on your way to or out of the Mammoth Lakes area. You'll see why Bishop calls itself the Mule Capital of the World if you arrive during Memorial Day weekend, when the streets are abuzz with mule and chariot races, jumping events, and myriad other equine-related activities. Approximately 40,000 mule lovers gather for what the *Guinness Book of World Records* called (in 1994) the world's longest-running nonmotorized parade. Call (760) 872–4263 for more information.

September in Bishop is a special event in itself thanks to the **Millpond Traditional Music Festival** (760-873-8014 or 800-874-0669) that takes place at Millpond County Park, sponsored by Inyo County and the Inyo Council for the

Arts. Featured are top performers of bluegrass, folk, and country music. Families will find this musical weekend ideal for picnics.

LAWS RAILROAD MUSEUM AND HISTORICAL SITE

A bit north of Bishop; (760) 873–5950; www.thesierraweb.com/bishop/laws.
This eleven-acre indoor/outdoor museum harks back to the rough-and-tumble pioneer days in the Owens Valley. Kids can climb into the cab of locomotive 9 to ring the bell, and explore the compartment cars of the 1883 Slim Princess narrow gauge train, which, says the sign, "began nowhar, ended nowhar, an' stopped all night to think it over." The museum is on the National Register of Historic Places. Check out the bell rack, featuring antique bells from Bishop-area schools; the Original Laws School, refurbished with local artifacts, and a country store with old-time school items and supplies on display.

PIONEER BUILDING OR BOTTLE HOUSE

Take U.S. Highway 6 north of Bishop 4.5 miles to the junction with Silver Canyon Road, turn right, drive a half mile to the compound. Open 10:00 A.M. to 4:00 P.M. daily in summer and weekends in winter. **Free.**
Repository of old bottles of every description. Antique mining equipment, an old country store, and a carriage house are other exhibits you can wander through. An hour or two here will give you a good impression of life in the 1880s, when mining, ranching, and farming were of utmost importance, and Los Angeles was twelve days away—by stagecoach.

ERICK SCHAT'S BAKERY

763 North Main Street, Bishop; (760) 873–7156.
This is a local institution. Home of the original "sheepherder bread," a hearty country loaf, Schat's also has delicious sweet rolls and a scrumptious luncheon buffet. You'll leave well fortified and ready to tackle another stretch of scenic California.

For More Information

Bishop Area Chamber of Commerce and Visitor's Bureau. *690 North Main Street; (760) 873–8504; www.bishopvisitor.com.* Request a copy of the Vacation Planner.

Annual Events

The following list of events in the Inland Empire and its environs was made available by the California Trade and Commerce Agency Division of Tourism. For a thirty-four-page list of events, contact the California Office of Tourism, P.O. Box 1499, Sacramento, CA 95812–1499.

FEBRUARY

Civil War Reenactment—Calico. *(800) TO–CALICO or (760) 254–2122.* Features living history displays, drills, and music.

Dickens Festival—Riverside. *(800) 430–4140, or (909) 781–3168.* Nineteenth-century play, plus kids' activities and a Victoria ball. You'll also enjoy a London-type marketplace with exhibits, carriage rides, and tours. **Free**.

Whiskey Flats Day—Kernville. *(760) 376–2629 or (800) 350–7393, fax (760) 376–4371.* Parade, carnival, rodeo, gunfighters, various contests, frog jumping, arts and crafts, a petting zoo, and much to eat. **Free**.

MARCH

Blake Jones Trout Derby—Bishop. *(760) 873–8405 or (760) 873–6999.* One-day trout derby with prizes, food, and beverages.

Calico Hullabaloo—Calico. *(800) TO–CALICO or (760) 254–2122.* Relive the rough-and-ready days of old Calico with greased-pole climbing, arm wrestling, and lots more.

Rock Bonanza—Boron. (760) 762-6862. A rock and mineral show. Tailgators demonstration and food booths. **Free**.

Hobby, Art and Craft Expo—Victorville. *(760) 245–5551, fax (760) 951–3804.* Demonstrations and exhibition of handmade crafts.

Redlands Bicycle Classic–Redlands. *(909) 798–0865.* Thousands of cyclists from around the world compete. **Free**.

Winterfest—Mammoth Lakes. *(800) 367–6572 or (760) 934–6643.* Winter celebration with cross-country ski races, snowmobile competition, and fun rides for the kids.

Citrus Harvest Festival—Highland. *(909) 864–4073, fax (909) 864– 4583.* Entertainment, historic home tour, children's games, car show, and contests.

APRIL–MAY

Scottish Gathering—Bakersfield. *(661) 328–0705.* A fabulous Scottish gathering. This Celtic cultural festival features bagpipe bands, clan tents, a dance competition, Scottish athletics, and entertainment.

Ramona Pageant—Hemet. *(800) 645–4465 or (909) 658–3111, fax (909) 658–BOWL.* Unique outdoor pageant portrays the lives of the Southern California mission-period Indians and Hispanics. Play adapted from Helen Hunt Jackson's 1884 novel *Ramona.*

Opening Day Trout Fair—Bishop. *(760) 873–8802.* Exhibits, instruction, and demonstrations.

Indian Pow Wow—Kernville. *(800) 350–7393 or (760) 376–2696.* A celebration of American heritage, dancers, drumming, Native American foods, arts and crafts. **Free.**

Orange Blossom Festival—Riverside. *(800) 382-8202.* This citrus celebration takes place in downtown Riverside. Besides three entertainment stages, citrus cooking demonstrations, and arts and crafts booths, the festival has a children's grove and a living history village.

MAY

Calico Spring Festival—Calico. *(800) TO–CALICO or (760) 254–2122.* Games, fiddle and banjo contests, a demolition derby, plus entertainment galore.

Cinco de Mayo—Victorville. *(909) 955–5000.* Mariachi music, dancing, ethnic food. **Free.**

May Trout Classic—Big Bear Lake. *(800) 4–BIGBEAR or (909) 585–6260.* Fishing competition.

Spring Aire Arts and Crafts Faire—Big Bear Lake. *(909) 585–3000, fax (909) 584–2886.* Show features hundreds of handcrafted items. Vendors, raffles, and loads of antiques.

JUNE

African American Celebration of the Emancipation Proclamation—Victorville. *(760) 243–7486.* Arts and crafts, music, ethnic foods. **Free.**

Huck Finn's Jubilee—Victorville. *(760) 245–2226.* River celebration and camp-out relives the life and times of Huckleberry Finn. Raft building, parade, big-top circus, hot-air balloon rides, music, crafts, and more. **Free.**

Hobie Cat Regatta—Big Bear Lake. *(909) 867–2864.* Competition for experienced and amateur sailors.

Whitewater Wednesday—Kernville. *(760) 376–2629 or (800) 350–7393, fax (760) 376–4371.* One- and two-hour white-water rafting trips down the wild and scenic Kern River.

JULY

All Nations Pow Wow—Big Bear. (800) BIGBEAR or (909) 584-9394. American Indians from across the United States participate in traditional dancing and crafts.

Chili Cook-off/Fireman's Muster—Redlands. *(909) 739–2546.* Vendor booths, music, a chili cook-off, and a firefighters' muster. **Free.**

Fourth of July Festivities—Mammoth Lakes. *(800) 367–6572, or (760) 924–2360.* Fireworks (of course!), a parade, a pancake breakfast, an arts and crafts show, a chili cook-off, a quilt show, and a horseshoe tournament. What, no barbecue?

July 4 Fireworks Over the Lake—Big Bear. *(800) BIGBEAR or (909) 866–2112.* Barbecue, entertainment, and spectacular fireworks.

Jazz Jubilee—Mammoth Lakes. *(760) 934–2478, fax (760) 934–2478.* World-class jazz bands perform outdoors.

Sierra Summer Festival—Mammoth Lakes. *(800) 367–6572 or (760) 934–3342.* Music festival spotlights master's classes, plus chamber, pop, and folk music.

Children's Fishing Festival—Mammoth Lakes. (800) 367-6752 or (760) 924-2360. Local fishing experts assist children in catching Alpers rainbow trout. **Free.**

AUGUST

Antique Car Club Fun Run—Big Bear Lake. *(909) 866–3938.* Classic, antique, and special-interest cars on display, show, and shine. **Free.**

TnT Drag Boat Races—Bakersfield. *(707) 664–0444.* More than one hundred boats race their engines out on Ming Lake.

Labor Day Arts and Crafts Festival—Mammoth Lakes. *(760) 873–7242.* More than seventy arts and crafts booths in an outdoor setting, along with entertainment, kids' activities, and lots of food.

Yodler Pavilion Concert Series—Mammoth Lakes. *(760) 466–2666.* Contemporary jazz, folk, country-western, and rock 'n' roll music performances.

SEPTEMBER

Apple Harvest—Oak Glen. *(909) 797–6833.* Southern California's top apple-growing region is the site for this event, with apple picking, a candy factory, hay rides, crafts on display, an art show, and (yum!) barbecues. **Free**.

Eastern Sierra Tri-County Fair and Wild West Rodeo—Bishop. *(760) 873–3588.* Old-fashioned country fair fun, with exhibits, a carnival, pig races, pony rides, a petting zoo, horse shows, and a PRCA rodeo.

Fall Festival Arts and Crafts—Big Bear Lake. *(909) 585–3000, fax (909) 584–2886.* Hundreds of handcrafted items on display.

Fiesta Days—Morongo Valley. *(760) 363–7242.* A small town fair that offers music, food, and arts and crafts. **Free**.

Festival of Roses—Wasco. *(805) 758–2616.* A carnival, pancake breakfast, tours of the rose fields, "fun run," parade, car show, art exhibits, entertainment, and (again yum!) barbecue.

Kern County Fair—Bakersfield. *(805) 833–4900, fax (805) 836–2743.* Family entertainment par excellence, a livestock show, a carnival, agricultural and floricultural exhibits, plus an auction.

Kern Valley Vulture Festival—Kernville. *(760) 376–2629, fax (760) 376–4371.* Guided nature tours, bird banding, plus Native American displays—all in celebration of California's biggest turkey vulture migration.

Rodeo Stampede—Barstow. *(760) 252–3093, fax (760) 252–3093.* PRCA rodeo.

Art and Wine Festival—Arrowhead. *(909) 337–3715.* Artists' displays and wine tastings on Lake Arrowhead's shoreline. **Free**.

Stater Brothers Route 66 Rendezvous—San Bernardino. *(800) TO–RTE–66 or (909) 889–3980.* Here's the original Route 66 nostalgia celebration. Car cruises and street fair feature more than 1,200 custom rods and cars, exhibits, plus a golf tournament and a poker run. **Free**.

OCTOBER

Calico Days Festival—Calico. *(800) TO–CALICO or (760) 254–2122.* Go back in time to Calico's glory years with a Wild West parade, a gunfight, stunts, burro races, rock pulling, and games circa the 1880s.

Grape Harvest—Rancho Cucamonga. *(909) 987—1012.* A celebration of the harvest of the vineyards that are located in the west end of San Bernardino County.

Desert Empire Fair—Ridgecrest. *(760) 375–8000.* Five-day event with 4-H competition, arts and crafts, entertainment, a rodeo, a demolition derby, and a livestock auction.

Film Festival—Lone Pine. *(760) 876–4444, fax (760) 876–4533.* Old West movie sets, a deep-pit barbecue, arts and crafts, guest stars, and a parade. Oh yes, and films.

Mardi Gras Parade—Barstow. *(760) 256–8657.* Halloween parade includes floats, bands, horses, clowns, costumed children, plus contingents from the military, fire, and sheriff's departments.

Maturango Junction—Ridgecrest. *(760) 375–6900, fax (760) 375–0479.* Chili cook-off, a pancake breakfast, entertainment, balloon rides, crafts, kids' activities, a car show, and a horseshoe contest. **Free**.

NORBA Bike Race—Ridgecrest. *(760) 371–1628.* Top pro bicyclists compete in mountain races. **Free**.

October Haunt—Calico. *(800) TO–CALICO or (760) 254–2122.* Visit China-town's haunted ruins and the Haunted Mine, along with pumpkin carving, costume competition, trick-or-treating, and ghost stories. Boo!

Oktoberfest—Big Bear Lake. *(909) 866–4607.* Music, singing, dancing, contests, arts and crafts, food, and games in a mountain setting. *Wunderbar!*

Wild West Daze Rodeo—Kernville. *(760) 378–3157.* Wild horse races, bull riding, saddle bronco-ing, bareback riding, steer decorating, barrel racing, and mutton busting. *No mas!*

NOVEMBER

Fine Arts Festival—Calico. *(800) TO–CALICO or (760) 254–2122.* Artists from throughout the Southwest display their works. Native American dances, tours of the historic town, programs around the campfire.

Gem and Mineral Society Show—Ridgecrest. *(760) 377–5192.* Dozens of gem and mineral exhibits, plus field trips. Educational.

Harvest Fair—San Bernardino. *(909) 384–5426, fax (909) 384–5160.* Re-creation of an 1881 Old West town, with a country/bluegrass show, crafts, and a unique car show.

Mission Inn Run—Riverside. *(800) 564–1255, or (760) 450–6510.* 5k and 10k runs, plus children's races and the invitational North American Challenge—with three-person teams from the United States, Canada, and Mexico competing.

DECEMBER

Children's Christmas Parade—Victorville. *(760) 245–6506, fax (760) 245–6505.* More than 150 holiday-theme floats, bands, novelty vehicles, and marching by equestrian units. **Free.**

Christmas Parade—Lone Pine. *(760) 876–4444, fax (760) 876–4533.* Old-fashioned Christmas parade with (you guessed it) Santa Claus.

Festival of Lights—Riverside. *(909) 683–7100 or (909) 683-2670.* Holiday lighting of the historic Mission Inn and surrounding downtown locations. Entertainment and specialty booths. **Free.**

The Deserts

The California deserts conjure up different images for different people. To some they suggest glittering resort cities, brilliant skies, and the verdant greens of impressive Palm Springs golf courses. To others they raise thoughts of a barren, even desolate, landscape of boulders, sand, and cacti lining the freeway from Los Angeles to Las Vegas. To yet others they inspire thoughts of pioneer history, rustic ghost towns, and abandoned gold mines. Whatever desert-related pictures may come to mind, however, one fact is indisputable: the desert is big. It is immense—stretching from the Mojave Desert and ultra-arid Death Valley National Park in the north to the Colorado Desert area that reaches south to the border of Mexico.

Although the region is strikingly—or starkly—beautiful, much of it is what some might call wasteland or others environmentally pristine. Either way, a good portion is off-limits to nonmilitary personnel. These two attributes certainly make it simpler for families who want to catch the desert's highlights but lack the time (or inclination) to explore every gully or gulch. As a matter of fact, vast tracts of the desert have no highways, and if something akin to a "road" exists, it can be rock-strewn, meandering, sign-less, and dusty, leading you and your clan (best-case scenario) to an old ghost town or some other remnant of long-gone Wild West days, or (worst-case scenario) to nowhere, nowhere at all.

If you are willing to take a modest chance, to be marginally adventuresome in checking out a few of the desert's endless nooks and crannies, you'll find that here, too. The Golden State is indeed a land of contrasts.

As its name suggests, Death Valley—at 282 feet below sea level, the lowest land surface in the Western Hemisphere—is about as dry as a place can get. In sharp contrast, much of Palm Springs and other resort communities of the Coachella Valley, some 150 miles to the south of Death Valley, are as verdant and lush as a tropical oasis—primarily because of irrigation, but partly because

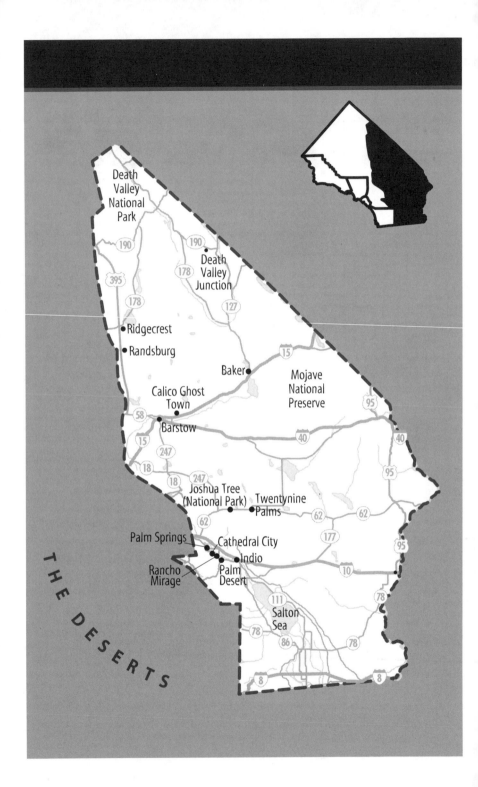

Death
Valley
National
Park

190

190

178

Death
Valley
Junction

395

178

127

Ridgecrest

Randsburg

15

Baker

Mojave
National
Preserve

95

Calico Ghost
Town

58

Barstow

40

15

247

40

18

95

18

247

Joshua Tree
(National Park)

Twentynine
Palms

62

62

62

Palm Springs

Cathedral City

177

95

Indio

Rancho
Mirage

Palm
Desert

10

78

111

Salton
Sea

78

78

86

T H E

D E S E R T S

8

8

of cool mountain streams that have flowed into the area for centuries. Even in summer, when 110-plus temperatures expose the desert's true personality, it's still a great time to visit. During the summer months, most all Palm Springs-area hotels reduce their rates 50 to 70 percent. And throughout the desert, summer seems to go by a little slower than elsewhere in California. Of course, the sun certainly shines brighter. It's almost as if nature is telling you to enjoy the offerings of the desert at a pace that suits you—and reminding you to bring along the sunscreen!

Palm Springs

Approximately 100 miles east of Los Angeles on Interstate 10 lies the Coachella Valley, home to the desert resort communities of Palm Springs, Rancho Mirage, Cathedral City, Palm Desert, Indio, and La Quinta. On the other (north) side of the freeway are the lesser-visited destinations of Desert Hot Springs, Yucca Valley, Morongo, Twenty-nine Palms, and Joshua Tree. Seen from an airplane window or hot-air balloon, these cities appear as rather artificial patches of green against a flat, arid landscape framed by mountain ridges.

If you drive into the valley from L.A., however, the first thing you'll notice are rows and rows of windmills protruding sentrylike from the hillsides. These are actually working wind turbines that generate electricity for nearly 100,000 homes.

Other desert areas may be more scenic (read: more barren), but the Coachella Valley (local population 329,500) has the monopoly on recreational attractions and leisure opportunities. Just consider a few valley stats: 600 tennis courts, 14,736 hotel rooms, and 102 golf courses, meaning more than one golf course per square mile in the desert resort area. Add to these numbers for tennis and golf 30,000 swimming pools, probably a zillion hot tubs (or spas), and 350 days of fun in the sunshine to the recipe, and it's a no-brainer why 3.5 million people visit the area every year. But the valley never seems crowded, even during the peak season (September through March) because things are so spread out.

World famous as "America's Premier Desert Resort," Palm Springs has ranked high on everybody's' Coachella Valley must-visit list since the 1930s, when the small town (current population 43,000) was a favorite playground for California's unofficial royalty—movie stars. Gone but not forgotten are Frank Sinatra and Liberace, who once had estates here. Bob Hope, Walter Annenberg, Suzanne Somers, Howard Keel, and Sidney Sheldon still call the desert home for at least part of the year. It doesn't take a rocket scientist to understand the valley's appeal. Average winter temperatures in the mid-seventies are enough to turn even Los Angelenos green (as in putting green) with envy. And the restaurants and resorts are truly world-class.

Palm Springs, part of the Coachella Valley, has an excellent newspaper, *Family News*, (760) 770–6357, which is published bi-monthly and is free. In it you'll find such features as "Now's the Time to Plan a Visit to Joshua Tree National Monument" and "Salton Sea Winter Boat Tours Planned." It's a useful source for desert happenings. Listings include such items as local hikes, museums (for instance, the **Children's Discovery Museum in Palm Desert**, 760-321-0602; the **General Patton Museum**, (760) 227-3483, at Chiriaco Summit for World War II memorabilia), various valley attractions, a daily calendar, and information on family-oriented events like the annual **Golf Cart Parade** (Palm Desert, first week of November). Check it all out at www.desert-resorts.com or www.palm-springs.org.

When driving on Interstate 10, you'll know you're near Palm Springs when your kids point out the 150-foot apatosaurus and 55-foot tall tyrannosaurus rex, the largest in the world. No, they didn't get lost trying to find the outlet mall and Casino Morongo down the road. They are known around these parts as the **Cabazon Dinosaurs,** and they haven't moved in years. Open 365 days a year from 9:00 A.M. to 8:00 P.M. Kids will enjoy dinosaur-related knickknacks at **Dinosaur Delights**, 50800 Seminole Drive, Cabazon; (909) 849-8309. Try DesertFun.com to get started.

WINDMILL TOURS

62950 20th Avenue North, Palm Springs; (760) 320–1365 or (877) 449–WIND. Tours daily between 8:00 A.M. and 4:00 P.M. Monday through Saturday. Summer hours may vary. $$$

Look for windmills (you can't miss them; some blades are more than 50 feet long!) and for signs on Interstate 10 at the San Gorgonio Pass, then hold onto your hats because it is very windy out here. There are more than 4,000 windmills "blowin' in the wind," generating pollution-free alternative energy. Experts tell us they provide enough energy to light up all the homes in Palm Springs. There are four 1.5-hour tours (the world's first windmill farm tours). Guests ride on electric golf carts, escorted by well-informed guides who enjoy their work (one is a retired dentist) and answering kids' questions. This is a terrific and painless way to introduce children to an unusual energy source with enormous future potential. And drop by the visitor center for a look at the world's biggest display of electric-powered vehicles (golf car fans will love this).

WHITEWATER TROUT COMPANY

9160 Whitewater Canyon Road, Whitewater. Drive north on Indian Canyon Drive to Interstate 10, west to the Whitewater exit. Continue 5 miles to the Whitewater Canyon exit. (760) 325–5570. It sounds fishy but there are tours, by appointment, at 9:00 A.M., Wednesday through Friday.

Driving on Interstate 10, watch for the Whitewater Trout Company sign; this is the epitome of fishing for the family that loves to fish together! The $3.00 set-up fee includes admission, license, tackle, and bait. Catch any fish? If you do and want to have a fish fry, the cost is $2.88 per pound, live weight. Call in advance for picnic reservations, and they will grill the fish for you.

MOORTEN BOTANICAL GARDEN

1701 South Palm Canyon Drive, corner of East Palm Canyon; (760) 327–6555.

Kids will learn about the diversity of desert flora at the world's first "cactarium," where 3,000 varieties of cacti flourish in a natural setting. Established in 1938, this unusual botanical garden bristles with cacti in all shapes and sizes. Ask the kids to look for colorful desert flowers because there's "always something in bloom."

Kid Flicks Thanks to Craig Prater, founder of the fabulous Film Noir Festival that debuted in Palm Springs in May 2000, children (the focus is on those two to eleven) have their own festival. The Children's Discovery Film Festival, one of the few in the world, enjoys a four-day run. Feature and short films, centered around children, enhance workshops on topics such as music and animation plus field trips for budding cinema fans. For information: (760) 327-2432 or crpk@webtv.net.

NORTEL NETWORKS PALM SPRINGS INTERNATIONAL FILM FESTIVAL

1700 East Tahquitz Canyon Way, Suite 3; (760) 322–2930; fax (760) 322–4087; www.psfilmfest.org; info@psfilmfest.org.

The year 2003 heralded the fourteenth annual film festival, which has become a mecca for buyers seeking films for distribution. The festival also presents an ideal opportunity for families to screen, with the help of an excellent guide, family films. Dennis Pregnolato, executive director, says there is a nice representation of family films, such as *Anton and Anna* (Germany) and *The Great Train Robbery* (United States). Films screened here include comedy, romance, experimental, animation, period pieces, suspense, and thrillers. You're sure to find a few family flicks among the offerings. Contact the box office at (760) 325–6565, open daily 12:00 to 9:00 P.M.

PALM CANYON THEATRE

538 North Palm Canyon Drive (in Frances Stevens Park); (760) 323–5123 (box office). Closed in the summer.

Palm Springs' newest theater group is located in a former elementary school auditorium. Strictly family-type plays like *The Secret Garden, Our Town,* and *Brigadoon* make this an ideal choice for a family matinee.

CELEBRITY TOURS

4751 East Palm Canyon Drive, in the Rimrock Shopping Center; (760) 770–2700 (reservations required). Tour A is a narrated one-hour drive including up to forty movie stars' homes. Tour B lasts two and a half hours and adds the Walter Annenberg Estate, country clubs, and the Eisenhower Medical Center. All tours are made in air-conditioned coaches. Pickups at Palm Springs hotels and the tour office.

If you've been wondering how to find Elvis's honeymoon hideaway or the place where Liberace entertained, book your family on an air-conditioned coach for a guided tour of the Las Palmas district (also known as the movie colony) and other areas where history was made. Well-rehearsed guides tell all, and you won't want to miss a word of their entertaining narrative. This is far better than a self-guided tour through the quiet neighborhoods of walled villas and winding streets— and it's the only way to get the lowdown on how Hollywood established itself in the desert.

Edward's Date Shoppe is next door to Celebrity Tours. Before or after your tour, try a deliciously rich date shake. The valley is a world-class date-growing area. Packaged assortments make zippy and inexpensive gifts the shop will ship for you.

TAHQUITZ CANYON

500 West Mesquite, Palm Springs; (760) 416–7044; www.tahquitzcanyon. com. $

One of the most picturesque points in the desert, the canyon is now open after being closed to the public for more than thirty years. Located on the Aqua Caliente Reservation, the canyon boasts a 60-foot waterfall, rock art, and ancient irrigation systems. Try a guided hiking tour. You'll also find a visitor center video, historical photos, a gift shop, and maps.

GOLF COURSES

If in L.A., the celebrities are all on the beach in Malibu; in Palm Springs they're probably on the golf course. Although many clubs are private, there are several beautiful courses open to the public. Some good courses open to the public and children are:

- **Tahquitz Creek Golf Academy.** 1885 Golf Club Drive; (760) 328-1005. Junior and adult clinics can be arranged. After the clinics, children can play at half the adult rate.
- **Desert Dunes Golf Club.** 19300 Palm Drive, Desert Hot Springs; (760) 251-5368, fax (760) 251-5368. $$$$
- **Cimarron Golf Club.** 67-603 30th Avenue, Cathedral City; (760) 770-6060; fax (760) 770-2876. Golfers of all ages will find the thirty-six holes at this recently opened club sheer paradise. There is a short and a long course. Inquire about golf clinics and other events. Tee times can be booked up to sixty days in advance. Check bargain twilight and standby fees as well. $$$$
- **The Golf Resort at Indian Wells.** 44-400 Indian Wells Lane, (760) 346-GOLF. Two Ted Robinson–designed championship courses. Rates range from $45 to $140. Tee times can be made up to seven days in advance.

*E*x*tra* *S*pecial *T*ip

Fab Family Golf If you have a budding Tiger Woods in the family or just want to practice your shot, visit the College Golf Center of Palm Desert at the College of the Desert, 73-450 Fred Waring Drive (760) 341-0994, open 7:00 A.M. to 10:00 P.M. A large bucket of balls is $8.00; a medium is $5.00. This is a driving range, and the manager, Dean Mayo, says kids like the junior golf clinics. Professional instruction available. The facility is excellent according to locals and tourists.

- **Desert Willow.** 38500 Portola Avenue, Palm Desert; (760) 346-0015. $$$$

- **Tommy Jacob's Bel Air Greens.** 1001 South El Cielo; (760) 322-6062; fax (760) 322-3126. Family-style golf during the season (January through April). Eighteen short holes on a beautiful course for adults and kids (they call it a putt putt course). This is an all par-three layout. The nine-hole Executive Course is ideal for juniors and adults. New is the ProTour Classic Short Game School, offering lessons. Children eighteen and under pay $5.00 for nine holes of golf.

- **Tahquitz Creek Palm Springs.** 1885 Golf Club Drive, Palm Springs; (800) 743-2211 or (760) 328-1005. Here is the place to enjoy resort golf "without paying for the rest of the resort." The club has two Arnold Palmer–managed courses, Resort and Legend, both rated four star by *Golf Digest* magazine. Rates range from $20 to $35.

The first people to fall under Palm Springs' spell were ancestors of the Agua Caliente band of Cahuilla (Kaw'-we-ah) Indians, who developed communities in the palm canyons at the foot of the San Jacinto Mountains. These canyons, along with other chunks of the Coachella Valley, were deeded in trust to the Indians in 1876. The Cahuillas control 42 percent of the valley, making them the wealthiest tribe in North America.

BIG HORN BICYCLE RENTAL & TOURS

302 North Palm Canyon Drive; (760) 325–3367; (760) 325–5585.

Bike it! Big Horn Bike Adventures has a four-hour 14-mile round-trip tour. Visit the Indian Canyons, bike on Palm Springs' Heritage Trail through the historic Tennis Club District, and stop to visit Moorton's Botanical Garden (see hundreds of cacti, look but don't touch!). At Palm Canyon there is a hike, then you'll head back to town via the Heritage Trail, topped off by an inimitable Palm Springs specialty, a date shake. You'll find Burley trailers for infants ten months and up at Bug Horns Palm Canyon location, along with children's bikes, multiple and single speed.

CANYON JEEP TOURS

15831 La Vida Drive; (760) 320–4600 or (760) 320–1365 for reservations. $$$$

Or Jeep it! If you'd rather see the Indian Canyons without any sweat, call Canyon Jeep Tours. All tours depart from the lobby of the Spa Hotel and Casino in Palm Springs at 100 North Indian Canyon. There is ample free parking in the casino lots across the street. The expedition starts at Whitewater Hill (elevation 2,500 feet) and makes its way through the Cahuilla Canyons of Snow Creek and Chino. Then it's on to the legendary Movie Colony, once a second home to Hollywood stars, including Elvis Presley and Jack Benny. There is a thirty-minute trek into Andreas Canyon and a drive into Palm Canyon. Before leaving the Indian Canyons, you'll visit an authentic trading post. It's filled with Native American souvenirs, maps, dream catchers, cassettes, and exquisite handmade turquoise jewelry. The variety of merchandise crammed into this shop is overwhelming! There is limited parking and a small menu for cold drinks. The most popular tour, the Bonanza, visits the windmills, canyons, and celebrity homes.

INDIAN CANYONS

Toll gate entrance, south end of Palm Canyon Drive; (760) 325–3400 or (800) 790–3398. Open fall and winter, 8:00 A.M. to 5:00 P.M.; spring and summer, 8:00 A.M. to 6:00 P.M. $$

Revenues from admission help fill the tribe's coffers, but this cluster of oases is a priceless natural jewel. With some of the thickest concentrations of palm trees in the world, thanks to the cool mountain streams that flow through them, the site provides a refreshing refuge from the heat of the desert. There are actually four separate canyons, comprising 32,000 acres: Palm, Tahquitz, Murray, and Andreas. All have trails for walking or hiking and well-maintained recreational facilities. The unusual rock formations in Andreas Canyon are the repository of ancient Cahuilla rock art. Tours operate Monday through Thursday, 10:00 A.M. to 1:00 P.M. and Friday, Saturday, Sunday, 9:00 A.M., 11:00 A.M., 1:00 P.M., and 3:00 P.M. For information, stop by the **Palm Springs Visitors Center**, 2781 North Palm Canyon Drive (just south of Tramway Road).

SMOKETREE STABLES

2500 Toledo Avenue; (760) 327–1372. Kids two to four can ride double. Ages five and up can ride their own horse, led by a guide. Open year-round except July and August, 8:00 A.M. to 4:00 P.M. (when days are longer, hours to 6:00 P.M.) To ride two hours, kids must be six or older.

In the same location for fifty years, the stables are next door to Fess Parker's former home (for the young 'uns, he played Davy Crockett). You can take a mini dude ranch vacation by hiring a horse.

PALAPAS OF ARABY COVE

3255 East Palm Canyon Drive; (760) 416–1818; www.palapas.net. **Free** *admission and* **Free** *parking.*

A fourteen-acre "hands on" village and garden center where artists demonstrate their techniques and exhibit their work. This serendipitous art-garden wonderland will delight kids and adults. Inquire about special events and workshops. A field trip includes children's art classes.

AQUA CALIENTE CULTURAL MUSEUM

219 South Palm Canyon Drive; (760) 323–0151, fax (760) 320–0350. Open Labor Day to Memorial Day 10:00 A.M. to 5:00 P.M. (Wednesday through Saturday), noon to 4:00 P.M. (Sunday). Summer hours Friday, Saturday, Sunday 10:00 A.M. to 4:00 P.M. **Free**.

Artifacts and historical photos from the early Cahuilla era, permanent collections on local history, changing exhibits (example, Cahuilla basketry), plus two shops with jewelry, clothing, music, and assorted Indian arts and crafts from tribes nationwide. One shop is in the museum, the other is in the lobby of the **Spa Hotel and Mineral Springs.**

PALM SPRINGS AERIAL TRAMWAY

Entrance on the north edge of town, at the end of Tramway Road, off Highway 111; (760) 325–1449 or (888) 515–TRAM; www.pstramway.com. Tram rides depart on the half hour, starting at 10:00 A.M. Monday to Friday, 8:00 A.M. weekends and holidays. Last ride off at 8:00 P.M. (9:45 P.M. during Daylight Savings Time). There are two new Swiss Rotair revolving tram cars with breathstopping views. Closed August. No advance reservations. $$$

If you'd like to know where all those mountain streams come from, take a ride on the spectacular tramway, a thrilling and manageable adventure for the whole family. Two eighty-passenger suspended cable cars whisk you from the parched desert floor up nearly 6,000 feet to the top of 10,800-foot **Mount San Jacinto** (Yah'-sin-toh) in a mere fifteen minutes. Up here there's not a palm tree in sight: This is pine tree country, some forty degrees cooler than the valley below.

From the **Mountain Station**, which has a gift shop and the Alpine Restaurant, there are breathtaking views of the sprawling valley floor and, off to the left, the unmistakable imprint of the San Andreas Fault. The station is at 8,516 feet.

MOUNT SAN JACINTO WILDERNESS STATE PARK

Behind you is the 13,000-acre park, with 54 miles of hiking trails. If it's winter, chances are you'll be able to cross-country ski, too. A **Nordic Ski Center**, open November 15 through April 15, rents equipment for adults and kids. So you can build a snowman and, back in Palm Springs, take a swim on the same day.

Other than driving, of course, there are four ways to explore the desert: covered wagon, jeep, bicycle, and hot-air balloon.

DESERT ADVENTURES (ages 6 and up)

(760) 324–JEEP or (800) 440–JEEP; www.redjeep.com. All two-hour tours leave from the office. Meet at 67-555 East Palm Canyon Drive, Suite A-106. Tours include Free *hotel pickup service for three- and four-hour tours only. Tours operate year-round.*

Now in its fifteenth year, Desert Adventures runs a Mystery Canyon tour, which lasts four and a half hours, covering the area where *Land of the Lost* was filmed. For families, the Santa Rosa Mountains National Scenic Area is the most popular, hands down. For a decidedly more twenty-first-century adventure, and a perfect way for families to explore the desert, consider hopping aboard a red, seven-passenger, four-wheel-drive jeep for one of the tour offerings. The San Andreas Fault tour, Indian Cultural Adventures, and Mystery Canyon jeep adventures are among the tour options. Mary Dungas, the owner, says the tours are perfect "for ages six to one hundred and six."

COVERED WAGON TOURS

(760) 347–2161; fax (760) 775–7570. Call first for directions, as schedule varies. Tour departs two hours before sunset to a palm oasis and the San Andreas Fault. Reservations required. $$$$

The pioneer-style tour (one hour and forty-five minutes) comes first, then a chuck wagon cookout dinner (barbecued beef, chicken, beans, coleslaw, garlic bread, and apple pie). Departure is two hours before dark.

TRI-A-BIKE

44841 San Pablo Avenue, Palm Desert; (760) 340–2840.

The third option is on two wheels. Tri-A-Bike is the oldest bike rental company west of the Mississippi. You'll find mountain and road experts here able to answer your questions about exploring the desert terrain. Tri-A-Bike rents assorted bikes (including mountain, road, tandem, and kids') for $19.00 a day (based on twenty-four hours) and $9.00 (and up) an hour for mountain or road bikes (be sure to ask about special family packages). Kids' (four and up) bikes rent for $4.00 an hour, $16.00 daily. Kids too young to ride? Tri-A-Bike has a trailer to pull the little ones. Along with that comes **Free** delivery and pickup of bicycles (depending on rental agreement), a lock, a helmet, and a map of the Coachella Valley Bikeway. This segmented route stretches from Desert Hot Springs all the way to the Salton Sea. The 4-mile-long Morning Side Loop passes by the Morningside and Springs Country Clubs.

Extra Special Tip

Santa Rosa and San Jacinto Mountains National Monument

Be sure to visit the **Santa Rosa Mountains National Scenic Area Visitor Center**, 51–500 Highway 784, Palm Desert (3.25 miles south on Highway 111 at the base of the mountain). The **Friends of the Desert Mountains Bookstore** at the visitor center, (760) 862–9084, stocks hiking and nature guides, giving you a fuller picture of what to expect in this rugged corner of Southern California. This area is under the stewardship of the **Bureau of Land Management**, (760) 862–9984. Open Friday through Monday 9:00 A.M. to 4:00 P.M. (except federal holidays). Walk along the Native Plant Garden Interpretive Trail and try the interactive exhibits dealing with natural and cultural resources of the Coachella Valley and surrounding mountain before you embark on exploring this area.

For many families, the most enjoyable aspect of Palm Springs is taking a stroll on palm tree–lined **Palm Canyon Drive,** the historic center of the city. This celebrated stretch of pavement is flanked by a seemingly endless array of cafes, restaurants, boutiques, and theaters.

While you're strolling along Palm Canyon, notice the celebrity stars on the sidewalks. They include such notables as Frank Sinatra, Sophia Loren, Leslie Caron, Elizabeth Taylor, Carol Connors (remember the song "Gonna Fly Now from Rocky"?), and Monty Hall (of *Let's Make a Deal* fame). Thank local star meister, Gerhard Frenzel, for making this star-studded sidewalk the walk and

*E*xtra *S*pecial *T*ip

Consignment Shopping Palm Springs is a veritable paradise for consignment shop fans. Take the kids by the hand when perusing the infinite displays of other people's treasures. Items range from rocking horses to Roy Rogers tin lunch boxes (kids, ask your parents if they have any in the attic. They go for at least ten times more than what your parents paid way back when!) A good place to start your meandering is at the Palm Springs Design Center, 2500 North Palm Canyon, (760) 416-0704, and fan out from there. And don't rush. This takes time! Ample *Free* parking in the area.

talk of the town. There seems no end to the Palm Canyon "star placing" ceremonies throughout the year. We've often encountered a ceremony going on in front of one of the stores. Of course, passersby are welcome to watch the festivities. It ain't Hollywood Boulevard, but it's still a kick. And as long as you are strolling along Palm Canyon with the kids, stop by **Dollsville Dolls & Bearsville Bears,** 292 North Palm Canyon; (760) 325-2241 (www.dollsville. com) just opposite the Hyatt Hotel. This charming shop is full of teddy bears and an astounding variety of Barbie collectibles. There are literally thousands of dolls and bears to peruse. As much a museum as a shop, it will impress parents and kids of all ages.

Until fairly recently, Palm Springs was not the most kid-conscious place in the world, unless the little ones happened to have a special affinity for golf, tennis, or sunbathing. Though the valley will never have the amusement park thrills to be found in L.A. or Orange County, it has many other diversions that kids adore.

THE FABULOUS PALM SPRINGS FOLLIES (ages 6 and up)

At the Plaza Theatre, 128 South Palm Canyon Drive; (760) 327-0225; www.psfollies.com. Evening and matinee performances beginning in November. $$$$

A Palm Springs original. Now in its twelfth season, this three-hour revue has a cast all over the age of fifty. From Gloria Loring and the Four

Lads to Carol Lawrence, they kick up a storm. This colorful, always humorous vaudeville-style program gives kids a feel for what showbiz used to be all about, despite a few harmlessly off-color jokes now and then.

*E*xtra *S*pecial *T*ip

Bus Around! The Sunbus will take you to most of the attractions we've tried and tested, from the Desert Museum to the movies, malls, and more. Rides cost 75 cents; $3.00 for a day pass. Contact Sunline Transit at (760) 343-3451 for **Free** personalized trip planning and information.

VILLAGEFEST

Palm Canyon Drive, between Baristo and Amado Roads; (760) 320–3781. Open every Thursday 6:00 to 10:00 P.M. except major holidays. **Free**.

The street fair transforms Palm Springs' main thoroughfare into a lively bazaar with street entertainers, live bands, food booths, 150 arts and crafts vendors, a farmers' market, pony rides, and a Kidzone with inflatable characters. This is your chance to buy anything from a quilted comforter that doubles as a pillow to scrumptious fudge. If you need to park, go early. Villagefest operates rain or shine.

*E*xtra *S*pecial *T*ip

Cooling Off When the temperature rises in Palm Springs, the best remedy is ice cream! And Palm Canyon Drive has just about any flavor you can create between two top ice cream shops. **Coldstone Creamery** at 155 South Palm Canyon Drive (760–327–5243) specializes in mix-ins; you select a size, choose a mix-in (such as Snickers candy bars, strawberries, or M&M's), decide on a waffle cone or a cup, and presto—your custom-made cone.

Then there is **Lappert's Hawaiian Ice Cream,** 110 South Palm Canyon Drive; (760) 778–1855. This is the home of giant snow cones, Hawaiian style cones (big enough to shave a few degrees off the desert heat), and non-calorie-controlled ice cream. It's desert dessert dining at its best. Flavors are fab, from mango and root beer to mint, pineapple, and coconut . . . It's better than air conditioning!

Extra Special Tip

Ship of the Desert The ship of the desert, none other than a Palm Springs camel, can take you on a desert tour. Operating seasonally from March through May and again from October to April, this expedition departs from the Oasis Date Gardens, 59-111 Highway 111, in Thermal (about 45 minutes from Palm Springs). Children must be six years old and ride on the same camel as the adult. A one-hour ride is $75 and must be paid in advance. Call (760) 399–5665 for information. Have a nutritious and delicious date shake while you're waiting for the camel to pick you up!

PALM SPRINGS DESERT MUSEUM

101 Museum Drive; (760) 325–0189; www.psmuseum.org. Open year-round, except Mondays and major holidays. Hours are 10:00 A.M. to 5:00 P.M. Tuesday through Saturday; noon to 5:00 P.M. Sunday. $$

The museum specializes in the Coachella Valley environment. It now has 20,000 more square feet with the addition of the new Steve Chase wing. One of its highlights: an anthropology collection of 39,000 artifacts, most representing the Agua Caliente band of Cahuilla Indians. There are also art exhibits. Kids will enjoy the exhibit of once live animals, with dozens of unusual reptiles and insects, plus a sculpture garden. The family programs are exceptional. Nature hikes depart Wednesday and Friday at 9:00 A.M. Five-day camp sessions are held in summer. Geared to first through eighth graders, programs include desert education and hands-on art activities.

Toor Gallery Cafe, adjacent to the **Annenberg Theater,** (760) 325–4490, (which has weekend concerts especially during the October through April peak season), serves sandwiches, salads, and desserts. *Hours 11:00 A.M. to 3:00 P.M. daily.*

THE VILLAGE GREEN

221 South Palm Canyon Drive; (760) 323–8297.

The oldest structure in Palm Springs, dating from 1884, the Village Green is a compact compound of museums. Desert pioneers are immortalized here. Museums include the McCallum Adobe (houses the Palm Springs Historical Society collection) and Miss Cornelia White's House (built in 1893 from railroad ties!). Next door is Ruddy's General Store Museum, admission fifty cents, where kids will see what a real general store looked like in the 1930s and 1940s—before the behemoth Wal-Marts and Home Depots emerged—complete with soapboxes and soup cans. The Agua Caliente Cultural Museum Center, 219 South Palm Canyons (760-323-0151; www.prinet.com/accmuseum), has Native American jewelry, basket exhibits, historic photos and documents, and a fifteen-minute educational video.

E_{xtra} S_{pecial} T_{ip}

Knott's Soak City Water Park 1500 South Gene Autry Trail, Palm Springs; (760) 327-0499 or (800) 247-4664. Museums, movie stars, and "date shakes at Hadley's" aside, here's why kids flock to Palm Springs. The park is an immaculately clean twenty-one-acre fantasy playground where cool water reigns supreme. There is amusement for kids of all ages at Oasis, from Squirt City and the tranquil Whitewater River inner-tube ride to more than a dozen other water slides, fourteen altogether, ranging from simple to simply outrageous. The Black Widow slide is a case in point. Those who dare coast in inner tubes along a 54-inch-wide, 450-foot-long slide that at certain points takes riders through total darkness and down a 50-foot drop—yikes! Plus there is stand-up surfing and body boarding. The three-man inner-tube ride is fast and furious! For the ultimate junior daredevil, Black Widow puts you in total darkness for 580 feet—enclosed in an inner tube!

The most surprising attraction—and arguably the most fun—is California's largest wave-action pool, a broad expanse of water that starts out calm but churns away every fifteen minutes to become a sort of Malibu-in-the-desert. Actually, giant fans create the artificial tide, but it feels like the genuine article. If your children are real water bugs, it might be hard to pry them away from this park at day's end. $$$. Children under three Free. Park closed November through mid-March.

PALM SPRINGS AIR MUSEUM

745 Gene Autry Trail; (760) 778–6262; www.air-museum.org. Open year-round 10:00 A.M. to 5:00 P.M., summer hours 10:00 A.M. to 3:00 P.M. $$

While you're on the Gene Autry Trail, visit the Air Museum for a close-up look at propeller-driven aircraft from an era your kids will know only from old movies, documentaries, and (perhaps) their history books. Vintage planes, many colorful and perfectly restored, recall the World War II era. The planes are on display to educate the public about aviation's role in winning the big war. Many guides are wartime vets whose knowledge will amaze you and the kids. The second floor has flight simulators (arrange to use them in advance) and a library. The gift shop carries a treasure trove of aviation gifts, books, and jewelry.

Lucky you if you're in the desert in July, because the Air Museum celebrates Cool Kids Month! with flying model airplane contests and other hands-on activities.

CHILDREN'S DISCOVERY MUSEUM OF THE DESERT

71–701 Gerald Ford Drive; (760) 321–0602. Open 10:00 A.M. to 5:00 P.M. Tuesday through Saturday; noon to 5:00 P.M. Sunday. $$

This 8,000-square-foot facility with more than fifty hands-on exhibits encourages kids to touch, explore, and discover. Youngsters can paint a Volkswagen Beetle, dig for Cahuilla Indian treasures, or make a pretend pizza in the Pizza Place. An ideal museum for children and parents who enjoy experiencing hands-on activities. Upstairs there are trunks and suitcases, costumes, and hats. Kids can dress up; this is a good photo opportunity!

Where to Eat

Capra's It's a Wonderful Italian Deli, *204 North Palm Canyon Drive; (760) 325–7073; fax (760) 322–3326.* Kids, ask your parents or grandparents if they recall those fab films from the 1940s to the 1960s such as *A Pocketful of Miracles* or *It's a Wonderful Life.* This cozy Italian deli is brimming with memorabilia recalling Frank Capra, the legendary Hollywood director who made movies that made the world smile. His family operates the deli, and they have framed Capra's 1942 Oscar in lucite.

When strolling along Palm Canyon, make a beeline for this deli where the Italian sandwiches are stuffed with everything from fresh roasted turkey to meatballs in marinara. The fettucine, spaghetti, and ravioli are just as good. Families will like the prices. Most every-

thing on the menu is $10 and under, and all items are available to go. Perfect for a picnic in the Indian Canyons. Mangia!

Simba's Ribhouse, *190 North Sunrise Way; (760) 778–7630; fax (760) 322–1985. Closed July through October. Closed Monday.* You'll find Simba in the kitchen cooking up her homemade specialties. Dinner means southern fried chicken, tender sliced turkey, corn bread, mashed potatoes, macaroni and cheese, and a lavish salad and fruit bar. Then there could just be chicken enchiladas, seafood pasta, yams, and catfish—all are Simba's pride and joy!

Top of the Tram Restaurant, *(760) 325–1391.* The closest you'll come to being in Switzerland without leaving

Palm Springs. Cafeteria-style lunch served from 11:00 A.M. Winter specialties include prime rib; summer brings barbecue beef, pork ribs, or chicken and vegetarian lasagna and roasted turkey. Kids will love the world's largest rotating tram car as it silently speeds to the 13,000-acre San Jacinto State Park, taking you from the palms to the pines. Upon arriving, view the film *Building on a Dream,* which explains how this daunting tram ride came about. This aerie is also the gateway to 54 miles of hiking trails. For camping information, call (909) 659-2067. Remember, no pets allowed in this sky-high paradise.

Tyler's, *149 South Indian Canyon Drive; (760) 325–2990. Open Monday through Saturday 11:00 A.M. to 5:00 P.M. Lunch only.* This tiny hamburger haven was once a bus station and then an A & W root beer stand. It reopened as Tyler's, serving, as far as this coauthor is concerned, the best hamburgers in town. The half-pound burger is $4.50 and

worth every cent.

Kids will like the sliders, three mini hamburgers that can be decorated with hot sauce, pickles, grilled onions, and ketchup. The menu is small, but the essentials are there, from chili dogs and egg salad sandwiches to homemade potato salad and coleslaw. Before noon every bar stool along the counter is taken with serious foodies. The root beer floats ($2.50) are divine, and the fresh lemonade ($1.50) is like grandma used to make.

During winter, Diana, the proprietor, prepares soups you dream about, from red pepper to fresh mushroom. On Fridays, ask for the clam chowder. There is a small patio in the back, but it's advisable to arrive early because this landmark beacon of comfort food, par excellence, fills up fast. You might try the takeout service if there is a long wait. And be sure to tell Diana, a whirlwind, that Pam sent you.

Where to Stay

Oasis Water Resort Villa Hotel, *4190 East Palm Canyon Drive, Palm Springs; (760) 328–1499 or (800) 247–4664; www.oasiswaterresort.com.* This hotel provides special packages, including condominium-style lodging,

𝕱ree admission to the water park, and complimentary breakfast. Two-bedroom, two-bath condos are spacious and convenient to the park. $$$$

Cathedral City and Rancho Mirage

The desert communities of Cathedral City and Rancho Mirage are small in population (40,087 and 11,500 respectively) but are host to many golf courses and resort communities, even more than in Palm Springs proper. Again, don't make the mistake of thinking all those emerald green courses are for members only. Many are open to the public and/or have reciprocal arrangements with specific hotels. Greens fees average $65. You can get golf lessons and use the driving ranges at many courses for nominal fees.

Extra Special Tip

Cathedral City is coming into its own. Once a sleepy, nondescript community on the way to somewhere else, it now offers many reasons to stop and spend a day. Ever imagined visiting Yankee Stadium, Fenway Park, and Wrigley Field all in one day? It's possible at the thirty-acre **Big League Dreams Sports Park,** 33–770 Date Palm Drive; (760) 324–1133 or (760) 324–5600, fax (760) 770–6541. Sports enthusiasts will go for the batting cage stations and sand volleyball courts. This is the nation's first amateur sports facility of its kind and merits at least a two-hour visit. There's a "Tot Lot" for the younger set.

And while you're in the neighborhood, try **Applebee's Neighborhood Grill & Bar,** 32400 Date Palm Drive; (760) 324–6911. Just a minute's drive from the Sports Park, this family-style restaurant has a kids' menu with all entrees under $3.99. All kids' meals come with a choice of soft drink, HiC fruit punch, or milk. The restaurant has a fascinating photograph exhibit of local history including Amelia Earhart's visit to Indio, plus memorabilia from local teams and sporting events.

The big news in Cathedral City is the big screen. "Learning at the Edge of your Seat" is what kids love at the Desert IMAX theater; the screen is 50 by 70 feet—that's six stories high! Show times are subject to change, so call first (760) 324–7333; www.desertimax.com. Free parking at the Cathedral City Civic Center. The theater is on the corner at 68–510 East Palm Canyon Drive at Cathedral Canyon Boulevard.

Extra Special Tip

Earth in Motion You've heard about it on the radio, you've seen it on television and probably the Internet—the infamous San Andreas Fault. Now there is a four-hour **Earth in Motion** tour designed by Jurassic Expeditions, taking visitors by bus to the world's most famous earthquake fault. This is "edu"-tainment at its best. The motor coach tour is produced and directed by Charles Watson, creator of "Seismo-Watch," a column read by millions weekly. The big Cardiff bus leaves from various pick-up points. Call (760) 862–5540 for reservations; www.jurassicexpeditions.com.

BOOMER'S FAMILY ENTERTAINMENT CENTER

67-700 East Palm Canyon Drive, Cathedral City; (760) 321–9893. Open 365 days a year; Monday through Thursday 11:00 A.M. to 10:00 P.M. (extended hours during the summer and on holidays); Sunday 10:00 A.M. to 10:00 P.M.; Friday 11:00 A.M. to midnight; Saturday 10:00 A.M. to midnight. Admission **Free**, *but inside fun is pay-as-you-play, with varying ticket prices for combinations. $$$*

For some decidedly nonprofessional-level golf action, take the tykes to the home of three fun eighteen-hole miniature golf courses. There are also bumper boats, go-carts, batting cages, a 10,000-square-foot games pavilion, 200 video and sports games, and a new laser tag and motion simulator.

Where to Eat

The River, *71–800 Highway 111, corner of Bob Hope, in Rancho Mirage.* For dining, strolling, movies, book browsing, or a scoop of ice cream, this latest desert mirage is the place to visit.

Where to Stay

Westin Mission Hills Resort, *At the corner of Dinah Shore and Bob Hope Drive; (800) 544–0287 or (760) 328–5955; www.westin.com.* The Cactus Kids Club program designed for children ages four to twelve offers a good mix of arts, crafts, nature walks, games, and swimming. Hours are Sunday through Thursday from 7:00 A.M. to 5:00 P.M. and Friday and Saturday from 7:00 A.M. to 8:00 P.M. There are rental bikes and in all guest rooms, the Sony Playstation. Kids love the 60-foot, S-curved waterslide, basketball, softball, and bicycle rentals. Then there are two golf courses and tennis courts. Inquire about the Summer Magic Getaway Package.

For More Information

Palm Springs Desert Resorts Convention and Visitors Bureau. *(800) 41–RELAX or (760) 770–9000; fax (760) 770–9001; www.desert-resorts.com or www.palmspringsusa.com for lodging information. Open 8:30 A.M. to 5:30 P.M. Monday through Friday.* Ask for an updated vacation planner. The bureau has the latest information on all the desert resort communities: Palm Springs, Cathedral City, Rancho Mirage, Palm Desert, La Quinta, Indian Wells, Indio, and Desert Hot Springs. You'll quickly realize how the area dazzles (in season) with celebrity golf tournaments, charity events, and chic benefits.

Palm Desert

In recent years Palm Desert, "where the sun shines a little brighter," has been something of a boomtown, with shopping and dining opportunities to rival—some would say surpass—those of Palm Springs. Palm Desert helps make the Coachella Valley the "golf capital of the world," not only on account of the many courses it boasts, but because golf carts are legal transportation on several city streets. There's even a **Golf Cart Parade** every November, in which a hundred carts decorated as floats parade along El Paseo, the "Rodeo Drive of the Desert."

Palm Desert is home to one of the most interesting street fairs in Southern California. Look for the College of the Desert Street Fair, 435 Monterey Avenue in Palm Desert—there's plenty of **Free** parking. Kids will love wandering through the farmer's market and checking out the endless vendors selling original art, jewelry, T-shirts, designer eyeglass frames, and faux designer purses. You name it...it's for sale here somewhere. Open Saturday and Sunday year-round. Don't miss it! And now, we will go from simple to "simply elegant" shopping, from the street fair to El Paseo.

The undisputed style center of the desert is a few blocks away on **El Paseo**, a 7-block drive between Highway 74 and Portola Avenue.

While strolling on El Paseo, stop at the **Daily Grill,** 73-061 El Paseo (on the corner), open 11:00 A.M. to 10:00 P.M. Monday through Saturday, Sunday from 10:00 A.M. (for brunch) to 10:00 P.M. (760) 779-9911. There's something for everyone, from a delicious cobb salad to a hearty serving of meat loaf and mashed potatoes. The children's menu has the usual—hamburgers, grilled cheese, and chicken fingers. Wash it down with a giant glass of fresh lemonade. At the **Gardens on El Paseo** (between San Pablo and Larkspur) sample a taste of the Caribbean at **Tommy Bahamas**, 73595 El Paseo (upstairs); (760) 836-0188. The conch fritters are truly a taste from the islands. Downstairs is a boutique with shirts in wild designs—chic but expensive.

If the adults want to slip away for a few hours, there is **Sullivans Steakhouse**, 73505 El Paseo, also on the upper level with a delightful twelve-ounce petite filet mignon for $19.95. The meal includes the best lettuce wedge (with diced tomatoes) in the desert. Reservations are essential. Call (760) 341-3560. If you take the kids, my advice is to go early, around 6:00 P.M. The noise level is a challenge even for kids!

 Pacifica in the Desert, 73505 El Paseo (upper level in the Gardens), 760-674-8666, www.pacificainthedesert.com, serves the "freshest fish in the desert." And for casual fine dining, with a lovely outdoor patio and with a gorgeous view to boot, it can't be beat. You'll find fresh seafood galore for lunch (daily except Monday) and dinner, seven days, at this family-friendly restaurant (complete with a kid-friendly menu with specialties selected by the owners' nine-year-old daughter). When you tire of fast food, eating here is a special event and the preparation is healthy, too. In other words, grilled and barbecue cooking replaces greasy and fried. There are Sunset Suppers, starting at $15. We think this is the best dining deal along this pricey stretch of desert real estate. $$$

LIVING DESERT WILDLIFE AND BOTANICAL PARK
47–900 Portola Avenue; (760) 346–5694. Open daily year round. $$

This 1,200-acre preserve lets parents and kids have a close-up look at everything from a desert cactus to a bobcat. Common desert inhabitants roam freely in addition to the world's smallest fox, bighorn sheep, gazelles, tortoises, and zebras. Although much of the desert fauna is nocturnal (cooler temperatures bring out the animals), you will surely encounter some of it, especially if you take a hike on one of the several trails on the premises. The family will enjoy the live animal shows daily in the outdoor Tennity Amphitheater. There is a fifty-minute guided tour via electric tram. One favorite: the Critter Close-Up, a daily event that permits kids to see and pet small desert animals. The

*E*xtra *S*pecial *T*ip

Sky Watcher Tours, (760) 345–2363, fax (760) 836–1942. Currently take place at the Desert Springs Marriott and the Hyatt Grand Champions. If the kids insist upon staying up late at night, consider Sky Watcher Tours as the solution. A sky guide leads a tour of the heavens using high-powered telescopes and sky binoculars. It's mythology mixed with astronomy and a stellar story kids will enjoy.

newest exhibit is Eagle Canyon, a lushly landscaped conservation center with more than thirty animal species, including mountain lions and golden eagles. At the Village Watutu, kids can get up close with camels, hyenas, birds, and a petting kraal. Stop for a cool drink at the **Thorn Tree Grill** and peruse the souvenirs at the Kumba Kumba Market.

During December, don't miss Wildlights, a marvelous display of illuminated Christmas symbols, and a fabulous outdoor electric train that zips around the desert. It's a desert original that fascinates kids of all ages.

*E*xtra *S*pecial *T*ip

The Renaissance Esmerelda Resort and Spa, 44400 Indian Wells Lane, Indian Wells; (760) 773–4444 or (800) 228–9290, www.renaissancehotels.com. At the Esmerelda, there is all a family could ask for, including a "sand" beach, three swimming pools, lots of space to spread out, and family-friendly rates. Up to five guests are allowed in each spacious room. Here is the place to kick back and relax; dad can try the links and mom can indulge in the stunning new Spa Esmerelda. Or, if there's a babysitter on hand, parents can have a 'couples' treatment in one of the private suites. The apple cinnamon creams and scrub is the next best thing to a homemade apple pie! $$$$

Extra *Special* *Tip*

Lake Cahuilla 58075 Jefferson Street, La Quinta. Riverside County Park offers day use, a swimming pool ($1.00 daily), camping, and fishing. A fishing license isn't required but fish stocking fees are charged. The sunsets on Lake Cahuilla are gorgeous, and there is plenty of space for kids to run around. A perfect break if you want to pause from driving and just relax. Lake Cahuilla now has genuine camel rides January through Memorial Day! Call the **Camel Safari** at (760) 398–1212 for an appointment for the one-hour ride, which at last camel check was $75.

Schedule your lakeside visit to allow time for lunch or dinner at **La Quinta Resort & Club**, *49499 Eisenhower Drive; (800) 598–3828; www. laquintaresort.com.* La Quinta is the ideal resort for families, with something for everyone. Parents can enjoy golf, a full-service spa, and spacious casitas and grounds. Children will like Camp La Quinta from 9:00 A.M. to 3:00 P.M. Programs include nature walks, arts and crafts, and miniature golf. The cost is $55 per day, per child. Evening programs are from 6:00 to 10:00 P.M., Friday and Saturday only, and the charge is $35 per progam per child. Up to two children stay **Free** in a casita with parents.

WESTFIELD SHOPPING TOWN

72–840 Highway 111; (760) 341–7979; www.westfield.com.

The largest mall in the Coachella Valley. The fully air-conditioned shopping center has more than one hundred stores and eateries, including a Resort Ten, for the latest films, and Charlotte Russe, an upscale young people's store. Look for family-friendly specialty stores such as the Disney Store.

MCCALLUM THEATRE

Bob Hope Cultural Center, 73000 Fred Waring Drive; (760) 340–ARTS; www.mccallumtheatre.com.

For the culturally inclined, the popular McCallum features theatrical, dance, classical, and celebrity events. The 2002–2003 season included *Sleeping Beauty,* produced by the American Family Theater.

Know Before You Go! Visitor information is best accessed at the official Palm Springs Visitor Information Center, 2781 North Palm Canyon Drive (at Highway 11), open daily from 9:00 A.M. to 5:00 P.M. Keep the complimentary copy of *The Visitor's Guide,* brochures, and local map with you as you cruise the views of this fabulous desert playground. There are some fascinating "firsts" here. The Palm Springs International Airport Terminal is the nation's first to open a Harley-Davidson Airport Rental Agency. Motorcycle fans will find a variety of models.

The First Friday—an event showcasing local art galleries, antiques stores, and gift shops in the Uptown Heritage District—is held the first Friday of each month. Participating stores from Amado to Tachevah on North Palm Canyon Drive stay open until 9:00 P.M. Call (760) 778-8415 or check the Web site at www.palm-springs.org for more information.

Where to Eat

Sammy's Woodfired Pizza, *73-595 El Paseo, in the Gardens, second level; (760) 836–0500; www.sammyspizza.com. Also located in Carlsbad, La Jolla, Mission Valley, Del Mar, Gas Lamp, Costa Verde, and Temecula.* Check out Sammy's for award-winning pizza and a family-friendly environment. There is a specially designed kids' menu with easy to eat entrees from pizza to pasta, many under $5.00. The Messy Sundae—a Sammy's original—is a masterpiece of vanilla ice cream, hot fudge, whipped cream, and nuts. $$

Where to Stay

Marriott's Desert Springs Resort and Spa, *74855 Country Club Drive; (760) 341–2211 or (800) 331–3112; www.marriott.com.* Among the many lodging options available in the Palm Desert area, this one stands out above the rest. As you enter this immense resort, you will be surrounded by the sounds of water flowing and birds calling. Marriott's preferred mode of transport? Gondolas, Venetian style. While some find this a bit Disneyland-esque, people still flock here for the dramatic ambience of this 1,200-room megaresort. A full-service spa, shopping complex, and golf course mean there is something to please every member of the family.

This sprawling resort is home to the Kid's Klub, where kids can spend quality time pursuing their own recreational activities while mom and dad are on the golf course or in the spa. Designed for ages five to twelve (kids under five require a baby-sitter, available through the concierge), the program operates seven days a week and features arts and crafts, putt-putt golf, boat rides, animal tours, lunch, and films such as *James and the Giant Peach*. Non-resort guests can also use the facility. Night Parties take place on holiday weekends between 6:30 P.M. and 10:00 P.M. The charge is $40 per child. There are different themes, such as a cooking party where kids make their own pizzas and desserts and a beach party, with sand-castle building and limbo contests, and play group games such as beach volley-ball. Kids are served hot dogs, hamburgers, and fries.

Extra Special Tip

More for Less! Why settle for a cramped hotel room when travel-ing with the children when you can call **Extra Holidays** at (800) 438-6493 and spread out in a spacious condominium. Extra Holiday Suites in Palm Springs can arrange your stay at the Vista Mirage, where two-bedroom, two-bathroom condo suites start at $93 a night. At the Plaza Resort & Spa, one-bedroom suites start at $79 a night. Palm Desert has the Desert Breeze Resort, with rates for Mediterranean-style villas starting at $79. Accommodations range from studios to two bed-rooms. Ask Extra about their two-night/third-night-free offer. Other condo locations in Southern California are near Legoland in Carlsbad and the Lagonota Lodge at Big Bear. And while we're on the subject of keeping those kids smiling, buy a copy of *TravelWise with Children: 101 Educational Travel Tips for Families* ($12.95) by Mary Rodgers Budren, Inprint Publishing. Check out Travel Tip 99: "When you travel, keep your eye out for mementos that might be helpful during a unit of study at school." Then there is *Family Fun's Games on the Go—250* travel games and tips from Lisa Stiepock and the experts at *Family Fun* maga-zine—Hyperion, New York ($13.95).

Indio

The first city in the Coachella Valley, Indio—also known as the Date Capital of the Desert—was founded in 1930. Fully 95 percent of the dates grown in the United States are cultivated in and around Indio.

This is truly the "city of festivals," beginning with the **National Date Festival,** which was founded here fifty years ago. Indio looks rather plain until you drive by the fairgrounds and glimpse the exotic entrance, which comes alive each February for the National Date Festival. The multicolored plaster domes, reminiscent of a scene from *Arabian Nights,* are sure to make your kids wonder if they have just seen Disneyland. But there's more on this stretch of highway!

CASTLE CITY FAMILY FUN CENTER
82–530 Highway 111 (at Arabia); (760) 775–6600. Open 11:00 A.M. to 11:00 P.M. daily. **Free**

This air-conditioned indoor entertainment center has a 160-seat animated theater, kiddie land, video games, and lots of snack food.

EMPIRE POLO CLUB AND EQUESTRIAN PARK
81–800 Avenue 52 (at Monroe); (760) 342–2762. Open 8:00 A.M. to 4:30 P.M. Monday through Friday. For a polo schedule call (760) 342–4133.

Indio is paradise for polo lovers. If you want to see polo in action, plan to have breakfast or lunch at the Empire Polo Club's Polo Grille Restaurant. This former horse shelter turned restaurant is open 11:00 A.M. to 7:00 P.M. Wednesday and Thursday and 11:00 A.M. to midnight Friday and Saturday. Off the beaten path at Avenue 50 and Monroe, the setting is peaceful and a far cry from the weekend crowds and traffic.

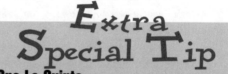

Extra Special Tip

Spa La Quinta Give mom and/or dad the day off! Spa La Quinta, 49–499 Eisenhower Drive in La Quinta; (800) 598–3828, will have the grown-ups feeling rejuvenated, relaxed, and revitalized . . . just what they need to maneuver their way around Southern California. The Restorative Break (a kind of facial that will put a sparkle back into mom's smile) is a good place to start. The spa experts can design a half or full day to include other goodies, such as a lavender wrap or a thermal mud bath!

The park covers 150 acres of landscaped grounds, including five world-class polo fields, a picturesque rose garden, and the tropical Medjhool Lake (named for the delectable dates that grow on the Indio date farms).

FEELING LUCKY?

Parents will notice Indio is home to two Vegas-style casinos, **Spotlight 29 Casino** (760-775-5566) and **Fantasy Springs Casino** (800-827-2WIN or 760-342-5695). Both face Interstate 10 and can be reached by taking the Auto Center Drive exit. There are no child-care facilities. Watch for big-name entertainment on selected evenings. We recently saw the Beach Boys and Olivia Newton John at Spotlight 29, and the concerts were well worth the $25 ticket. Just opened at Fantasy Springs is a state-of-the-art bowling center. Open 9:00 A.M. to 2:00 A.M. at 84245 Indio Springs Parkway, north of Interstate 10 at Golf Center Parkway. For information call (760) 342-5000, ext. 3181 or 3180. Rates are $3.25 per game, Monday through Friday from 9:00 A.M. to 5:00 P.M. If you've always wanted to try a neon bowling ball (they range in weight from six to sixteen pounds) in orange, red, green, blue, or purple, this is the place to make it happen!

RIVERSIDE COUNTY FAIR AND NATIONAL DATE FESTIVAL

Riverside County Fairground, 46–350 Arabia Street, Indio; (800) 811–FAIR; www.datefest.org. $$

For ten days each February, Indioites celebrate their principal crop—the tasty, versatile date. The festival is held in conjunction with the annual Riverside County Fair. The festive ambience attracts families for rides, food, games, local entertainment, and camel rides. Don't miss the Arabian Nights Musical Pageant at 6:45 P.M. daily.

If you're heading south from Indio, explore the 35-mile-long **Salton Sea**, the largest body of water entirely in California and saltier than the ocean. A haven for bird life, it is part of the vast (36,527-acre) **Salton Sea National Wildlife Refuge and Imperial Wildlife Area** (760-393-3052). In the **Salton Sea State Recreation Area**, boating and saltwater fishing are the order of the day. Several campsites and nature trails are located around the "sea" shores.

OASIS DATE GARDENS

59–111 Highway 111, Thermal; (760) 399–5665. Open 7:30 A.M. to 5:30 P.M. daily.

This is a 250-acre working date farm, where you can take a guided tour of the groves, have a picnic in a palm garden, or simply partake of the offerings at the Country Store. There are always **Free** samples available (ask for a **Free** date shake). If you like dried fruits and nuts, this is the place to stock up.

Where to Eat

Cosmos Italian Kitchen, *73-155 Highway 111, Palm Desert; (760) 674–3431.* For reasonable prices and homemade Italian standbys, from spaghetti and meatballs to pizza, this is the best choice. Large booths and tables are served by a friendly waitstaff. The desert is rife with expensive pasta places, but why outspend yourself for lunch or dinner when you can dine on hearty portions at half the prices charged by nearby restaurants. Mama Mia! Try Cosmos' and you'll see what we mean when that giant pepperoni, mushroom, and tomato pizza hits your table.

Joshua Tree National Park and Chiriaco Summit

Even if your kids have never been to **Joshua Tree National Park** before, they will probably recognize the short, bristly, and oddly contorted trees that thrive here from the cover of the popular U2 album, *The Joshua Tree.* It was actually Mormon settlers who named the trees. They thought their thick branches, which protrude toward the sky, resembled the biblical Joshua praying. The south entrance to the park is at Cottonwood Spring, about 25 miles east of Indio off Interstate 10. The **Cottonwood Visitor Center** is open 8:00 A.M. to 4:00 P.M. daily except Christmas. There are nine campgrounds at the park, with fireplaces, tables, and toilets. Permits required. Day-tripper admission $10.00.

Less than an hour's drive north of the Coachella Valley, and worth at least a half-day detour, Joshua Tree is where the southern Colorado Desert (elevation less than 3,000 feet) meets

Extra *Special* *Tip*

Gublers Orchids If anyone in the family is fascinated by orchids, by all means stop by **Gublers Orchids,** 2200 Belfield Boulevard, Landers, CA 92285; (760) 364–2282, fax (760) 364–2285. You'll find it "off the map" when traveling on Highway 62 toward Joshua Tree National Park. This state-of-the-art orchid farm is in the middle of nowhere, it seems. However, once you see the gorgeous display of orchids, marvel at the climate-controlled greenhouses and the solar greenhouses, and peruse the bromeliads, ferns, and yes, even carnivorous plants, you'll be glad you went out of your way. Complimentary tours Monday–Saturday 10:00 A.M. and 4:00 P.M.

the vast expanse of the Mojave (high desert). The park, formerly a national monument, covers 794,000 acres (850 square miles) and in some places affords unobstructed views of more than 50 miles. The park ranks fourth on the list of "Top Ten National Park Facilities in Caifornia," based on 1998 visitations. The highlight for many kids will be scrambling about the lower portions of giant quartz-monzonite boulders and monoliths in the Mojave Desert portion of the park. See if you (or they) can spot remnants of the 2,000 mines and prospect holes throughout the area, left behind by late-nineteenth-century miners. There are also six hiking trails, nine interpretive trails, three visitor centers, and eight family campgrounds to keep you busy.

Try to schedule your visit to Joshua Tree around a sunset. The photographic opportunities here are unparalleled, especially when the shadows dance on the colossal rock formations and the cholla cacti and Joshuas seem to glow in the fading sunlight. The whole place has the feel of a rather eerie lunar landscape, a boundless place in which to take time out and wonder. It's not a geographical experience anyone in your family will soon forget. For more information, call the Joshua Tree National Park Scenic Tour (760–285–1608).

Visit the **Park Center,** 6554 Park Boulevard, Joshua Tree (take Interstate 1 to Highway 62, turn right at Park Boulevard in Joshua Tree) at the west entrance to the national park. Open 9:00 A.M. to 5:00 P.M. Sunday to Thursday and 8:00 A.M. to 8:00 P.M. Friday and Saturday. The Park Center is forty-five minutes from Palm Springs, two and a half hours from Los Angeles and San Diego. Stop here to purchase maps, books, souvenirs, handcrafted gifts, and fine art. You can also visit a sculpture garden. The bakery opens at 6:00 A.M. and sells freshly prepared sandwiches and pastries.

GENERAL PATTON MEMORIAL MUSEUM

(760) 227–3483; open 9:30 A.M. to 4:30 P.M. daily. $

Thirty miles east of Indio and 70 miles from the Arizona stateline is a museum not to be missed. Exit at Chiriaco Summit and look for the American flag. You are at what was once the entrance to Camp Young, the famous Desert Training Center. This is the site chosen by Major General George Smith Patton, Jr., in March 1942 as a training center for desert warfare. Nearly one million American servicemen and -women trained here. Patton commanded the camps for four months, departing in August 1942 to lead Operation Torch, the allied assault on German-held North Africa. The camp closed on April 30, 1944. The museum has an excellent twenty-six-minute video, plus exhibits. Many of the artifacts were donated by servicemen and -women. There are armored tanks on display, along with memorials and a small outdoor chapel.

Next to the General Patton Memorial Museum is the **Chiriaco Summit Coffee Shop,** (760) 227-3227, owned by the Chiriaco family. There is a U.S. Post Office here and a service station, as well.

The General Patton Museum was established through the tireless efforts of Margit Chiriaco Rusche and the Bureau of Land Management. Margit recalls seeing the tanks from her front yard as a five-year-old, when the Desert Training Center was in full swing. Be sure to have breakfast, lunch, or dinner at this charming coffee shop, where comfortable booths have looked out on the desert since 1934. Margit bakes the best chocolate cake, slathered with chocolate frosting and walnuts, for miles! On the menu is the DTC (Desert Training Center) burger, made with Spam (kids, ask your grandparents about that!). There are also corn dogs with chips and lots of sandwiches kids will enjoy. The Traveler's Special breakfast costs $3.95, and that includes two each of pancakes, eggs, sausage patties, and bacon. It's worth driving out to Chiriaco Summit for this breakfast bargain!

Where to Stay

Oasis of Edon Inn and Suites, *56377 Twenty Nine Palms Highway; (800) 606-6686; www.desertgold.com/eden.html.* If you've had a dream about spending a night in a Grecian, Roman, safari, or Oriental suite, make a reservation at the one and only Oasis of Eden Inn and Suites, where high desert hospitality means a full or studio kitchenette with adjoining rooms (perfect for a family), deluxe complimentary continental breakfast, Free in-room movies, including HBO and Disney, and a marvelous large heated pool, surrounded by a colorful, hand-painted mural. This is a one-of-a-kind hideaway with a personality.

Spin and Margies, *Off Route 62, and ten minutes from Joshua Tree National Park;*

(760) 366-9124; www.deserthide away.com. This adorable little property has a fun Southwest feel. With only four suites with kitchens, there is definitely a "get away from the hustle and bustle of city life" feeling here. There are videos in the rooms for the children when they are through discovering the desert for the day. $$$

The Twenty Nine Palms Inn, *73950 Inn Road; (760) 367-3505.* Founded in 1928, this is another high desert discovery. Its cozy restaurant serves lunch and dinner. Yes, you are slightly off the beaten path, but the high desert air is invigorating and kids will find the spacious grounds perfect for exploring. Guests spending the night enjoy a complimentary continental breakfast.

Brunch is served on Sunday from 9:00 A.M. to 2:00 P.M. Desert cottages are roomy and ideal for a family; the decor is authentic with vintage furnishings. You may want to linger an extra day.

But you're almost at the entrance of Joshua Tree National Park, an 850-square-mile plant and wildlife sanctuary, worth another full day of exploration.

Extra Special Tip

Magical Mystery Tour En route to Joshua Tree Monument, if you've exited from Interstate 10 to Highway 62, you'll be on a stretch of highway that takes you through some fascinating scenery and worthwhile places to stop. This is a two- to three-hour trip in itself, especially if you stop for lunch and visit a few museums and art galleries along the route.

The high desert sweeps the vast area straddling San Bernardino and Riverside Counties. You know you've arrived when the temperature dips about ten degrees from that of the stunning sun-dappled mountains of the ritzier side of Interstate 10, that being Palm Springs. Families head for the high desert when they want to explore a portion of the 800,000-acre Joshua Tree National Park.

Along the way you'll pass Morongo Valley and Yucca Valley prior to arriving at Joshua Tree. The Yucca Valley lies at the gateway to the Mojave Desert's Morongo Basin.

At the Community Center Complex, 57116 Twentynine Palms Highway, you'll find the **Hi-Desert Nature Museum** (open Tuesday through Sunday, 10:00 A.M. to 5:00 P.M., Free.) This is a family-oriented facility related to the Hi-Desert's unique natural and historical environments. The museum shop has nature theme gifts and children's science gifts (open 10:00 A.M. to 5:00 P.M. Tuesday through Sunday). Kids can interact with resident snakes, insects, or spend some time on arts and crafts.

Twenty Nine Palms is home to the Marine Air Ground Task Force Training Command Marine Corps Air Ground Combat Center. While this immense military base, rivaling the size of the state of Rhode Island, is not open to the public, it is the site on occasion of military events on the parade ground, such as the Battle Color Ceremony presented by the Marine Corps.

While in the area, make it a point to stop at **Pappy & Harriet's Palace and Motel** on Pioneertown Road ("eatin', drinkin', and sleepin' in an old western town" says their ad). Enjoy live country music at the restaurant Friday, Saturday, and Sunday (760) 365–5956; pioneertown.com/palace. Breakfast at Pappy & Harriet's is served Saturday 10:00 A.M. to noon and Sunday 8:00 A.M. to noon. Lunch Friday, Saturday, and Sunday is from 11:00 A.M. to 5:00 P.M. Dinner is served nightly. Closed Monday and Tuesday. This is a far cry from any chain restaurant. The ambience is authentic; Old West, rustic, and noisy. Local characters looking like vintage cowboys are often sitting around. There's so much going on here with dinners and western entertainment that a monthly schedule is published.

Pioneertown, 4 miles out of the Yucca Valley, was founded by Gene Autry, Roy Rogers, and Dick Curtis in 1946 and was used as a filming location. The kids may not remember the film *Gunfight at the OK Corral*, but a few parents and grandparents might. This was filmed here along with many other stories of the Old West. This area is truly a time warp, but it's the real McCoy.

Several hiking trails start here, such as the 2-mile Water Canyon Trail and the Pipes Canyon Trail, where you can see the original "pipes," or springs, that attracted the first settlers.

As you enter the town of Twenty Nine Palms along the **Twenty Nine Palms Highway** (it's the alternative route to Arizona, the Colorado River, and Las Vegas, by the way), look for the magnificent historical murals painted on the sides of eleven buildings throughout the town. They depict Indians, miners, homesteaders, and ranchers. One mural kids might find interesting is found on the south wall at 6308 Adobe Road, *Jack Cones the Flying Constable*.

Bet you never thought there was so much to see and do along the way. Like an experienced travel writer once said, "Value the journey as well as the destination."

Mojave National Preserve

Many visitors to Southern California are surprised to learn how extensive the state's desert lands really are. Unless you consider yourself to be a true desert rat, you may want to make only a detour to the **Mojave National Preserve**, more loosely known as the East Mojave National Scenic Area. This 14,000-square-mile tract—twice the size of New Jersey—lies roughly between Interstates 40 and 15, well east of Barstow. Some of the most prominent natural features in the preserve are the **Kelso Dunes,** situated in the southern section. Rising to 600 feet, the dunes are the third highest in the United States. Shifting sands on the steep side of the dunes create a unique rumbling sound that has given these mobile mounds the alias "the singing dunes." The dunes are ringed by high mountain ranges, and the overall effect is one of a great, stark beauty. A red-tailed hawk soaring above may be the only reminder that this is Southern California, not Mars.

PROVIDENCE MOUNTAINS STATE RECREATION AREA
(805) 942–0662, in the northern portion of the preserve.

Some three dozen ancient volcanic cinder cones are scattered throughout the area. Bighorn sheep are often sighted near the visitor center, which is close by the limestone **Mitchell Caverns**. Park rangers lead visitors on ninety-minute tours of the caves. The star attraction of this area, however, is the **Cima Dome,** a geological formation created by volcanic action that rises 1,500 feet above the desert floor and measures 10 miles in diameter. Covered with the largest Joshua tree forest in the world, the dome is best viewed from Mid Hills, several miles away. Several designated state scenic roads, including the Kelso-Cima Road, Essex Road, and Lanfair-Ivanpah Road, crisscross the preserve.

For More Information

California Desert Information Center. *831 Barstow Road, Barstow, 92311; (760) 255–8760.* The center provides maps and other information about the Mojave National Preserve and other scenic desert drives.

Barstow Area

The western portions of the Mojave, though as desolate as the lands to the east, offer a very different kind of experience. Barstow, once a railroad cross-roads and transportation center, lies halfway between L.A. and Las Vegas at the junctions of Interstates 15 and 40. Right in the center of the Mojave, it's the traditional base from which to explore Calico Ghost Town, Rainbow Basin, and Mitchell Caverns.

CALIFORNIA WELCOME CENTER AT TANGER OUTLETS

The state of California has nine official welcome centers placed strategically throughout the state. The Barstow Center is located at 2796 Tanger Way, Suite 106; (760) 253-4782. California welcome centers provide information on all twelve regions. Other welcome centers are located in Rohnert Park, Pier 39 in San Francisco, Carlsbad, Santa Ana, and the Shasta-Cascade region, to name a few. Check out the state's tourism Web site at www.visitcalifornia.com for locations of all welcome centers.

BUN BOY

1890 West Main Street; (760) 256-9118. $-$$

One of the main attractions in Barstow itself is stopping for lunch at a more-than-fast-food-but-less-than-a-restaurant kind of eatery, where all Southern Californians seem to have had a burger at some point in their lives. It's the kind of place you might imagine Jack Kerouac pulling into for a quick bite before waxing beatific about the experience. There is another Bun Boy in Baker, off Interstate 15 North, and here you will find the world's highest thermometer—and probably some of California's hottest weather as well! Nevertheless, families will enjoy giant-sized servings of homemade peach, strawberry, and apple pie. Both Bun Boys open at 6:00 A.M. and close at 10:00 P.M.

Once you've filled your gas tank (and your tummy tank), it's time to leave civilization behind again. You won't miss the sounds of the city one bit as you head north on Fort Irwin Road, out of Barstow, and enter the realm of **Rainbow Basin** *(760-252-6000)*, a national natural landmark, where the colors of the rainbow decorate gorge walls housing an inestimable quantity of fossilized remains that are ten- to thirty-million years old. And may the force be with you as you drive through the rock-strewn, otherworldly landscape of **Owl Canyon,** where the movie *Star Wars* was filmed. If your kids don't know R2D2 from C3PO, this would be the place to fill them in.

CALICO GHOST TOWN

Located minutes off Interstate 15, east of Barstow, (800) TO–CALICO or (760) 254–2122; www.calicotown.com. Open daily 7:00 A.M. to dusk (shops, playhouse, and railroad hours 9:00 A.M. to 5:00 P.M.).

A not-to-be-missed item on your Mojave itinerary, the ghost town—the most celebrated of many such once-booming settlements that pepper the Mojave—contains remnants of the flourishing mining culture of over a century ago. As you approach, keep a lookout for small cavelike openings in the mountains above the town. These once were the entrances to the miners' homes. In the town's heyday in the 1880s, some 4,000 people called this dusty outpost home. Before you begin to feel too sorry for them, remember they made fortunes from silver mines that yielded $65 million worth of rich ore. One interesting nugget of information: The town was prosperous enough to keep twenty-two saloons in business.

In 1896 the price of silver plummeted, as did the town's fortunes. In the bat of an eyelash, Calico went from boom to bust. Today, the restored mining town lives on after a fashion as part of the San Bernardino County Regional Park. A stop in Calico is about as close to time travel as you'll ever get. Some of the town's original buildings, such as **Lil's Saloon, Lucy Lane's House,** and the **General Store,** have been restored so well that western-theme movies continue to be filmed here.

But Calico is more than atmospheric building facades. You can actually enter Lil's or the **Top of Hill Cafe and Ice Cream Parlor** for some modern-day refreshment. There are twenty-three shops along Main Street—the only street—a favorite being the 1880s-style candy store. You and the kids also might hop aboard a narrow-gauge train for a ride to the silver mine areas north of town.

At **Maggie's Mine,** the very adventurous can get an inside look at the miner's workplace, the 30-mile network of tunnels and mine shafts beneath Calico, by taking a guided tour. Maybe you'll even spot a wedge of silver. But if you're like us, you'll stay above ground and pan for gold, boo the villain at the town playhouse, or dress up like an 1890 pioneer and have your portrait taken. This is one ghost town that is very much alive!

Festivals in Calico take place throughout the year. Palm Sunday weekend, for example, is **Calico Hullabaloo** time, when "horseshoe pitchin', stew cookin', and tobacco spittin' " are the order of the day. But you can take a walking tour with "Lefty," the town historian, or listen to Sheriff "Lonesome George" spin a yarn throughout the year. Camping is another option; facilities are located in the narrow canyons below the town, with six cabins equipped with beds and air-conditioning.

Ridgecrest

While Barstow is the crossroads of the Mojave as a whole, little Ridgecrest, a town of some 30,000 about 70 miles to the northwest, is the best base camp for branching out to explore the natural wonders and attractions of Mojave's northwestern portions.

Ridgecrest is the hub high desert community for visiting the natural attractions of **Mount Whitney** and **Death Valley**, a two-hour drive away. For further information, contact the **Ridgecrest Area Convention and Visitor's Bureau,** 100 West California Avenue; (800) 847–4830 or (760) 375–8282; fax (760) 371–1654; racvb@ridgecrest.ca.us.

You've seen Ridgecrest in dozens of movies, television shows, and videos. Over 500 television commercials have been filmed here since 1990. Think back to *Star Trek V, Flight of the Intruder, ET,* and *Dinosaur,* which was filmed on location at the Trona Pinnacles. Jawbone Canyon has seen the likes of *Wayne's World II, Desert Blue,* and *Woman Undone.* And Olancha Sand Dunes hosted *Star Trek V.*

▉ MATURANGO MUSEUM
100 East Las Flores Avenue, at China Lake Boulevard; (760) 375–6900; fax (760) 375–0479. Open 10:00 A.M. to 5:00 P.M. Monday through Sunday. $

The museum was established in 1962 to tell the story of the northern Mojave Desert. There are exhibits showcasing animals, birds, paleontology, and Native American displays. The hands-on Discovery Area appeals to children of all ages. The museum is also home to the Death Valley Tourist Center and the Northern Mojave Visitor Center.

Three miles east of Ridgecrest, off Highway 178, a right turn just as the road reaches the top side of the rise brings you to the **Bureau of Land Management's Wild Horse and Burro Corrals.** This is where the animals are held, fed, and prepared for adoptions locally and throughout the country. It is open Monday through Friday, 7:30 A.M. to 4:00 P.M. Closed in July. For further information call (760) 446–6064.

CHINA LAKE EXHIBIT CENTER, AT THE CHINA LAKE NAVAL WEAPONS CENTER

East end of Blandy Road in the old Officer's Club building; (760) 939–3530. Open 7:30 A.M. to 4:00 P.M. Monday through Thursday.

This center is constantly expanding thanks to hardware and photos from various China Lake projects. It has been a research, development, and test site since 1943 and covers more than a million acres in Southern California's Mojave Desert. The museum focus is on technical advances in the defense industry made at China Lake. Soon to come: the refurbishment of an FA-18 Hornet aircraft, the first of twenty prototypes manufactured for China Lake in the late 1970s. Kids can see missiles, free-fall weapons, and a variety of other intimidating weapons of war such as a Tomahawk submarine, a Shrike, and a Maverick. More benign is the Lunar Soft Landing Vehicle. Kids should find the actual Sidewinder missile to be especially awesome.

On quite a different note, the China Lake Naval Weapons Center houses the largest cache of ancient Native American rock art in North America. If you want to feel like an anthropologist for the day, call the museum at least two months in advance to register for an interpretive tour to Little Petroglyph Canyon, on the grounds of the center. All-day excursion $20 per person. Unlike the rest of the base, the center is open to the public Monday through Friday, 7:30 A.M. to 4:30 P.M., and Saturday 10:00 A.M. to 2:00 P.M.

Head east out of Ridgecrest on Highway 178 and take in the panorama of the **Panamint Mountains**, which frame **Death Valley**. About 20 miles up the road, the **Trona Pinnacles** pierce the clear desert sky. The pinnacles, more than 500 in number, are composed of tufa (a porous rock formed as a deposit from springs and streams) and reach heights of 150 feet. It's easy to see why portions of the movie *Star Trek V* were filmed here.

Where to Eat

Texas Cattle Company, *1429 North Chinalake Boulevard, Ridgecrest; (760) 446–6602; fax (760) 446–2378; www.texascattlecompany.com.* This family-oriented restaurant is adorned with a train that runs around the ceiling and a toy chest ready for waiting children. $$

Where to Stay

The Heritage Hotel, *1050 North Norma Street; (800) 843–0693 or (760) 446–6543.* The hotel offers 170 comfortable guest rooms and features complimentary American breakfast for guests. Film crews stay here often, as do many military personnel from nearby China Lake Naval Air Weapons Center.

Randsburg Area

Twenty-two miles south of Ridgecrest, off Highway 395, is the home of the living ghost town of Randsburg. While not as well known as Calico Ghost Town, Randsburg shared much the same fate as its desert neighbor. Today, visitors can stop for a snack, browse among antiques stores, and take a peek at the bullet slug still lodged in one of the local bars. When you turn off Highway 395 at the sign to Randsburg, the first building you will see is the old jail to your left. Park your car and browse among the vintage structures. This area is desolate but photogenic and has been used as a location for movies and television productions.

 DESERT TORTOISE NATURAL AREA
South of Randsburg; (760) 384–5400.
You've come this far, so don't miss the Desert Tortoise Natural Area (DTNA), just southwest of Randsburg. This 40-square-mile chunk of land has been reserved for the protection and preservation of the largest known population of the shy desert tortoise, an endangered species. There is an information kiosk and self-guided interpretative trails. If you want to see this desert reptile (California's official reptile) at its most active, make your 𝐅𝐫𝐞𝐞 visit in April or September.

 RANDSBURG GENERAL STORE
35 Butte Avenue, Randsburg; (760) 374–2418.
One of the few places in town that stays open during the week and probably the only joint where you can order a delicious chocolate phosphate.

RED ROCK CANYON STATE PARK

This is a favorite site for filmmakers, and the beginning scene of *Jurassic Park* was filmed here. There is a self-guided nature trail beginning near campsite 50, offering a good introduction to indigenous plants, animals, and awe-inspiring vistas. If you'd like to see more breathtaking desert-scapes, cross over to Highway 14, which skirts red, pink, orange, and white-colored canyons that seem to change color as the light shifts.

Death Valley National Park

It's awesome to imagine that twenty-seven acres of "empty" California desert comprise what we now know as Death Valley. The region is one of 265 areas worldwide recognized and preserved by the Man and the Biosphere organization. This one, the **Mojave and Colorado Desert Biosphere Reserve**, is the ideal place to share with your children the importance of environmental protection. Death Valley National Park was rated fifth on California's list of Top Ten National Park Facilities, luring 1,177,800 visitors in 1998.

Before you enter the dazzling desolation of Death Valley, consider making a stop in **Darwin Falls**, a little bit off Highway 178 before the valley. The whole family can manage the half-mile hike to the oasis of lower Darwin Falls. The upper falls aren't far behind. Your memories of green will serve you well as you head into Death Valley, the lowest point in the United States and reportedly the hottest place on earth. Average summertime highs are 115 degrees, and with scarcely a tree in sight, there isn't much shade to cool off in. If you happen to come here between June and September, remember to take it easy and drink water frequently—dehydration is dangerous and can happen faster than you think.

But don't let the heat deter you from visiting. Or the intimidating name, for that matter. With a rich mining heritage dating back to 1849 and modern tourist facilities, Death Valley can actually be a very lively place. Geological wonders have, however, always been at center stage. You can see the famous ones in a day or so, but savor the barren beauty slowly.

AMARGOSA OPERA

(760) 852–4441. Doors open 7:45 P.M.; show starts 8:15 P.M. Saturday only during October, December, and January through mid-May; Saturday and Monday during November, February, March, and April. Children under five not allowed. $$
Plan your trip so that you can visit this site in the ghost town of Death Valley Junction. Performances star Marta Becket, who plays all of

the characters. Murals depict gypsies, revelers, clerics, and Spanish royalty. Eccentric, yes, but charmingly unusual.

Extra Special Tip

Thunder and Lightning While you're in the desert, check with the *Palm Springs' Life Desert Guide* (Free and available at most hotels and restaurants) to see if there are any powwows scheduled during your visit. The entire family will find these colorful events a living history lesson. Adding to the pagentry are the dozens of artisans selling Native American jewelry and arts and crafts. And of course, Indian fry bread is readily available. The **Morongo Band of Indians** holds an **annual powwow** adjacent to the Casino Morongo that features gourd dancing, drum contests, exhibitions, and ceremonies that showcase Native American traditions.

The costumes, with feathers and fabulous beading, are a sight to behold. Bird songs, a means of aesthetic expression among the Cahuilla people, are preserved and sung at this powwow. There are other Native American events organized by the **Twenty Nine Palms Band of Mission Indians,** such as an intertribal powwow.

For more information on powwows, check the *Palm Springs Visitor's Guide,* the official publication of Palm Springs Bureau of Tourism (760-778-8415, 800-347-7746; www.Palm-Springs.org) or pick up a Free copy of the *Palm Spring's Life Desert Guide* (760-325-2333) and check the "Calendar of Events" section.

For the absolute latest on the powwow scene or other Native American-related events, check the Palm Springs Desert Resort Communities' Web site at www.desert-resorts.com.

If you have any input or questions, try the e-mail at PSDRCVB@earthlink.net or call (800) 41-Relax. And remember to ask for the Vacation Planner, which includes "R&R Club" discount offers for resorts, restaurants, and retail shops.

BORAX MUSEUM
109 Furnace Creek Road; (760) 786–2345.

The museum chronicles the history of Death Valley and has an extensive collection of minerals.

If you stay at Furnace Creek and can tear yourself away from the many pools and restaurants, some spectacular scenery awaits. You may want to leave the driving to:

- **Death Valley Tours, Furnace Creek**, *(760) 786–2345, ext. 222*. The old television series *Death Valley Days* recounts tales of this vast region. Today kids get a fresh spin on these wild and woolly tales from well-versed guides. Stories of the Donner Party and courageous pioneers in covered wagons will fascinate youngsters of all ages.

- **Fred Harvey Transportation Company** operates air-conditioned vans, ideal for families. Affiliated with the Furnace Creek Ranch Resort.

- Then head for **Artist's Palette Drive**, a famous byway that winds through pastel-colored hills laced with minerals. Early morning is the best time to take photographs from **Zabriskie Point**, which overlooks ancient lake beds. By contrast, **Golden Canyon** is at its best in the afternoon. In between, you could investigate the bizarre salt formations of the **Devil's Golf Course** and get an elevated perspective from 5,474 feet up at **Dante's View**, where the Panamint Mountains and snowcapped Mount Whitney will be visible.

Extra Special Tip

Historic Hotels Children will cultivate an appreciation for the golden age of travel if you take the time to reserve a night or two at one of the eight hotels in Southern California holding membership in Historic Hotels of America.

Historic hotels range from large, refined hotels to country resorts surrounded by tranquil hills. Kids will find the anti–high tech hospitality a far cry from standard rooms and look-alike lobbies of chain lodging.

Historic hotels in Southern California are: Furnace Creek Inn in Death Valley, La Valencia in La Jolla, Mission Inn in Riverside, The Georgian in Santa Monica, Ojai Valley Inn and Spa in Ojai, Hotel Del Coronado in San Diego, Regal Biltmore Hotel in downtown Los Angeles, and The Argyle in Hollywood. For reservations at any of these distinctive hotels call (800) 678–8946. There's no better way to combine hospitality and history than with a one-of-a-kind hotel; and be sure to find out about the National Trust for Historic Preservation while you're staying at one of these hotels—and share their fine magazine, *Preservation*, with your kids.

SCOTTY'S CASTLE

(760) 786–2392. $$

Located in the northern part of the valley in an area known as Grapevine Canyon, this Spanish Moorish–style mansion was the creation of Walter Scott (and some of his desert friends), who built his home in the 1920s at the cost of $200 million. The building took ten years to complete, but you can see it inside and out in considerably less time. Save your visit here for the second day of your Death Valley tour. Near the castle is the Ubehebe Crater and the Sahara-scale sand dunes.

Where to Eat and Stay

Furnace Creek Inn and Ranch Resort, *(760) 786–2345; www.furnace-creekresort.com, or call Historic Hotels of America at (800) 678–8946 for reservations; www.historichotels.com. Inn open October through mid-May; ranch open all year.* Make your temporary headquarters this sixty-six-room, family-friendly inn in Furnace Creek—Death Valley's nearest approximation to a town and a beehive of activity during the season. Deluxe surroundings are drenched with history at this handsome Spanish-tiled resort, perched elegantly atop a lush oasis surrounded by soaring palm trees. The inn's warm spring-fed swimming pools and tranquil views are irresistible. In addition to newly refurbished digs at Furnace Creek, there are tennis courts, horses to ride, and a golf course at 214 feet below sea level, the lowest eighteen-hole golf course in the world.

Adjoining the course's registration area is an outdoor snack bar, accessible via golf cart and filled with the aroma of onions frying on the grill. You can order thick, delicious hamburgers topped with onions, chili peppers, and more. It's just one of the unexpected finds in this part of the desert. If it's really hot, the kids can take refuge from the rays in the air-conditioned video arcade.

After taking in the sights, at least some members of the family will probably clamor for another dip in the pool. And why not? There's no better way to appreciate the spectacular California desert than by cooling off from the legendary (and intense) desert heat! This is truly a perfect family destination, complete with stunning sunsets, star-filled nights, and action-packed days.

For More Information

Visitors Center in Furnace Creek. Should you decide to explore the valley on your own, you'll have to pay a $5.00-per-car fee at the center, which also provides maps and information.

Annual Events

The following list of events planned in the deserts was made available by the California Trade and Commerce Agency Division of Tourism.

JANUARY

Nortel Networks Palm Springs International Film Festival—Palm Springs. *(760) 322–2930, fax (760) 322–4087.* More than 150 international films with a special awards gala honoring industry greats.

South West Arts Festival—Indio. *(800) 44–INDIO or (760) 347–0676, fax (760) 347–6069.* Marketplace for contemporary and traditional southwestern art; 150 acclaimed artists showcase fine and craft art.

FEBRUARY

McCormicks Exotic Antique Car Show and Auction—Palm Springs. *(760) 320–3290, fax (760) 323–7031.* Display and auction of 300 classic, antique, and special-interest cars.

Riverside County Fair and National Date Festival—Indio. *(800) 811–FAIR or (760) 863–8247, fax (760) 863–8973.* The festival features exhibits of dates and produce; fine arts; floriculture; gems and minerals; a livestock show; and pig, camel, and ostrich races.

MARCH

La Quinta Arts Festival. *(760) 564–1244, fax (760) 564–6884; www.LQAF.com.* Takes place at Center for the Arts (south of Highway 11). This annual juried art show attracts art lovers of all ages. Merv Griffin is the festival's lifetime honorary chairman. This art extravaganza is now in its twenty-first year. Kids alert: During the festival there is a **Children's Art Center** (Saturday and Sunday), usually from 10:00 A.M. to 4:00 P.M. with art activities for children ages seven to twelve (they must be accompanied by an adult).

State Farm Cup and Newsweek Champions Cup—Indian Wells. *(760) 340–3166, fax (760) 341–9379; www.champions-cup.com.* Prestigious tennis event featuring top male and female professionals.

Indio Powwow—Indio. *(800) 827–2946 or (760) 342–2593, fax (760) 347–7880.* Featuring Native American dance, traditional food, and arts and crafts.

Wildflower Festival—Yucca Valley. *(760) 369–7211, fax (760) 369–1605.* Annual display of desert wildflowers; tours. 𝐅𝐫𝐞𝐞.

MAY

Desert Tortoise Days—California City. *(760) 373–4955.* Children's fishing derby, evening dance, arts and crafts, live entertainment, parade, golf tournament. 𝐅𝐫𝐞𝐞.

Grubstake Days—Yucca Valley. *(760) 365–6323, fax (760) 365–0763.* Parade, carnival events, dancing, demolition derby, games, food, hometown crafts booths, children's activities. 𝐅𝐫𝐞𝐞.

DECEMBER

Festival of Lights Parade—Palm Springs. *(760) 778–8415 or (800) 927–7256.* Illuminated bands, floats, and automobiles make this one of the desert's top holiday events.

Tamale Festival—Indio. *(760) 342—6532 or (800) 44–INDIO.* This very popular food festival is held the first weekend in December. Tamale Land has children's activities. A carnival is open throughout the event.

Golf Cart Parade—Palm Desert. *(760) 346–3263 or (800) 873–2428.* More than one hundred golf cart floats with dazzling decorations.

Joshua Tree National Park Festival—Twenty Nine Palms. *(760) 367–5522.* Exhibits and sales by more than twenty artists.

San Diego County

What does summer vacation mean to your family? How about one with plenty of outdoor recreation—boating, hiking, biking, picnicking, swimming, golfing, baseball, surfing, or sunbathing on miles of beach? Does it include excursions to great parks full of wildlife and sea life, exciting museums with hands-on displays of fun things from outer space to automobiles, old sights with new twists, all surrounded by the Pacific Ocean, mountains, and desert and capped by a clear blue sky with mega-sunshine? The year-round answer is San Diego County, Southern California's endless summer vacation destination, encompassing metropolitan San Diego, the coastal areas of North County including Oceanside, and to the east, the mountains and desert of the Back Country, featuring Julian and Anza-Borrego.

San Diego County's location at the extreme southwest corner of the contiguous United States not only helps explain its temperate climate (an average year-round temperature of seventy degrees) but also its friendly spirit. In this geographically varied, 4,205-square-mile region, you can head west out to sea, south into Mexico, east into forested mountains that receive more rain and snow than Seattle and deserts that are hotter and drier than Phoenix, and north into 70 miles of sandy, palm-lined beaches that rival Florida. You will find country kitchens and apple farms, cosmopolitan bistros and burger joints, craft shops and giant retail malls, high-rises and bungalows, dirt roads and ten-lane freeways—inhabited by 2.9 million culturally and ethnically diverse people. Their sheer numbers make San Diego America's seventh most populous area and the Golden State's second-biggest metropolis, after Los Angeles.

Kudos! San Diego came out a big winner in the Family-Friendly 2001 Travel Awards, published in the April 2001 issue of *Family Fun Magazine*. For the second consecutive year, San Diego was named the "coolest city" in the south-

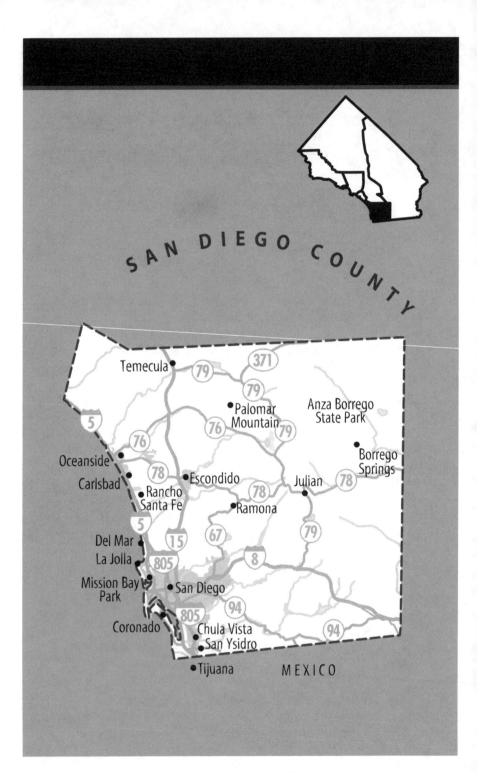

SAN DIEGO COUNTY

Temecula
79
371
79
Palomar
Mountain
76
Anza Borrego
State Park
79
5
76
Borrego
Springs
Oceanside
78
Julian
78
Carlsbad
Escondido
Rancho
Santa Fe
78
Ramona
5
67
79
Del Mar
15
La Jolla
805
8
Mission Bay
Park
San Diego
805
94
Coronado
Chula Vista
94
San Ysidro
Tijuana
MEXICO

western United States, and the magazine gave San Diego's beaches and the San Diego Zoo highest scores. Plus, the San Diego Zoo and SeaWorld San Diego were both listed among the top twelve nationwide favorite attractions.

Metropolitan San Diego

Touring the greater San Diego area is best accomplished by automobile. Your choices of activities and attractions are incredibly diverse. Many families start in the Mission Bay area at SeaWorld and are entertained by the penguins, sharks, and killer whales. Or you might begin at the world-famous San Diego Zoo with its exotic and rare species of animals and plants. Or the San Diego Wild Animal Park may beckon, where the animals roam free and really wild. Balboa Park's museums, art galleries, and theaters provide you with some fantastic cultural attractions. If outdoor recreation is your family's favorite, there are hundreds of beaches, parks, sailing, and fishing options. We like to begin at the beginning by visiting the Old Town State Historic Park and Presidio district, then touring the first California missions, downtown's restored Gaslamp Quarter, or Point Loma's Cabrillo National Monument that commemorates the first European to set sight on San Diego Bay. But no matter how you divide and conquer it, you will find incredibly fun things to see, do, and taste throughout metropolitan San Diego.

CABRILLO NATIONAL MONUMENT

1800 Cabrillo Memorial Drive, State Route 209, off Interstate 5; (619) 557–5450. Open 9:00 A.M. to 5:15 P.M. daily, possibly extended in summer. $$

Cruising the Pacific Coast north of Mexico in 1542, explorer Juan Rodriguez Cabrillo first landed at Point Loma, a 400-foot-high peninsula separating San Diego Bay from the ocean. He claimed it (and everything else in sight) for Spain. Today you can marvel at the same view Cabrillo had of the southernmost tip of this narrow finger of land. On Point Loma's plateaulike surface are two military reservations, a cemetery, and informative attractions for young and old alike. You can get your bearings at the visitor center, tour the monument's small museum, and take in a **Free** film or a ranger-sponsored program in the auditorium. Then let the kids climb Old Point Loma Lighthouse, with its breathtaking panorama of the city meeting the sea. This is a superb spot for winter whale-watching.

🏛 OLD TOWN SAN DIEGO STATE HISTORIC PARK AND PRESIDIO PARK

Located in a six-block area bounded by Wallace, Juan, Twiggs, and Congress Streets, sandwiched between Interstates 5 and 8; (619) 220–5422. Open daily 10:00 A.M. to 5:00 P.M. **Free** *admission.* **Free** *guided walking tours depart the Robinson–Rose House daily at 2:00 P.M. All buildings are closed New Year's Day, Thanksgiving, and Christmas.*

In 1769, a mere 167 years after Cabrillo arrived, Gaspar de Portola established the first **Presidio Royal** (military fort) while Father Junipero Serra founded the first in a string of twenty-one California missions. Since both the fort and the mission were built in San Diego, they earned the city the moniker "birthplace of California." This is, of course, California-ish hyperbole, because for centuries before de Portola or Serra, Native Americans—quite successfully, in fact—had prospered from the area's fertile lands and bountiful seas.

The fort and mission were located originally in what today is called **Old Town.** The cluster of adobe buildings at the base of Presidio Hill has swollen over time into a fascinating complex of historic landmarks, museums, art galleries, shops, and ethnic restaurants. These include the **Black Hawk Smith & Stable,** the **Colorado House/Wells Fargo Museum,** the **Courthouse,** the **Johnson House, La Casa de Estudillo,** the **Machado-Stewart Adobe,** the **Mason Street School,** the **Plaza,** the **Robinson–Rose Building,** the **San Diego Union Newspaper Museum, Seeley Stables,** and the **Whaley House.** Our best advice is just to go, park, walk, and enjoy this family-friendly district.

🖼 JUNIPERO SERRA MUSEUM

2727 Presidio Drive, in Presidio Park; (619) 297–3258. Open Tuesday through Saturday from 10:00 A.M. to 4:30 P.M., Sunday from noon to 4:30 P.M., closed major holidays. $$

This museum stands above the sites of the eighteenth-century presidio and Father Junipero Serra's first mission in Alta, California. It's a great place to learn about San Diego's early Spanish and Mexican periods. Exhibits include artifacts from archaeological excavations at the site.

🏛 MISSION BASILICA SAN DIEGO DE ALCALA

10818 San Diego Mission Road (east on Interstate 8, exit Mission Gorge Road north to Twain Avenue, then drive west to San Diego Mission Road); (619) 281–8449. Open 9:00 A.M. to 5:00 P.M. daily except Thanksgiving and Christmas. $

Father Serra's first mission, relocated east to its present location in 1774, was burned down by Indians the following year. Rebuilt in 1781, the fully restored mission remains an active parish. Behind the chapel is a small museum containing robes, relics, and original records in Serra's own handwriting.

Extra Special Tip

Who Was Alonzo Horton? For some years after California won statehood in 1850, San Diego remained a relatively quiet community with a Spanish and Mexican flavor. That changed dramatically when Alonzo E. Horton arrived in town from San Francisco in 1867. Buying up some 960 acres of waterfront land, he began the process of developing what was to become today's downtown area. The **Gaslamp Quarter,** bounded by Broadway, Fourth, and Sixth Streets and Harbor Drive, is the historic sixteen-block quarter where Horton made his first land purchase and where his legacy lives on. A twenty-year restoration and cleanup campaign to return the Gaslamp Quarter to its gay 1890s splendor has paid off: The area sparkles with period street lamps, old-time trolley stops, and, of more recent vintage, trendy restaurants, hotels, offices, artists' studios, and nightspots. *For complete information including walking tours and audiotapes, contact the Gaslamp Quarter/Historical Society Museum, 410 Island Avenue; (619) 233–4692. Open Monday through Friday, 10:00 A.M. to 2:00 P.M., Saturday 10:00 A.M. to 4:00 P.M., Sunday, noon to 4:00 P.M.*

HORTON PLAZA

Between Broadway, First, and Fourth Avenues and G Street, downtown; (800) 214–7467. Open Monday through Saturday, 10:00 A.M. to 9:00 P.M.; Sunday, 11:00 A.M. to 7:00 P.M. Hours adjusted seasonally and during holiday periods.

Named after Alonzo Horton, but opened in 1985, this five-story, lavishly decorated and landscaped open-air mall houses more than 150 shops and restaurants, fourteen movie theaters, and two live performance stages. Parking is available at an adjacent garage. Kids will love the festive atmosphere and food courts.

OLD TOWN TROLLEY TOURS

(619) 298–8687. Every thirty minutes, daily, beginning at 9:00 A.M. $$$$

Two-hour narrated tours of most of the key San Diego sites are available on propane-powered vehicles. You can exit and reboard anytime during the day at any of the ten fun stops (like Balboa Park, Horton Plaza, Gaslamp Quarter, Seaport Village, Embarcadero, Old Town, and Coronado) along the route. This is a wonderful way for the entire family to become acquainted with the city without the hassles of driving and parking your own car.

SAN DIEGO TROLLEY SYSTEM AND THE TRANSIT STORE

102 Broadway, near Horton Plaza; (619) 233–3004 or (619) 685–4900. Runs daily 5:00 A.M. to 1:00 A.M. every fifteen minutes. One-way fares start at $1.00; day-tripper passes (unlimited use of all types of public transit) are $5.00 per day.

An electric trolley run by the Metropolitan Transit System. the North-South Line runs from downtown San Diego to the Mexican border at San Ysidro; the East-West Line runs along the bay and includes Seaport Village, the Gaslamp Quarter, downtown, and El Cajon.

Extra Special Tip

San Diego Art & Soul An unprecedented cooperative partnership formed between the San Diego Convention and Visitors Bureau, the City of San Diego Commission for Arts and Culture, and hundreds of organizations and businesses to promote the rich cultural diversity of the area. For an updated daily list of events, links to hundreds of art, music, and cultural Web sites, and a free color brochure, access www.sandiego artandsoul.com or call (619) 533–3050.

FIREHOUSE MUSEUM

*1572 Columbia Street; (619) 232–3473. Open 10:00 A.M. to 4:00 P.M. Thursday through Sunday; closed major holidays. All firefighters **Free**. $*

Admire antique fire equipment and helmets from around the world in San Diego's oldest firehouse.

MUSEUM OF CONTEMPORARY ART–SAN DIEGO

*1001 Kettner Boulevard at Broadway; (619) 234–1001. Thursday to Tuesday, 11:00 A.M. to 5:00 P.M. (**Free** to all the first Tuesday of every month.) $*

In the spectacular thirty-four-story America Plaza, the museum features four galleries on two levels with permanent and changing exhibits of modern paintings, sculpture, and designs. The all-glass exterior gives dramatic views of the San Diego Trolley Station, Amtrak Depot, and the skyline. Call for current exhibitions.

San Diego by the Sea

San Diego by the Sea The **Embarcadero,** located at the west end of Broadway, is the thoroughfare forming the heart of downtown San Diego's waterfront action. It's home to the **Broadway Pier,** with berths for cruise ships and freighters, a debarkation platform, U.S. Customs offices, and a cool observation deck. Definitely plan on taking the kids on one of the San Diego Bay excursion cruises to view all the action around Harbor Island, Shelter Island, Point Loma, and Coronado Island. Dinner cruises and whale-watching trips also depart here. Here are some options:

 The Original San Diego Harbor Excursions. *1050 North Harbor Drive; (619) 234–4111.* $$$. Dinner cruises also available. Scheduled departures vary seasonally. Generally they are daily between 10:00 A.M. and 5:30 P.M. Sights you will enjoy include the Navy fleet and the stunning Coronado Bay Bridge.

Orion Sailing Charters. *3842 Liggett Drive; (619) 574–7504.* $$$$. Guided sailing and whale-watching cruises.

San Diego–Coronado Ferry. *1050 North Harbor Drive; (619) 234–4111.* Operates daily beginning at 9:00 A.M.; last trip 9:00 P.M. $. Every hour on the hour departs San Diego and takes you to Ferry Landing Marketplace in Coronado. Reservations not necessary. This is a super way to do Coronado for the day!

 Hornblower Cruises and Events–San Diego. *1066 North Harbor Drive; (619) 686–8715.* $$$. Reservations required for one- or two-hour cruises, brunch, and dinner/dancing excursions aboard these deluxe vessels.

SAN DIEGO CHILDREN'S MUSEUM/MUSEO DE LAS NINOS DE SAN DIEGO (ages 2–12)

200 West Island Avenue on the corner of Front Street (just a block from the Convention Center); (619) 233–5437 (visitors' line) or (619) 233–8792 (administrative offices). Open Tuesday through Saturday, 10:00 A.M. to 5:00 P.M.; closed Monday except during holidays. $$

This facility has dozens of interactive, hands-on exhibits that spark the imagination in you and your kids. Kids can play basketball in Virtual Hoops, a virtual reality–based contest or paint on the Curious Canvas, even go on stage at the Improv Theatre.

MARITIME MUSEUM OF SAN DIEGO

1492 North Harbor Drive; (619) 234–9153. Open daily 9:00 A.M. to 8:00 P.M.
$$

The museum will really get your family in a seafaring mood. You can explore three ships: the square-rigged *Star of India,* launched in 1863 and the oldest merchant vessel afloat; the ferry boat *Berkeley,* circa 1898; and the *Medea,* a steam-powered luxury yacht built in 1904.

SEAPORT VILLAGE

West Harbor Drive and Kettner Boulevard; (619) 235–4014. Open daily 10:00 A.M. to 9:00 P.M.

Encompassing fourteen acres, this village looks like a transplanted New England fishing town, complete with a carousel, lighthouse, and clock tower along with almost 100 shops, theme eateries, and restaurants. The Loof Carousel, circa 1890, is worth a whirl. You could easily spend most of the day here wandering the waterfront and enjoying a harbor cruise.

BALBOA PARK

Just northeast of the downtown business district; (619) 239–0512 for general information.

In 1868 some farsighted city leaders set aside 1,200 acres of barren pueblo land for a city park. Now that land contains the world-famous San Diego Zoo and thirteen museums (the largest concentration outside the Smithsonian in Washington, D.C.). The best way to see the rest of Balboa Park's attractions is on foot. Park at the Plaza de Panama lot (by Laurel Street near the Cabrillo Bridge crossing) or take the 𝐅𝐫𝐞𝐞 tram from the Inspiration Point parking lot (the tram has eleven stops through the park).

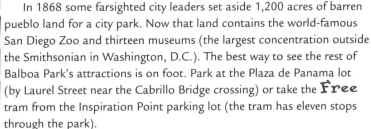

Extra Special Tip

Passport to Balboa Park Is a Great Value There are so many incredible things to see and do in Balboa Park, it would probably take you a week to do it all! The **Passport to Balboa Park** is designed with that in mind. Experience up to twelve Balboa Park museums for $21 (a $56 value). This Passport to Balboa is valid for seven days. Obtain yours at any of the museums or the Balboa Park Visitor Center House of Hospitality at 1549 El Prado. Call (619) 239–0512 for more information.

SAN DIEGO ZOO

In Balboa Park. From Interstate 5, take Pershing Drive exits and follow the signs; (619) 234–3153; www.sandiegozoo.org. Opens at 9:00 A.M. every day; closing hours vary by season so be sure to call ahead. $$$

Let the zoo be your San Diego headquarters for at least two days of family adventure. The Spanish Colonial buildings here were built originally along El Prado (the Promenade) for the 1915 Panama-California Exposition. Part of the exposition was a modest menagerie, which a certain Dr. Harry Wegeforth took over, expanded, and turned into what is now one of the world's rarest collections. The zoo's size is formidable: more than 4,000 animals; more than 900 species; and 100-plus magnificently landscaped acres with 6,500 exotic plants.

Animals are "on display" outdoors year-round. Viewing is enhanced by many exhibition areas having no bars. Areas include Gorilla Tropics (with incredibly humanlike primates), the Tiger River section, a tropical rain habitat, the Sun Bear Forest, a Southeast Asian jungle, a Hippo Beach (with underwater viewing to see how graceful a swimmer this huge land mammal can be), and the largest koala exhibit outside of Australia. (Get ready for new stuffed teddy bear requests after this particular show!)

The Children's Zoo is user-friendly, with more chances for your kids to pet animals than you can wave a carrot at, plus an incubator for baby chicks and an animal nursery. The Skyfari tram is a great way to see the zoo by air. Our recommendation for "doing the zoo" is the Deluxe Tour, which includes admission to the big zoo, a 45-minute double-decker bus tour (marvelous view), the Children's Zoo, and a Skyfari aerial tramway ride.

REUBEN H. FLEET SPACE THEATRE AND SCIENCE MUSEUM

In Balboa Park, 1875 El Prado; (619) 238–1233. Open daily 9:30 A.M.; closing times vary. $$

This awe-inspiring facility features a planetarium, hands-on exhibits, and the incredible OMNIMAX, which features new IMAX films. From birds to the Wright brothers to jets, you and the kids will thrill to the history and magical science of flight. Don't miss this!

SAN DIEGO HALL OF CHAMPIONS SPORTS MUSEUM

In Balboa Park; (619) 234–2544. Open daily 10:00 A.M. to 4:30 P.M., closed major holidays. $

Offers a fascinating peek into local sports history via photographs, memorabilia, video tapes, and audiotapes.

SAN DIEGO AEROSPACE MUSEUM & INTERNATIONAL AEROSPACE HALL OF FAME

In Balboa Park, in the Ford Building; (619) 234–8291. Open daily 10:00 A.M. to 4:30 P.M., closed major holidays. Admission is **Free** *to all on fourth Tuesday of every month. $$*

Check out the replica of Lindbergh's **Spirit of St. Louis** and an A-12 Blackbird. The hall of fame honors heroes of aviation and space flight.

SAN DIEGO MODEL RAILROAD MUSEUM

In Balboa Park in the Casa de Balboa Building; (619) 696–0199. Open Tuesday through Friday and some holidays 11:00 A.M. to 4:00 P.M., Saturday and Sunday 11:00 A.M. to 5:00 P.M. Admission is **Free** *to all on first Tuesday of the month. $*

Four scale-model railroad layouts detail the geography and development of the railroad industry in Southern California. Your kids will love the hands-on model railroad.

SAN DIEGO MUSEUM OF ART

In the center of Balboa Park; (619) 232–7931. Open Tuesday through Sunday 10:00 A.M. to 4:30 P.M.; closed major holidays. $$

The lovely facility has a permanent collection of Italian Renaissance works, Spanish baroque Old Masters, and American, Asian, and Native American art and culture.

SAN DIEGO MUSEUM OF PHOTOGRAPHIC ART

1649 El Prado, in Balboa Park; (619) 239–5262. Open daily, 10:00 A.M. to 5:00 P.M. Admission is **Free** *on second Tuesday of every month. $$*

Devoted exclusively to the photographic arts. Year-round changing exhibitions display everything from fine art photography to images from around the world.

SAN DIEGO MUSEUM OF MAN

In Balboa Park, the group of buildings around the California Quadrangle; 1350 El Prado; (619) 239–2001. Open daily 10:00 A.M. to 4:30 P.M., closed major holidays. Admission is **Free** *on third Tuesday of the month. $$*

These multifaceted exhibit halls explore the origins of humankind and feature the cultures of American Indians, ancient Egypt, Mexico, and Latin America. Special features on folk art, textiles, and early man.

SAN DIEGO NATURAL HISTORY MUSEUM

East end of Balboa Park; (619) 232–3821. Open daily 9:30 A.M. to 5:30 P.M.; hours may be extended seasonally. Admission is **Free** *on first Tuesday of the month. $$*

Houses both permanent and changing exhibits and displays detailing the plants, animals, and geology of San Diego County as well as Baja California. Be sure to call for current displays.

TIMKEN MUSEUM OF ART

1500 El Prado, in Balboa Park; (619) 239–5548. Open Tuesday through Saturday 10:00 A.M. to 4:30 P.M., Sunday 1:30 to 4:30 P.M., closed major holidays. **Free** *admission and tours.*

This charming gallery contains Old Masters, eighteenth- and nineteenth-century American paintings, and Russian icons.

BOTANICAL AND FLORAL GARDENS, BOTANICAL BUILDING

In Balboa Park; (619) 235–1100. Gardens are open year-round. Building is open 10:00 A.M. to 4:00 P.M. daily except Thursday. **Free**.

Revitalize yourself and give the kids some fresh air by heading into Balboa Park's magnificent display of botanical wonders. Included are more than 7,600 trees, 67 kinds of palms, 2,200 rose bushes, plus desert cacti, lilies, ferns, orchids, bamboo, and other oxygen-rich flora. Tour the building (an old Santa Fe railroad station) for explanations of what you've just encountered.

QUALCOMM STADIUM

9449 Friars Road, in Mission Valley; home to the National Football League's San Diego Chargers (619–280–2121 for schedules) and Major League Baseball's San Diego Padres (619–283–4494 for tickets and game times).

This venue, formerly known as Jack Murphy Stadium, was the site of the Super Bowl in 1998 and 2003, and hosts many other events during the year.

Extra Special Tip

Other Things to See and Do in Balboa Park

Museums, galleries, and gardens are not the only things going on in Balboa Park for your family. The forty-eight-passenger **Miniature Railroad** will take you and yours into a bygone era. The **Carousel** will set you spinning. The **Starlight Bowl,** where the San Diego Civic Light Opera Association presents delightful musicals, is a sure hit, so call (619) 544–7827 for current schedules. The **Spreckels Organ Pavilion** has Free concerts on weekends. The pavilion houses the world's biggest outdoor pipe organ; call (619) 235–1100 for program information. The **Morley Field Sports Complex,** in the northeastern section of the park, can satisfy just about every recreational need your family can dream of (no matter how complex), with a tennis club, two golf courses, a swimming pool, a kiddy pool, some bocce courts, a fitness center, a playground, an archery range, a couple of baseball diamonds, assorted picnic areas, two recreation centers, and a zippy eighteen-hole Frisbee golf course.

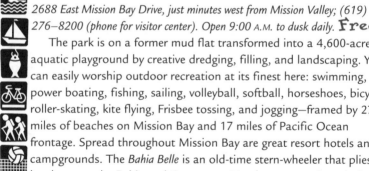

MISSION BAY PARK

2688 East Mission Bay Drive, just minutes west from Mission Valley; (619) 276–8200 (phone for visitor center). Open 9:00 A.M. to dusk daily. Free.

The park is on a former mud flat transformed into a 4,600-acre aquatic playground by creative dredging, filling, and landscaping. You can easily worship outdoor recreation at its finest here: swimming, power boating, fishing, sailing, volleyball, softball, horseshoes, bicycling, roller-skating, kite flying, Frisbee tossing, and jogging—framed by 27 miles of beaches on Mission Bay and 17 miles of Pacific Ocean frontage. Spread throughout Mission Bay are great resort hotels and campgrounds. The *Bahia Belle* is an old-time stern-wheeler that plies the bay between the Bahia and Catamaran Hotels most evenings during the summer and weekends in the winter.

SEAWORLD SAN DIEGO

1720 South Shores Road, on Mission Bay; (619) 226–3901 or (800) SEA–WORLD; www.seaworld.com. Open daily 10:00 A.M., earlier in the summer; closing hours change daily and seasonally. Be sure to call for current times. Parking is $7.00 per car. $$$$

For kids, this is probably the number-one reason to visit San Diego. Opened in 1964, this celebrated 166-acre marine amusement park features trained killer whales, ponderous sea lions, playful otters, and lovable dolphins. You can take in five different shows and more than twenty educational exhibits, including the Penguin and Shark Encounters, containing the world's largest collection of these species. How about Forbidden Reef, an underwater cave with eels and bat rays, and the not-to-be-missed whale and dolphin Petting Pool? Of course, you've got to see Baby Shamu, only the sixth killer whale to be born in a zoo in a fantastic performance alongside other killer whales. You and the kids will scream with laughter at the crazy antics of Clyde and Seamore, the infamous sea lion duo. Try out the new family adventure land, Shamu's Happy Harbor, where you get to crawl, climb, jump, and definitely get wet in a dozen or so play areas. In 1999 Shipwreck Rapids opened as the park's first adventure water ride—a wet and wild experience for sure! Shipwreck Reef Cafe will handle any castaway's appetite (the best dining among twenty or so food options.) The Sky Tower and the Aerial Tram ($2.25 each or $3.50 for both) are great ways to see the park.

BELMONT PARK

3146 Mission Boulevard, Mission Bay; (619) 491–2988. Open every day, but hours vary with the season. **Free** *admission to amusement park, but you pay as you go for your choice of rides and games.*

Fun, fun, and more fun. Take a ride on the **Giant Dipper,** a completely restored and rowdy 2,600-foot-long wooden roller coaster, first put into service in 1925 (current cost is $2.50). Then take another dip in **The Plunge,** the world's largest indoor swimming pool. **Pirate's Cove** is an indoor playground designed for children two to twelve, accompanied by parents. The arcades and Virtual Reality Zone will send everyone for another loop.

E*xtra* S*pecial* Tip

Diversity Dining From to ethnic takeout to historic hangouts to oceanfront glimmer, San Diego chefs use the region's freshest ingredients to create hearty and intriguing dishes. The county's estimated 6,400 restaurants offer everything from new taste sensations to traditional favorites and are attracting some of the nation's top culinary talents. You can sample the tastes of Thailand one evening and Mexico the next, and snack on local favorites like fish tacos and smoothies in between. Best bet? Ask your hotel's front desk for nearby favorite dining spots or contact the San Diego Convention and Visitors Bureau for its list of restaurant members (more than 250 choices). Contact www.sandiego.org.

Extra Special Tip

Hotel Circle Drive and Mission Valley

Mission Valley is a suburban area of metro San Diego that is bisected by Interstates 8 (east-west) and 805 (north-south). **Fashion Valley Center** and **Mission Valley Center** are mega-malls in this district that can provide you and your family with plenty of dining and entertainment options. They are conveniently located next to a big concentration of accommodations at Hotel Circle Drive, where you will find an abundant selection of family-friendly properties like the Comfort Inn & Suites at Hotel Circle (619-881-6800); Ramada Plaza Hotel (619-291-6500); Doubletree Club Hotel (619-291-8790); and Red Lion Hanalei (619-277-1101).

Where to Stay

Shelter Pointe Hotel & AJ's Restaurant, *On Shelter Island, 1551 Shelter Island Drive, San Diego, 92106; (619) 221-8000 or (800) 566-2524; www.shelter pointe.com.* Located on thirteen acres of spectacular beachfront property, only five minutes from San Diego International Airport, this hotel features 206 guest rooms and suites—all with bay and marina view balconies or patios. There are two heated pools and spas, a fitness club, a sand beach with volleyball, bicycle and boat rentals, and a 524-slip marina. **AJ's American Grille and Bar** serves breakfast, lunch, and dinner daily. You'll love the location for the water vistas, as well as easy accessibility to everything you want to see in San Diego. Other highlights are outstanding value packages, plus a $3 million renovation completed in January 2002. $$$

Sommerset Suites Hotel, *606 West Washington Street, San Diego, 92103 (just west of State Route 163, near Balboa Park and San Diego Zoo); (619) 692-5200 or (800) 962-9665; www.sommerset suites.com.* Eighty one-bedroom suites with fully equipped kitchens. Complimentary continental breakfast and evening refreshments. Outdoor pool, spa, BBQ area. Very family-friendly environment; call for special rates and packages. $$$

Town & Country Resort Hotel, *500 Hotel Circle North, in Mission Valley, San Diego; (619) 291-7131 or (800) 77-ATLAS; www.towncountry.com.* This thirty-two-acre resort has 1,000 rooms and suites of every motif and configuration to suit your family's particular needs. There are four swimming pools and spas, nine restaurants and lounges, an eighteen-hole golf course, tennis courts, and a shopping village. Best of all, kids stay **Free**, and there are innumerable package plans that include tickets to nearby SeaWorld and the zoo. A venerable choice for your San Diego headquarters. $$$

For More Information

San Diego Convention and Visitors Bureau. *401 B Street, Suite 1400, San Diego, 92101-4237. (619) 232–3101; www.sandiego.org.*

San Diego International Visitor Information Center, *11 Horton Plaza, First Avenue and F Street, downtown. (619) 236–1212.* Experienced, multilingual staff members are super helpful to all visitors, especially foreign travelers. *Open 8:30 A.M. to 5:00 P.M. Monday through Saturday year-round. In the summer, open on Sunday from 11:00 A.M. to 5:00 P.M.*

Chula Vista

Located in the southern tip of San Diego County, the suburb of Chula Vista offers an interesting variety of visitor attractions, all less than twenty minutes from downtown and twenty minutes to the Mexican border.

ARCO/U.S. OLYMPIC TRAINING CENTER
Eight miles east of Interstate 805 at Telegraph Canyon Road and Wuente Road; (619) 482–6103. **Free** *hourly tours are available daily from 10:00 A.M. to 3:00 P.M.; holidays excluded, varies seasonally.*

This is the nation's first warm-weather, year-round, multi-sport Olympic training complex, which complements the U. S. Olympic Committee's other training centers at Colorado Springs, Colorado, and Lake Placid, New York. The 150-acre training site includes a fifty-lane archery range and support building; a six-bay boathouse and a 2,000-meter course for canoeing, kayaking, and rowing; a cycling course and support building; a synthetic surface field hockey pitch and support building; four regulation grass fields and support buildings for soccer; a four-court complex and support building for tennis; a 400-meter track and support building; and a separate, dedicated five-acre throwing area for field events. In the Copley Visitors Center, a short film captures the dedication and emotion involved with the Olympic movement. After the film, you'll be taken on a narrated tour of the 150-acre campus. Inspiring!

KNOTT'S SOAK CITY U.S.A.—SAN DIEGO
2052 Entertainment Center (next to the Coors Amphitheater), Chula Vista; (619) 661–7373. Open daily Memorial through Labor Day; Saturday and

Sunday only during May, September, and October. Hours of operation vary; be sure to call ahead on your preferred day to splash. $$$$

Thirty-two waterlogged acres packed with twenty-two of the most intense water rides imaginable and appointed with a 1950s San Diego surf theme. Body slides, tube slides, wave pools, beaches, and a kiddy play zone will supply your youth with a water wonderland filled with surprises. Food and snacks available on the premises.

For More Information

Chula Vista Chamber of Commerce. *233 Fourth Avenue; (619) 420–6603; www. chulavistachamber.org.*

Coronado

The beaches of Coronado (translated as Crown City) lie between San Diego Bay and the Pacific. Many people call this an "island," but it is actually a peninsula connected to the mainland on the south by a long, narrow sandbar, the Silver Strand. However, you will want to enter this picturesque city, immensely popular for its boating, swimming, golf, tennis, and sunbathing, by way of the dramatic San Diego–Coronado Bay Bridge. This 2-mile expanse of graceful splendor dates back to 1969. The **Ferry Landing Marketplace** has plenty of shopping and dining options to handle your family's needs if you come over by ferry (another pretty option, especially if you just plan on spending the day).

 BIKES & BEYOND
1201 First Street at the Ferry Landing Marketplace; (619) 435–7180. Rates vary; call for current hours and schedules.

Your family's source for rental bicycles, skates, and surreys in Coronado. A super way to explore Crown City.

Where to Stay

Hotel Del Coronado, *1500 Orange Avenue, Coronado; (619) 435–6611 or (800) 468–3533.* "The Del," as the hotel is known here, has attracted the rich and famous, including thirteen U.S. presidents, since its opening in

1888. The turrets, tall cupolas, hand-carved wooden pillars, and Victorian filigrees of this stunning, magnificently restored 691-room national historic landmark resort have served as the backdrop for many movies and films. So much history has unfolded within the Del's walls that a cassette walking tour has been made available. For example, at its opening over a century ago, it was the largest structure outside New York City to be electrically lighted, and the installation was supervised by Thomas Edison himself!

Today the Del offers a wide variety of accommodations to suit any family's taste and pays close attention to the needs of children, with special programs, baby-sitting services, and children's menus. Choose from the formal main dining room, two restaurants, and a twenty-four-hour deli. The Del's beach provides great swimming and sunbathing, plus rental boats, windsurfers, and paddleboats. Just watch out for some of the smaller, original rooms, and you'll be in grand shape at this venerable place. World-renowned and definitely worth a visit! $$$$

Loews Coronado Bay Resort, *4000 Coronado Bay Road, Coronado; (619) 424–4000 or (800) 815–6397.* Located on a private, fifteen-acre peninsula named Crown Island, surrounded by water and astonishing views of the downtown San Diego skyline and marina. Five guest-room towers feature 438 very deluxe guest rooms with mini-bars and fax machines. There are three outdoor pools, whirlpools, and decks, five tennis courts, an exercise club, and a private eighty-slip marina with rentals galore— sailboats, paddleboats, Wave Runners, Jet Skis, and beach equipment.

Most important for your family is the outstanding year-round program called the **Commodore Kids Club,** offering supervised educational and entertaining options for ages four to twelve provided by fully licensed caregivers. Offered seven days a week, activities change daily and include nature walks, sand-castle building, face painting, arts and crafts, and G-rated video screenings. Full-day, half-day, and evening programs are available. Families with more than one child get the second child at half price. Call for current rates.

Kids also enjoy the game room with pinball, video, and Ping-Pong. This program is a real winner. We think your family will enjoy it enormously. Be sure to call for special holiday programs and value packages that combine Sea-World and other attractions' tickets, too. A very helpful staff is ready and waiting for your family. Like the slogan says, "Loews Loves Kids," and it shows! $$$$

For More Information

Coronado Visitors Bureau. *1047 "B" Avenue, Coronado, 92118–3418. (619) 437–8788, (800) 622–8300; www.coronado.ca.us.*

La Jolla

Heading up the coast along Pacific Coast Highway 1 from Mission Bay and Pacific Beach will lead you directly into the toney suburb of La Jolla (say la-hoy-ya; it's Spanish for "the jewel"). This truly precious area is home of the University of California-San Diego (UCSD) and the distinguished Salk Institute for Biomedical Research. There is also some fabulous real estate along the beaches, coves, and caves; and trendy shopping and dining along downtown's Prospect Avenue, the Rodeo Drive of San Diego.

SCRIPPS INSTITUTION OF OCEANOGRAPHY AND STEPHEN BIRCH AQUARIUM-MUSEUM

2300 Expedition Way, off La Jolla Village Drive, on the campus of UCSD, overlooking La Jolla and the Pacific; (858) 534–3474. Open daily except Thanksgiving and Christmas 9:00 A.M. to 5:00 P.M. $$

These facilities are among the most prestigious world leaders in research and instruction. Opened in 1992, they replaced a smaller facility that had been operating since 1951. Inside the aquarium you can see more than 3,000 fish in thirty tanks, including a two-story, 70,000-gallon kelp forest with species from the waters of the West Coast, Mexico's Sea of Cortez, and the South Pacific. There is also a man-made interpretive tide pool. The innovative and interactive museum introduces the world's largest oceanographic exhibition, *Exploring the Blue Planet*. The bookshop has educational souvenirs and books for all ages on the science of the seas. This attraction strikes an educational counterpoint to the frenetic action of SeaWorld.

MUSEUM OF CONTEMPORARY ART, LA JOLLA

700 Prospect Street, La Jolla; (858) 454–3541. Open 11:00 A.M. to 5:00 P.M. daily except Wednesday. Hours change seasonally.

Children can enjoy the outdoor sculpture garden and food court. Everyone will view outstanding examples of minimalist, conceptual, and California art in a beautiful setting.

LA JOLLA WALKING TOURS

910 Prospect Street; (719) 535–9636. Departs seasonally from the Colonial Inn. Call for current times and schedule.

Offers ninety-minute to two-hour walking tours of historic buildings and the La Jolla Cove area, teeming with sea and shore life.

For More Information

La Jolla Town Council, *7734 Herschel Avenue, Suite F; (858) 454–1444; www.lajolla tc.org.*

North County—Coastal Communities

Just north of La Jolla along the ocean, be sure to take the drive up Pacific Coast Highway 1/U.S. Highway 101 for a relaxing trip through some classic Southern California beach communities, inhabiting what the locals call North County. The charming seaside hamlets of **Solana Beach, Cardiff-by-the-Sea, Encinitas, Del Mar,** and **Leucadia** have miles of sandy beaches with rocky coves, cliffs above, and lots of friendly folks waiting to welcome you at the small shops, restaurants, and inns in these charming enclaves.

TORREY PINES STATE BEACH AND RESERVE

North Torrey Pines Road, Del Mar; (858) 755–2063. Open daily 9:00 A.M. to dusk. $

This beach/reserve stretches between La Jolla and Del Mar. Enjoy one of just two places in the world where the Torrey pine tree grows (the other is Santa Rosa Island, near Santa Barbara). A visitor's center has interpretive displays, and there are miles of great hiking and nature trails. The beach below is a favorite for swimmers; the cliffs above are a popular take-off spot for hang gliders.

Hot-Air Ballooning North County is also famous for its hot-air balloon rides. Several companies offer sunrise and sunset flights that feature scenic views of the coastline, rolling hills, and reservoir-dotted valleys. Most companies fly year-round, weather permitting. Rides depart early in the morning or just before dusk and last about an hour. All pilots are FAA certified. Fares start around $135, but package and family plans are offered. Not advised for children eight and under. A Skysurfer Balloon Company (858) 481–6800; and California Dreamin' Balloon Adventures (760–438–3344). Call for current prices and schedules.

DEL MAR FAIRGROUNDS & RACE TRACK

2260 Jimmy Durante Boulevard, Del Mar; (858) 755–1141; www.delmarfair.com.

This is where "the turf meets the surf" with two attractions. The **San Diego County Fair** runs here June 15 through July 4. Then thoroughbreds are off and running July through September. The combined facility is a gorgeous, 350-acre historic site overlooking the Pacific. More than a hundred events are held here each year. Call for this year's schedule.

QUAIL BOTANICAL GARDENS

230 Quail Gardens Drive, just east of Interstate 5, Encinitas; (760) 436–3036; www.qbgardens.com. Open daily 9:00 A.M. to 5:00 P.M., closed major holidays. First Tuesday of every month is **Free**. *$$*

The gardens contain one of the world's most diverse plant collections, including California natives, exotic tropicals, palms, and bamboo. This site was formerly owned by avid plant collector and naturalist Ruth Baird Larabee, who donated her thirty-acre estate to the public in 1957. The gardens are open for self-guided tours as well as a super chance to see the namesake resident quails in a natural bird refuge.

For More Information

Del Mar Chamber of Commerce. *1104 Camino del Mar; (858) 755–4844.*

Encinitas Chamber of Commerce. *138 Encinitas Boulevard; (760) 753–6041 or (800) 953–6041; www.encinitas.org.*

Rancho Santa Fe

If you've had it with hype and just want to reeee-laaaax, the postcard perfect Spanish Colonial–style village of Rancho Santa Fe is known for its quiet, peaceful setting. Go 6 miles inland, amid magnificently fragrant eucalyptus trees. They were planted by the Santa Fe Railroad in hopes they would make great railroad ties—but the wood was too soft to even hold a spike! Today these trees provide a magnificent backdrop for the family-welcoming upscale village.

Where to Eat and Stay

Inn at Rancho Santa Fe, *5951 Linea Del Cielo; (858) 756–1131 or 1-800-THE-INN-1; www.theinnatranchosantafe.com.* Third-generation hotelier Duncan Royce Hadden manages this family-owned and family-friendly inn. On the twenty-two manicured acres there are twenty-three cottages with eighty-nine individually styled accommodations, including many family suites—all set against a magnificent backdrop of eucalyptus. The entire clan can enjoy tennis, croquet on the front lawn, or a swim in the heated outdoor pool. The gym has your basic workout gear, and you can dine in the coffee shop, main dining room, or poolside. The inn even maintains a private guest cottage on the sand at Del Mar. You will feel like rich natives when you and your kids spend a day at the beach, then retreat to the inn. $$$$

Carlsbad

The picturesque beach community of Carlsbad (named for the famous Karl-bad spa in Europe) is home to many coves and beautiful lagoons, as well as golf resorts, bistros, inns, and antiques emporiums. LEGOLAND California, a must-do family experience, opened in 1999.

LEGOLAND CALIFORNIA (ages 2 to 12 recommended)
One Legoland Drive (just off Interstate 5, exit Cannon Road or Palomar Airport Road and follow signs); (760) 918–LEGO or (877) LEGOLAND; www.legoland.com. Open daily, hours vary seasonally, call for times. $$$$
      Opened in March 1999 to well-deserved acclaim, this 128-acre park is the first LEGO-themed facility in the United States. Thirty million plastic LEGO building blocks were used to create the 5,000 models that decorate the park. You and your kids won't believe what can be created out of those little blocks of plastic—and there's lots of opportunity for you to create, too! LEGOLAND is a hands-on, interactive experience for the entire family. No thrilling, chilling rides here—just forty attractions in nine themed "blocks" (The Beginning, Village Green, The Ridge, The Lake, Fun Town—our fave, The Garden, Castle Hill, Miniland, and Imagination Zone), plus restaurants and shops that mix education, a little bit of adventure, and a lot of fun! Be sure to schedule a day to really enjoy LEGOLAND at your kids' pace.

BIPLANE RIDES AND AERIAL DOGFIGHTS/BARNSTORMING ADVENTURES

6743 Montia Court; (760) 438–7680 or (800) SKY–LOOP; www.barn storming.com. Open year-round during daylight hours. Call for prevailing winds, schedules, and fees.

Open-air flights in vintage cockpit biplanes and mock aerial combat in military-style aircraft could make for an unforgettable family adventure. Better for older children, we think, but use your own judgment.

FLOWER FIELDS AT CARLSBAD RANCH

East of Interstate 5 at Palomar Airport Road and Paseo del Norte; (760) 431–0352; www.theflowerfields.com. Open March through April generally, during daylight hours. $$

Wear comfortable walking shoes as you and the kids traipse through more than fifty acres of gently sloping hillside covered with a rainbow of buttercups. An incredible sight!

CHILDREN'S DISCOVERY MUSEUM OF NORTH COUNTY (ages 2 to 12)

300 Carlsbad Village Drive #103, in the Village Faire shopping center, corner of Carlsbad Village Drive and U.S. Highway 101; (760) 720–0737. Open Tuesday through Sunday, generally noon to 5:00 P.M., with schedules varying seasonally. Be sure to call ahead. $

North County's first children's museum, this 3,000-square-foot facility opened in 1994 with a kids' supermarket, a medieval castle complete with costumes, and a variety of interactive displays. You'll also find a solar-powered toy train.

Where to Eat

Tip Top Meats & Deli, *6118 Paseo Del Norte, just off Interstate 5 at Palomar Airport Road; (760) 438–2620. Open daily, 6:00 A.M. to 8:00 P.M.* Don't be fooled by the name—this local favorite offers the best value for miles around. A full breakfast starts at $2.98 (one egg, home-fried potatoes, toast and ham, bacon or sausage); burgers are $1.98; dinners start at $4.49 (prime rib roast, potatoes, cabbage, sauerkraut, soup or salad, and roll is only $6.98). Just enter through the market and proceed to the deli area, where you'll place your order. Pick a seat in the dining room and wait for your number to be called—and dig in to a tip-top meal! Say hi to owner "Big John" Haedrich for us! $

Where to Stay

Four Seasons Resort Aviara, *7100 Four Seasons Point, Carlsbad; (760) 603–6800. $$$$.* Located on a plateau overlooking the Batiquitos Lagoon, a wildlife sanctuary, and the Pacific Ocean, this opulent 331-unit property opened in August 1997 and is rated five-diamond by AAA. The adjacent Aviara Golf Club, designed by Arnold Palmer, opened in 1991 and is ranked in the top ten nationally by golf magazines. Your family can take part in three- or four-day golf academies to see if you've got a Tiger Woods in the making!

Part of a 1,000-acre master planned community, the resort will remain more than 50 percent open space. In the Spanish Colonial-style main hotel, standard guest rooms are large (average 540 square feet) and feature five-star amenities.

The best feature for families is undoubtedly the Four Seasons' **Kids for All Seasons program** for ages five to twelve. Upon check-in, kids receive a personal invitation to visit the center and take part in kite flying, swimming and beach games, lagoon nature trail exploration, table games, and other supervised activities. Your kids will receive a welcome cookie and milk turndown treat on their first night as well as children's menus in all the restaurants. Cribs, strollers, high chairs, and playpens are all complimentary, along with a selection of toys to check out. The **California Bistro** serves three meals daily and should be your choice for the family. Or just indulge in twenty-four-hour room service. You deserve it!

Grand Pacific Palisades Resort & Hotel, *5805 Armada Drive (exit Palomar Airport Road east from Interstate 5); (760) 827–3200; www.grandpacificpalisades.com.* Across the street from LEGOLAND, overlooking the Carlsbad Flower Fields and the Pacific Ocean, this should be your family's headquarters for fun in North County. You can leave your car in the hotel parking lot and walk across the street to the side entrance to LEGOLAND. Return during the day for naps and lunch breaks—an ideal way to plan your stay. The contemporary Mediterranean architecture of the hotel encloses ninety spacious hotel rooms and a seventy-one-unit time-share resort. A full-service restaurant, room service, two inviting outdoor heated pools and whirlpools, concierge services, a social activity director, a game room, and a fitness center—all staffed with friendly, helpful people—make this a grand place! $$$

For More Information

Carlsbad Convention and Visitors Bureau. *P.O. Box 1246, Carlsbad, 92018; (760) 434–6093 or (800) 227–5722; www.carlsbad.ca.org.*

Oceanside

Bustling Oceanside, at the mouth of the San Luis Rey Valley, is home base to the U.S. Marine Corps' Camp Pendleton (approximately 125,000 acres) and the ever-popular Municipal Pier—California's longest, which planks in at a whopping 1,942 feet. Check out the great fishing, seafood restaurants, and ice-cream shop located on this wooden wonder.

CALIFORNIA SURF MUSEUM

223 North Coast Highway, Oceanside. (760) 721–6876; www.surfmuseum.org. Open Thursday to Monday from noon to 4:00 P.M. (unless the surf is awesome!). Call for special events and seasonal operating hours. **Free** *admission.*

Everything you wanted to know about surfing—for the novice to learn and for the experienced to enjoy. A real kicked-back gem.

HELGREN'S SPORTFISHING

315 Harbor Drive South; (760) 722–2133. Open year-round, call for times and fees.

Take your choice of charter fishing vessels; half-day, full-day, and overnight trip options, as well as whale-watching cruises between December and February.

MISSION SAN LUIS REY

4050 Mission Avenue, 4 miles east of town on State Route 76; (760) 757–3651. Open Monday through Saturday 10:00 A.M. to 4:30 P.M. and Sunday, noon to 4:30 P.M. $

This "king of the missions" is number eighteen in the famous chain of twenty-one California churches begun by Father Serra. It's also the largest and has wooden double-dome construction. Picnicking facilities are available on the attractive grounds.

Where to Eat

101 Cafe, *631 South Coast Highway; (619) 722–5220; www.mainstreetdata. com/101cafe. Open daily from 6:30 A.M. to midnight.* Established in 1928, this family diner serves up traditional American-style home-cooked meals. The hamburgers are the best and the milk shakes a dream. There's a great 1950s jukebox and historic photos all over the walls. $

Where to Stay

Oceanside Marina Inn, *2008 Harbor Drive North; (760) 722–1561 or (800) 252–2033. www.omihotel.com.* Secluded at the tip of Oceanside's bustling harbor, the inn offers sixty-four one- and two-bedroom units with kitchens. Wonderful water views; many units have fireplaces and balconies. A pool, spa, and barbeque area are other highlights. This perfect family waterfront stopover is close to many North County attractions. $$

For More Information

Oceanside Visitor and Tourism Information Center. *928 North Coast Highway, Oceanside, 92054; (760) 721–1101 or (800) 350–7873; www.oceansidechamber.com.*

Escondido and Vicinity

Inland from the Pacific, the north-south Interstates 5 and 15 run several miles apart, embracing gently rolling hillsides, forests, and streams that will make you pinch yourself and wonder, "Are we still in California?" In the center of it all is the city of Escondido. Other scenic communities scattered through inland North County include Fallbrook, San Marcos, Poway, Rancho Bernardo, La Costa, Vista, and Valley Center.

HERITAGE WALK AND ESCONDIDO'S HISTORICAL SOCIETY MUSEUM

321 North Broadway in Grape Day Park, Escondido; (760) 743–8207. Open Thursday through Saturday 1:00 to 4:00 P.M. **Free.**

Includes a Victorian house, Indian metate (grinding stones), a circa 1888 Santa Fe Railroad depot, and the Bandy Blacksmith Shop.

CALIFORNIA CENTER FOR THE ARTS

340 North Escondido Boulevard, Escondido; (760) 839–4138 or (800) 988–4253. Call for current programs, schedules, and fees.

This center located on a twelve-acre campus has an art museum, a 1,500-seat concert hall, and art education programs for young people in a world-class facility.

ICEOPLEX

555 North Tulip, Escondido; (760) 489–5550; www.iceoplex.com. Open daily at 8:30 A.M., closing times vary. $$

This is a massive facility that boasts two Olympic-size ice-skating rinks, a fitness center, a spa, an Olympic lap pool, a Jacuzzi, a sauna, and a training room. You can chill out here after all your fun in the sun!

NORTH COUNTY FAIR MALL

272 East Via Rancho Parkway at Interstate 15, Escondido; (760) 489–2332. Open daily, call for seasonal hours.

With its 180 specialty shops, fifteen restaurants, and five major department stores, this is one of the largest indoor retail centers in the county. Your family will discover plenty to see, do, and eat here. (We think it makes a great stopover on the way to or from the Wild Animal Park.)

SAN DIEGO WILD ANIMAL PARK

15500 San Pasqual Valley Road, located 5 miles east of Interstate 15 on State Route 78, just outside Escondido; (760) 747–8702 or (760) 234–6541; www.sandiegozoo.org. Open every day beginning at 9:00 A.M. Closing times vary by season. $$$$

On 2,100 acres of prime sanctuary land, and without a doubt the showpiece of North County, the park was designed originally as a breeding facility for the San Diego Zoo (its sister facility). You and your family will want to spend a day here to see more than 3,000 wild animals roaming freely in settings that resemble their native habitats. Designed for the animals first and foremost, it is the only zoo where the guests are put in cages (specifically, into the comfortable Bush Line electric monorail, which glides above the habitats), while the animals roam unrestrained. You will see large herds of antelopes, gazelles, deer, rhinos, and exotic sheep and goats. Flocks of flamingos, pelicans, cranes, geese, ducks, herons, ostriches, vultures, and storks live in the big enclosures as well. Even the single-species exhibits—herds of African and Asian elephants, families of gorillas and chimpanzees—are large and natural.

The seventeen-acre **Nairobi Village** holds most of the visitor facilities, including restaurants, gift shops, and picnic areas. Plan to attend the bird show, wild animal show, and elephant demonstrations held here. And make some new friends in the petting kraal.

The **Kilimanjaro Hiking Trail** is a 1.75-mile walking safari where you can see rhinos, tigers, elephants, cheetahs, and giraffes up close and personal. Special photo caravan safaris will take you right into the middle of the habitats in a large, open-air truck for an additional fee. We cannot recommend this activity highly enough. The chance to pet a rhino or feed a giraffe as it bends over your head is a thrill of a lifetime. We really were impressed and amazed here.

THE WAVE WATERPARK

161 Recreation Drive off Broadway, Vista, 7 miles inland on State Route 78; (760) 940–WAVE; www.ci.vista.ca.us/wave. Open Memorial Day through Labor Day, 10:30 A.M. to 5:30 P.M. $$$

The state-of-the-art wave maker is called Flow Rider, one of only three in the United States. Your family's dudes (and dudettes) can body surf all day long and never have to wait for that perfect wave—because they're all perfect! Four wild water slides, an underwater playground, an Olympic-size pool, and a picnic area make this inland water spot a great experience. It's a great value, too.

SAN PASQUAL BATTLEFIELD STATE HISTORIC PARK AND MUSEUM

15808 San Pasqual Valley Road, Escondido; (760) 737–2201. Open Friday through Sunday 10:00 A.M. to 5:00 P.M. **Free**.

The museum honors those who participated in the 1846 San Pasqual Battle during the Mexican-American War. See videos and exhibits regarding that historic time. A dramatic reenactment is held every December.

ANTIQUE GAS AND STEAM ENGINE MUSEUM

2040 North Santa Fe Avenue, Vista; (760) 941–1791 or (800) 5–TRACTOR; www.agesem.com. Open daily from 10:00 A.M. to 4:00 P.M. $

Weekend threshing bees in June and October are really fun! Our kids were impressed with the blacksmith. Catch a bit of history at the museum. Forty acres of turn-of-the-century farming equipment, all maintained in working order. Kids can see actual corn, wheat, and oat crops harvested from the field and into the kitchen.

Where to Eat

Bates Nut Farm, *15954 Woods Valley Road, 3 miles east of Valley Center; (760) 749–3333; www.batesfarm.com. Open daily 9:00 A.M. to 5:00 P.M.* This is a family favorite because of its **Free** petting zoo, shady picnic grounds, fresh pro-duce, and terribly tasty array of fruits, nuts, and candy. There are arts and crafts fairs each April and November; pumpkins predominate in October, and fir trees in December. $

Where to Stay

Lawrence Welk Resort, Museum, and Dinner Theatre, *8860 Lawrence Welk Drive, 7 miles north of Escondido off Interstate 15; (800) 932–9355 or (760) 749–3000. Museum open daily at 10:00 A.M., closing times vary.* **Free** *admission to museum. Dinner theater performances offer musical variety for the whole family. Call for times, programs, and ticket prices.* Not just for Grandma and Grandpa, with their memories of the legendary band leader, this 1,000-acre hideaway with only 132 spacious rooms has all the amenities for a super family vacation retreat. They include on-site golf, tennis, swimming pools, spa, and restaurants featuring kids' menus and all-you-can eat buffets. Perfect for that multi-generation reunion! $$$$

For More Information

San Diego North County Convention and Visitors Bureau, *720 North Broadway, Escondido, 92025-1899. (800) 848–3336 or (760) 745–4741; www.sandiegonorthcounty.com.*

Temecula Valley

The town of Temecula was founded in 1882 and served as an important stop on the Butterfield Stagecoach Route between San Bernardino and San Diego. Today it is a fast-growing community nestled between San Diego and Riverside Counties with some award-winning vineyards, fourteen wineries, horse ranches, seven golf courses, harvest festivals, and superb antiques shops.

OLD TOWN TEMECULA

Front Street between Moreno Road and Third Street. Open daily, hours vary. Get a walking tour map and visit the Welty Building, jail, First National Bank, and G. Machado's store. Many of these historic build-

ings are antiques malls now, sure to delight shoppers. But there's no predicting how long they will grab your kids' attention (before they start acting like the proverbial bull in a china shop). Probably a half hour will do it.

🏛 MISSION SAN ANTONIO DE PALA

Pala Mission Road, north of State Route 76, Pala; (760) 742–1600. Open Tuesday through Sunday 10:00 A.M. to 3:00 P.M. $

A branch of the Mission San Luis Rey, it was built in 1816 as part of an inland chain of missions that never really developed. The chapel, gardens, and mineral room have all been restored. Very quaint.

Where to Stay and Eat

Pala Mesa Resort, *2001 Old Highway 395, off Interstate 15, Fallbrook; (800) 722–4700 or (760) 728–5881; www.palamesa.com.* This spacious golf resort is ideal for families with its 133 connecting rooms, views of rolling hills, eighteen-hole golf course, and irresistible family-size swimming pool. You'll find plenty of outdoor recre-ation, including horseshoes, croquet, volleyball, tennis, badminton, a whirlpool, and a spa. **Alexander's Restaurant** is open 6:00 A.M. to 2:00 P.M. and 5:30 to 10:00 P.M. with a nice golf-course view. The early California decor will make you appreciate the reasonably priced children's menu even more. $$$$

For More Information

Temecula Valley Chamber of Commerce. *27450 Ynez Road #104, Temecula, 92591. (909) 676–5090 or (888) TEMECULA; www.temecula.org.*

The Mountains (Back Country)

Don't miss the eastern portion of San Diego County, affectionately known by locals as the Back Country. Bisected by three main roads—State Routes 76, 78, and 79—the Back Country offers mountain peaks rising more than 6,000 feet, dazzling foliage in fall, snowfalls in winter (and sometimes even in April!), and desert flora year-round. This land of contrasts has fabulous hiking, biking, camping, and fishing options for your active times and plenty of bucolic beauty for your off-tour hours.

PALOMAR MOUNTAIN OBSERVATORY AND STATE PARK

From Oceanside, off State Route 76 (about 11 miles inland on County Road S6; (760) 742–2119. Daily 9:00 A.M. to 4:00 P.M. **Free**.

For a grand perspective, ascend Mount Palomar (elevation 6,140 feet) to the observatory. Inside this striking white-domed structure, you'll find one of the world's largest scientific instruments—the 200-inch **Hale Telescope.** You and the kids can watch its inner workings and see a video at the museum nearby describing all the functions of this scientific wonder. Along with the observatory, enjoy the completely uncrowded **State Park** (760-742-3462 for general information) with thickly forested areas, wildlife, fishing, camping, and hiking trails.

For More Information

San Diego East Visitors Bureau. *5005 Willows Road, Suite 208, Alpine, 91901; (619) 445–0180 or (800) 463–0668; www.visitsandiegoeast.com.*

Julian and Vicinity

For a piece of living history, continue toward the interior of North County along State Route 78, and you'll arrive at Julian. In the hills only 60 miles inland from Oceanside, Julian lies in the heart of the Cleveland National Forest. Beautiful downtown Julian looks much as it did a century ago. It was founded in 1870 by settlers Drew Bailey and his cousin Mike Julian, hence the name. A gold strike yielding nearly $5 million made the town of Julian famous back in the 1870s. When the gold rush ended, apples became the cash crop of choice. Now Julian is famous for hillside acres of apple orchards (Julian is known as Southern California's apple capital) and beautiful fields of spring wildflowers. The two-block-long Main Street and surrounding area has everything you'll want within easy walking distance. Yes, you are still in Southern California (just an early 1900s version!).

EAGLE MINING COMPANY

North end of C Street, downtown; (760) 765–0036. Daily 10:00 A.M. to 3:00 P.M., weather permitting. $$

Guided tours through this old gold mine will show you how those shiny, precious flakes were extracted from Mother Earth. A fascinating journey into the mountainside for the entire family.

JULIAN PIONEER MUSEUM

2811 Washington Street; (760) 765–0227. Tuesday through Sunday 10:00 A.M. to 4:00 P.M. April through November, on weekends the rest of the year. $

Housed in a late 1800s structure, the museum shows you and the kids what life in early Julian was like.

CUYAMACA RANCHO STATE PARK

15027 Highway 79, south of Julian; (760) 765–0755. Open daily year-round. $$

Twenty-five thousand acres of beautiful terrain include pine, oak, and cedar trees; meadows; lakes; streams; and the Green Valley waterfall. Explore via ten miles of trails for mountain biking, hiking, and horseback riding. You can see more than a hundred species of birds in the area, or perhaps even a mule deer or coyote. The park has a visitor center, gift shop, and a museum depicting the gold rush days at the Stonewall Mine during its 1886–91 peak. We love just going for a simple picnic.

MISSION SANTA YSABEL

23013 Highway 79, Santa Ysabel; (760) 765–0810. Daily 7:00 A.M. to dusk. Free.

You can take a self-guided tour of this charming satellite mission built in 1818. There is also an Indian burial ground and museum. It's a pleasant stopover on your way to Julian.

*E*xtra *S*pecial *T*ip

Seeing Julian in Slow Motion Our favorite way to see Julian is by way of **Country Carriages** (760-765-1471), located right downtown on Main Street. To get your bearings on the area, begin with a ride on a horse-drawn carriage, all hitched up and ready to go. A thirty-minute clop-clop trip around town costs $25 per couple with two children—worth it for the history lesson alone. After your buggy ride, stay in the old-fashioned mood with an ice-cream treat at **Ye Olde Soda Fountain** at the **Julian Drug Store.** Kids of all ages love the chance to sit on the old-fashioned stools and see how such classics as an egg creme or black cow are made by hand.

Where to Eat

Dudley's Bakery and Snack Bar, *On Highway 78 in downtown Santa Ysabel; (760) 765–0488; www.dudleysbakery.com. Open Wednesday to Sunday, hours vary seasonally.* Here you will find an incredible selection of seventeen famous breads, plus cookies, pies, and yummy pastries. This is a great place to have breakfast or lunch with your family and pick up treats for later. Don't miss this place. It's usually jammed, so you won't be able to! $

The Julian Grille, *2224 Main Street; (760) 765–0173.* Housed in a homey cottage, the restaurant serves lunch daily and dinner Tuesday through Saturday. The menu features steaks, pasta, and seafood your family will savor. $$

Where to Stay

Julian White House Inn, *3014 Blue Jay Drive; (800) WHT–HOUSE or (760) 765–1764; www.julian-whitehouse-bnb. com.* The most family-friendly of the several bed-and-breakfast inns in the area, it features five guest rooms in a petite southern mansion in the woods. It has been owned and operated by Mary and Alan Marvin, along with their daughter, Alexandra, since 1989. $$$

Pine Hills Lodge and Dinner Theatre, *2960 La Posada Way, Julian; (760)* 765–1100. *Call for schedule and admission prices.* A must-stop for vintage Back Country food and family entertainment. Every Friday and Saturday evening, a fantastic barbecue dinner of baked chicken and baby back ribs is accompanied by locally cast Pine Hills Players musical presentations. A variety of rustic and recently refurbished accommodations are offered in eighteen lodge and cabin units at reasonable rates. $$$

For More Information

Julian Chamber of Commerce, *2129 Main Street; (760) 765–1857; www.julianca.com.*

Borrego Springs

This peaceful resort community is located inside the Anza-Borrego Desert State Park and has a wide variety of lodging, camping, dining, golf, and recreation options. The community hosts a Grapefruit Festival in April. The Borrego Days Festival in October includes a parade and an arts and crafts fair to welcome back snow birds for the warm winter season. We think the best time to visit the area is during the spring, when desert wildflowers are in magnificent bloom.

ANZA-BORREGO DESERT STATE PARK

Approximately two hours east of downtown San Diego, just west of County Road S22 and surrounding the quaint town of Borrego Springs. The visitor center is located at 200 Palm Canyon Drive; (760) 767–4205 for general information or (760) 767–4684 for recorded wildflower information. Open daily October through May 9:00 A.M. to 5:00 P.M.; rest of year open only on Saturday and Sunday. Camping fees vary and reservations are strongly suggested. $

This is the biggest state park in the United States, with 600,000 acres of wildly rugged mountains (highest elevation 6,000 feet) and desert (elevation 40 feet), along with flora, fauna, and fossils dating back 540 million years. You will see mesquite, yucca, and smoke trees, cacti, and thousands of native plants and flowers.

Start your visit at the magnificent 7,000-square-foot visitor center, built into the hillside, with exhibits, maps, natural history books, a twenty-minute video presentation, and volunteers who are eager to help your family plan your desert experience. There are nature walks, campfire programs, fossil programs, and guided hikes to choose from. The park is geared for off-road travel and exploration. The most dramatic and popular attraction is the spring wildflowers. Our favorite hikes

Extra Special Tip

Finding Hotel Values San Diego Hotel Reservations (800–SAVE-CASH; www.savecash.com) or Sights of San Diego Hotel Reservations (800–434–7894; www.booksandiego.com). Super helpful hotel reservation assistance at no charge. Firms represents 200-plus properties in the entire county and can book the price range, location, and style of hotel that's perfect for your family.

include the Borrego Palm Canyon Nature Trail, a gentle 3-mile round trip, as well as the Pygmy Trail, a 1-mile round trip that leads to fifty short palm trees. Among the park's many other points of interest: the **Box Canyon Historical Monument, Coyote Canyon,** the **Culp Valley Overlook,** the **Elephant Tree Discovery Trail,** the **Mason Valley Cactus Garden,** and the **Vallecita Stagecoach Station.**

Extra Special Tip

Anza-Borrego Junior Ranger Program

This program will deepen your seven- to twelve-year-olds' appreciation of nature. It is the ultimate outdoor adventure for kids since parents are NOT allowed! On Saturday and Sunday during winter and spring, you can drop off your children at the visitor center for supervised activities in the park. Kids receive a log book to record their visit. Best of all, the Junior Ranger program is Free! Call the park for current times and a schedule at (760) 767–4205.

San Diego County, with its rich Spanish and Mexican heritage and American spirit, is a world-class destination with an ideal climate, fantastic natural wonders, and enough excitement to create a wonderfully satisfying family adventure. Adios!

Where to Eat and Stay

La Casa Del Zorro Desert Resort, *3845 Yaqui Pass Road, Borrego Springs; (760) 767–5323 or (800) 824–1884; www.lacasadelzorro.com.* Any of the two- or three-bedroom *casitas* (homes) will have you and your family feeling totally relaxed within hours at this forty-two-acre resort. Each bedroom has its own bath (such an advantage) and some casitas even have a private pool. This historic desert resort started in 1937 and is renowned as a haven of rest and tranquility. It is rated with four stars by Mobil and four diamonds by AAA. You can't go wrong choosing from any of the seventy-seven accommodations, in the value season starting as low as $60 per night. On the property, you'll find a putting green, three heated pools, whirlpools, and six lighted tennis courts. The restaurant serves all three meals daily, surrounded by beautiful views and early California decor. It's a great family destination getaway. $$$$

For More Information

Borrego Springs Chamber of Commerce. *P.O. Box 420, Borrego Springs, 92004. (760) 767–5555 or (800) 559–5524; www.borregosprings.org.*

Tijuana (Baja California, Mexico) Tourism and Convention Bureau. *P.O. Box 434523, San Diego, 92143–4523, or call the office in Mexico direct by dialing 011 52 66/84–05–37 or access www.tijuana.com.*

Extra Special Tip

Crossing the Border into Mexico at Tijuana Fifteen miles south of downtown San Diego is the border town of San Ysidro, California, the U.S. gateway to Tijuana, Baja California, and the rest of Mexico. San Ysidro, with its largely Hispanic population, provides services to American travelers bound for Baja as well as Mexican nationals leaving and entering California. This highly commercialized sector has signs in both English and Spanish. San Ysidro Boulevard leads directly to the border crossing. It's filled with Mexican-style stores, eateries, auto insurance dealers, pawn shops, and money-exchange houses. (Even though the U.S. dollar is widely accepted in Tijuana, you will need pesos farther into Mexico.) Keep in mind that Tijuana is the world's busiest port of entry with more than 60 million border crossings each year. The city itself is bursting with more than 1.2 million people in a semi-developed country with rapidly changing economics and politics.

You can cross the border on foot (we recommend you leave your car in one of the secured parking lots) or by car (not recommended for day trips, since you need to purchase Mexican auto insurance). The San Diego Trolley (Blue Line) from downtown provides the easiest access since it terminates at the San Ysidro border crossing. The cost is only $2.50 each way (phone 619-234-1060 for schedules). Interstates 5 and 15 also terminate at the border, along with many of the amenities we take for granted.

Tijuana is a duty-free zone, which makes the city very popular for bargain shoppers seeking hand-crafted jewelry, pottery, and leather products. U.S. residents may return home with up to $400 worth of merchandise, including one liter of alcoholic beverages, 100 cigars, and 200 cigarettes (providing the person is twenty-one). Some merchandise, particularly fruits and vegetables, is not allowed into the United States. Tijuana's diverse shopping, dining, and entertainment options are not necessarily geared for everyone in your family, but the city does offer a sampling of cultural diversity and exposure to a bustling Mexican border town.

Annual Events

The following list of events in the San Diego County area was provided by the California Trade and Commerce Agency.

MARCH

Shamrock Festival—San Diego. *(619) 233–4692, fax (619) 233–4148.* St. Patrick's Day block party in San Diego's Gaslamp district with live music, Irish entertainment, food, and face painting. **Free**.

APRIL

Santa Fe Market—San Diego. *(619) 299–6055, fax (619) 296–1570.* Festival of southwest American Indian arts and crafts including guest artists and cultural demonstrations. **Free**.

Encinitas Street Fair—Encinitas. *(760) 943–1950.* More than 300 vendors, children's rides, face painting, clowns, arts and crafts. **Free**.

MAY

Fiesta Cinco De Mayo—San Diego. *(619) 299–6055, fax (619) 296–1570.* Mexican celebration in Old Town includes nonstop entertainment and food booths. **Free**.

Carlsbad Village Faire—Carlsbad. *(760) 434–8887.* One-day street fair features 800 booths; arts, crafts, antiques, international foods, and live entertainment.

JULY

San Diego County Fair—Del Mar. *(858) 792–4262, fax (858) 792–4453.* Annual county fair featuring world-class entertainment, rides, exhibits, livestock, and food.

Fourth of July Parade and Celebration—Coronado. *(800) 622–8300.* Includes fireworks and demonstrations by the U.S. Navy. **Free**.

Independence Day Celebration—Julian. *(760) 765–1857, fax (760) 765–2544.* Annual event includes old-fashioned parade, staged bank robbery, live country music, arts and crafts, ongoing raffle. **Free**.

An Old-Fashioned Fourth of July—San Diego. *(619) 220–5423.* Activities include hayrides, music, entertainers, dancing, sack races, and pie-eating contests. **Free**.

Fourth of July Freedom Days—Oceanside. *(760) 722–1534, fax (760) 722–8336.* Parade, street fair, festivities, fireworks, and music at the outdoor beach amphitheater. **Free**.

AUGUST

Latin American Festival—San Diego. *(619) 299–6055, fax (619) 296–1570.* Latin American crafts, artists, demonstrations, entertainment, and food booths. **Free**.

Longboard Surfing Contest—Oceanside. *(800) 350–7873 or (760) 721–1101.* Join the legends of surfing as they participate in the original surfing contest. **Free**.

SEPTEMBER

Fall Fiesta—Old Town San Diego. *(619) 220–5422.* Celebrating the Hispanic heritage of Alta California with foods, crafts, music, and dance. **Free**.

International Friendship Festival—El Cajon. *(619) 441–1753, fax (619) 588–1190.* One hundred and ten booths featuring international cuisine and cultural displays, crafts, a fine arts exhibit, entertainment, children's activities, and an American Indian celebration. **Free**.

Harbor Days—Oceanside. *(760) 721–1101, fax (760) 722–8336.* Celebrate a festival of crafts and events at the beautiful Oceanside Marina and Harbor. **Free**.

OCTOBER

Oktoberfest—Carlsbad. *(800) 227–5722 or (760) 434–6093.* Patriotic, traditional German music; children's games and lots of German food.

NOVEMBER

Community Tree Lighting—Julian. *(760) 765–1857, fax (760) 765–2544.* Old-fashioned Christmas tree lighting, costumed carolers, living Nativity pageant, and horse-drawn carriage rides. **Free**.

Festival of Lights—San Diego. *(619) 299–6055.* Celebration includes dances from around the world and dramatic Nativity scene lighting. **Free**.

DECEMBER

Holiday of Lights—Del Mar. *(858) 755–7161, fax (858) 792–4453.* Holiday light display featuring more than 200 themed entries including Santa's elves, Twelve Days of Christmas, and a magical forest. **Free**.

Holiday in the Park—San Diego. *(619) 220–5422, fax (619) 220–5421.* Candlelight tours of museums and historic homes featuring period decorations and entertainment.

Mission Christmas Faire—Oceanside. *(760) 721–1101, fax (760) 722–8336.* More than 200 booths, amusement rides for children, and entertainment. **Free**.

Harbor Parade of Lights—Oceanside. *(760) 721–1101, fax (760) 722–8336.* Lighted boat parade through the oceanside harbor. **Free**.

Index

About the Authors

o-authors Laura Kath and Pamela Price have over fifty years combined travel and life experience in sunny Southern California. Pamela resides in Palm Springs when she is not traveling and writing/broadcasting about her experiences. She is the author of *100 Best Spas of the World* (Globe Pequot Press, 2003) and is a member of the California Restaurant Writers Association.

Laura is the author of ten nonfiction books and president of Mariah Marketing, her Santa Barbara County–based consulting business. She is a member of the International Food, Wine & Travel Writers Association and the Society of Incentive Travel Executives.

This dynamic duo blends the best of real-life family travel experience with the most up-to-the minute visitor information—making this book a must-read.